Titta Ruffo

Titta Ruffo is the first volume in a subseries to Contributions to the Study of Music and Dance entitled Opera Biographies, Editor, Andrew Farkas, Associate Editors, William R. Moran and Thomas G. Kaufman.

TITTA RUFFO
AN ANTHOLOGY

EDITED BY
ANDREW FARKAS

With a Foreword by Tito Gobbi
and a Discography by William R. Moran

Contributions to the Study of Music and Dance, Number 4
OPERA BIOGRAPHIES

Greenwood Press
Westport, Connecticut • London, England

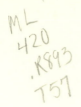

Library of Congress Cataloging in Publication Data

Main entry under title:

Titta Ruffo : an anthology.

  (Contributions to the study of music and dance,
ISSN 0193-9041 ; no. 4) (Opera biographies)
  Bibliography: p.
  Includes index.
  Discography: p.
  1. Ruffo, Titta, 1877-1953. 2. Singers—Italy—
Biography. I. Farkas, Andrew. II. Title. III. Series:
Contributions to the study of music and dance ; no. 4.
IV. Series: Opera biographies.
ML420.R893T57   1984   782.1'092'4 [B]   83-10681
ISBN 0-313-23783-2 (lib. bdg.)

Copyright © 1984 by Andrew Farkas

Library of Congress Catalog Card Number: 83-10681
ISBN: 0-313-23783-2
ISSN: 0193-9041

First published in 1984

Greenwood Press
A division of Congressional Information Service, Inc.
88 Post Road West
Westport, Connecticut 06881

Printed in the United States of America

10 9 8 7 6 5 4 3 2 1

To Dr. Ruffo Titta, Jr.,
in appreciation for his generous help,
his encouragement, and his friendship

Contents

Appendixes

Illustrations

Foreword

TITO GOBBI

Titta Ruffo, along with Enrico Caruso and Fedor Chaliapin, stands beyond human limitations, bordering on myth, illuminating forever the operatic firmament.

The source of his incandescence was not only the rare, perhaps unique, beauty of the sound of his inexhaustible natural gift, but also the psychological penetration of his characterizations, his interpretations, and his carefully researched makeup and costume.

He showed the way to a long line of singing actors and will remain in the history of opera for many, many years—unapproachable, unsurpassable, and inimitable, even to those who would try.

It is a mistake to imitate, even for gifted artists. It is more important to find oneself, to expand one's own limitations and to remain within them. Yet the temptation is great. I remember the irresistible fascination the leonine voice of Titta Ruffo had on me. I listened to his records for hours with my mouth open and imagined that within me I could feel the vibrations of that superhuman voice. I widened my mouth as in a yawn to give it more space. Fortunately, I never tried to imitate him, but the grandiosity and serenity of his phrasing remained an inspiration and an example for me.

My teacher, Giulio Crimi, told me once that one evening, when Caruso was singing, he stood in a loge with Titta Ruffo. "What do you think of Caruso?" he asked Ruffo. "He is extraordinary.... I am afraid of him!" came the reply. A few nights later when Titta Ruffo was singing and Crimi found himself in the loge with Caruso he posed the same question. "He is extraordinary.... I am afraid of him!" was Caruso's identical response.

Translated by Andrew Farkas.

They were afraid of each other, they challenged one another, but they respected each other!

I never heard Titta Ruffo in the theater, but I had the good fortune to meet him for a few minutes. I was singing Rigoletto in Pisa and I was told that "the Maestro" was in the audience. It was very exciting. I certainly could not compete with him in the generous outpouring of sound, and so I sought to give my best in sweetness of tone and all the *mezza voce* Verdi asked for in his music. At the end of the performance I waited in my dressing room, and like a king with his court, Titta Ruffo made his entrance. With a calm, thunderous voice, like a satisfied lion, he pronounced his verdict: "In this theater of my city only two baritones may sing Rigoletto: Titta Ruffo and Tito Gobbi. Bravo!"

I was knighted Rigoletto by the King of All Baritones.

Acknowledgments

I am greatly indebted to Dr. Ruffo Titta, Jr., son of the late baritone, for the contribution of his own writings, his generosity in placing at my disposal rare photographs, manuscripts, and the updated chronology, and for his untiring help in correcting the errors that crept into the manuscript.

I also owe thanks to several friends and colleagues, first and foremost to my associate, William R. Moran (La Cañada, California), for his definitive discography of Titta Ruffo's recordings and valuable advice about the anthology; Tom Kaufman (Boonton, New Jersey) for the numerous additions and corrections to the chronology and for locating several important reviews; Howard C. Sanner, Jr. (Hyattsville, Maryland) and Henry Wisneski (New York City) for editorial and research assistance; Ted Fagan (Palo Alto, California) and George L. Nyklicek (San Francisco) for translations; Kurt H. Binar (San Francisco) and Horacio Sanguinetti (Buenos Aires) for lending photographs, and Paul Karabinis (Jacksonville, Florida) for copying all the photographs lent; and last but not least, Jack S. Funkhouser (Jacksonville, Florida) for invaluable assistance in the final preparation of the manuscript.

I also want to thank those individuals and corporate entities who so generously gave their permission to reproduce their work. Without the collective assistance of all these individuals this book would not have been possible.

1. Titta Ruffo in 1912
   Photo: Zuretti & Fiorini
   Courtesy of Ruffo Titta, Jr.

Titta Ruffo

ANDREW FARKAS

Titta Ruffo has often been called the Caruso of the baritones. The comparison undoubtedly came about because of the singularity of their voices, and because of the tenorile qualities of Ruffo's baritone and the much-acclaimed baritonal coloring of Caruso's golden tenor. But there the parallel ends. Their artistic personality, life style and career patterns bear little resemblance to one another. Caruso's lighthearted sunny Neapolitan disposition strongly contrasts with the sombre, brooding personality of Ruffo. The difference is conspicuous in their interpretations. Comparing the two on common grounds, in the Italian song repertory, one finds Caruso's renditions gay, playful, or heartbreaking; Ruffo's are meditative, introspective, or melancholic. Both artists make valid statements, but their approach, the way they *feel* the music, is worlds apart. At the same time the listener is overwhelmed by the magnificence of their voices, knowing instinctively that as there has been only one Caruso, it is equally unlikely that future generations will hear the like of Titta Ruffo.

Ruffo Cafiero Titta (an enterprising impresario reversed the family and given names before his debut) came from humble origins. Born in Pisa, on June 9, 1877, he never attended school. He was kept as a "little domestic" at home and started to work before his teens. He became a highly skilled iron worker and spent many years in his father's shop, continuing his trade almost up to the time of his debut. Having no aspirations to a musical career, he discovered his voice by accident. His older brother, Ettore Titta, who later became a successful composer and music teacher, took him one evening to a performance of *Cavalleria rusticana*. It was sung by the husband and wife team, Roberto Stagno and Gemma Bellincioni, creators of the roles of Turiddu and Santuzza. The performance made a profound impression on young Ruffo. Upon returning home from the theater he begged Ettore to play the "Siciliana" on his flute. Almost unaware of what he was doing, he began to sing, as retold in his memoirs "in a tenor voice of such beauty and spontaneity that when the music ended we looked at each other with astonishment. He [Ettore] could not explain where my voice came from, and clasping his flute with trembling hands exclaimed: 'This is a miracle!' "[1]

Many years later no less an authority than Giuseppe de Luca said the same thing of Ruffo's baritone: "That was no voice—it was a miracle!" And so it seemed to the generations of listeners who heard him in person, and to us, grateful heirs to his recorded legacy.

One would imagine that the discovery of a voice of Ruffo's caliber enabled him to find helpful singing teachers, and that through rapid progress with his studies he soon made a triumphant entry into the profession. Unfortunately, it happened otherwise. His training had to wait, as much on account of his youth as his poverty. When he was eventually admitted to the Accademia di Santa Cecilia of Rome he had to continue to work in his father's shop to earn a living. His hands were so rough and his fingers so rigid from hammering wrought iron that the piano teacher of the Academy sent him away, saying that any attempt to teach him to play the piano—a requirement for graduation—was a waste of his time as well as Ruffo's. The ritualistic, antiquated methods of his voice teacher, Persichini, and the latter's stubborn insistence that he was not a baritone but a bass, made his life miserable. His classroom attendance forced him to be away from work several hours each week. He always had to endure his father's lifelong animosity but his absence now made the old man's inexplicable antagonism intolerable. After having spent about half a year at the Academy in a class whose star pupil was, incidentally, none other than Giuseppe de Luca, he left after a scandalous confrontation with Persichini. Shortly thereafter he became the pupil of a retired baritone who earned his living from giving voice lessons. Unable to pay his teacher in the third month of his training, he was forced to suspend his training once more. Soon after that Titta senior and junior completed a two-year project for an American millionaire. Being paid off by his father, young Ruffo set out for Milan with three hundred hard-earned lire in his pocket that had to sustain him for months. Once there, he presented his letter of introduction to a professionally active singer and voice teacher, Lelio Casini. Since the young man had no financial resources, Casini offered to give him voice lessons without payment as his engagements and travels allowed. After months of misery, sickness, starvation and intermittent voice lessons, Ruffo finally confronted his teacher with the bare facts: he would either make his debut immediately and start to earn money, or he would have to return to the forge and hammer and permanently give up the dream of a singing career.

Casini understood. A seemingly endless series of auditions finally led to his first engagement. He made his debut on April 9, 1898, at the Teatro Costanzi of Rome, as the Herald to the Lohengrin of Francisco Viñas, to excellent reviews. The performance was attended by his ever-skeptical father, two of his sisters (Ettore, who was in the army, couldn't get a leave), and his beloved mother who always encouraged him and never lost faith in his eventual success. Ruffo was twenty-one years old, and though aware of his inadequate musical training, began his career as a professional singer.

After a slow start in the lesser theaters of Italy, a career he did have, a meteoric one: blazing, comet-like, with a rapid ascent, a brilliant peak, and a long *coda* of accelerated decline. As others carry through a lifetime the inalienable treasure of a solid foundation, Ruffo's immense gifts were flawed by the absence of adequate schooling. Prodigious but improper use put undue strain on his magnificent voice. He sang too much, giving always the most he was capable of giving. Unprotected by a dependable vocal technique his voice did not enjoy the longevity it could have had. Eventually it became frayed, diminished in brilliance, and the lower notes of his range, which were never more than adequate, became less serviceable. He continued to sing until his early fifties; the audience reception was mostly warm, but the reviews became increasingly "mixed."

In its prime the legendary Ruffo voice was a formidable instrument. It combined clarion power, a bronze-hued helden-baritone timbre, a range up to a recorded A flat and a reported high C, a fine, ingratiating resonance, and an incisive vibrato not unlike the sound produced by a master cellist on one of Stradivari's rare cellos. His singing was further enhanced by exemplary diction and an absence of obtrusive mannerisms. He was particularly proud of his uncommonly beautiful enunciation of Italian; his two published recordings of Hamlet's monologues—Shake-speare's, not Thomas'—are a pleasure to hear, despite the unidiomatic presentation, contrary to what Anglo-Saxon ears are accustomed to.

In the absence of formal schooling or adequate specialized training, his characterizations were rooted in his inborn intelligence and artistic instinct. His rapid rise in the world of opera made him conscious of the position he had attained. Determined to maintain it, through hard work, self-education and with the help of some fellow singers he became and remained a conscientious artist who always did his homework in preparing for his roles.

A chronological analysis of his recordings discloses the curious fact that he arrived at a definitive interpretation of his roles early in his career. Once he had formed a character to his own satisfaction, he would seldom deviate from the model. He might change some of the details, but the overall conception would remain unaltered. His recordings of "Largo al factotum" are all different yet all similar despite the many years that separate them. His introverted, prayer-like "Dio possente" from 1915 may have a more moving immediacy, yet this Valentin is the twin brother of the one who recorded the same aria in 1922 with minor changes and only slightly less emotional involvement.

Every Ruffo recording thrills the listener with the magnificence of the voice the same way it must have thrilled an audience in the theater. The palpable, sensuous beauty of the stupendous voice shaking the rafters must have been an exciting experience. At times it gives the impression that the music serves the voice and not the other way around. The records amply demonstrate the reasons for his universal success and his enduring fame. But the same records also disclose some shortcomings suggesting that the criticisms leveled at his interpretations were by and large justified. His Rigoletto is impressive and powerful but not moving, his Iago more nasty than evil, his Don Giovanni gallant but not seductive. He glories so much in the impact and natural beauty of his large voice that he is often oblivious to some of the fine details of the music. For this reason he was generally more successful with straightforward, un-complicated characters with simple, well-defined emotions: his Escamillo is swaggering, his Nabucco imperious, his Nelusko taunting. The some-times monochromatic effect of his interpretations is well—if uninten-tionally—brought out by Vincent Sheean: "When I think of Ruffo it is of a frightening presence and some equally frightening tones—*Rigoletto*, nothing else, and perhaps I never saw him in anything else."[2]

At the same time there is written and recorded evidence that there were numerous exceptions to this apparent rule. When he threw himself heart and soul into a role, he was able to find all its subtleties and convey unsuspected depths of characterization. He successfully captured the many moods of the title role of Thomas' *Hamlet* despite the limitations of the music. It was, by all accounts, one of his best roles, a personal favorite and often, though not always, an artistic and critical triumph. His Tonio was also an acclaimed, almost clinical portrayal of a retarded man victimized by the powerful emotions of lust, frustration and re-venge. The model of his characterization was a half-wit he met by chance on a mountain road in Italy and whom he observed on several successive days as he passed along the same path each day. (This utilization of a live model for the creation of a stage personality is described by Ruffo's good friend, Fedor Chaliapin; he based his Don Basilio on an unkempt Spanish priest who once sat across from him on a train in Spain.) Ac-cording to all contemporary accounts it was a masterful interpretation, both vocally and histrionically. Posterity is the poorer that its visual as-pects were not captured on film and that the "Prologue" is the only recorded excerpt of the role. Outstanding as it is, it cannot possibly suggest, much less recapture, his conception and delivery of the role in its entirety.

Titta Ruffo is remembered and admired more for his life's work than for a particular interpretation. There is no operatic character exclusively associated with him, with the possible exception of Hamlet, a role he "owned" during the best years of his career. He recorded most of Hamlet's music and with his retirement the opera virtually disappeared from the international repertory, leaving insufficient opportunity for live or recorded comparisons. That Ruffo failed to set unattainable standards in his best roles, and was not entirely successful with some others, was owing to his limitations rather than to laziness or a lack of effort. He is remembered as a scrupulously conscientious, hard-working artist, who gave the same attention to acting, costume and makeup as to musical matters. If any discussion of Figaro first brings Stracciari to mind, if one tends to identify Rigoletto with Gobbi, it does not reflect negatively on Ruffo. The artists of these two convenient examples had the benefit of leaving to posterity a complete recording of their best roles on disk and, in the case of Gobbi, also on film. Yet the enthusiastic, glowing reviews Ruffo consistently earned in such disparate roles as Hamlet, Rigoletto, Figaro and Tonio speak of his abilities and versatility as a singing actor. It also deserves mention that the majority of his recordings were made relatively early in his career, without the benefit of the maturing process the repetition of a role gives an artist. He recorded most of Rigoletto's and Hamlet's music when he was barely thirty years old, the latter within a year of undertaking the role for the first time. The two excerpts he rerecorded in 1920, "Pari siamo" from *Rigoletto* and the *Hamlet* "Brindisi", show an interpretation enriched by many subtleties during the intervening years.

Rating Ruffo below the supreme exponents of the roles in his repertory still keeps him close to the top, within the small and distinguished group of all-time greats. His position in the history of great operatic singing is also assured by the fact that any mention of the baritone voice *per se* makes one think of Titta Ruffo, first and foremost, the same way as Enrico Caruso has been and will remain *the* tenor. In coloring and resonance Ruffo's voice was a unique, matchless organ; in its prime it had a haunting beauty, unmistakable and unforgettable timbre, exciting brilliance and formidable power like none other.

Much of Titta Ruffo's private life is well documented in his literate and candid autobiography, *La mia parabola*. This book, written by a man—as it has already been mentioned—without any schooling, has been continuously praised ever since it was first published in 1937. As recently as 1975, the well-known Italian musicologist, Eugenio Gara called it in his *Cantarono alla Scala* "maybe, and without maybe, the most fascinating and best written autobiography left by an Italian singer to his admirers."[3] Even though as the title clearly implies, the singer was aware of the parabolic nature of his career, the critical acclaim notwithstanding, he is guilty of omission in his autobiography. He only writes about his long, arduous ascent, but he is disappointingly laconic about his engagements past his apprentice years, and about artistic and interpretative matters in general. It may have been modesty that compelled him to silence about his brilliantly successful middle period, and regrets that withheld his pen from narrating the details of his years of decline. The narrative ends in 1924, and left without the descending curve of the *parabola*, the reader does not get the full story of his career from the singer himself.

Another subject notably absent is any mention of his political views. It is not surprising if one contemplates the omnipotence of the fascist regime at the time the book was published and the singer's well-known antifascist attitude. His most painful experience with the evils of the fascist state was through a family tragedy, when his brother-in-law, the Socialist leader Giacomo Matteotti, was abducted and murdered by the Fascisti. As reported in the August 21, 1924, issue of the *New York Times* (p. 2, col. 3) the baritone was singing Rigoletto in Bogotá when a cablegram reached him about the disappearance of Matteotti. As no understudy could be found, he finished the performance, but wanting to be near his sister, he left immediately for Europe. Arriving in time for Matteotti's funeral, he was a pallbearer for his slain brother-in-law, just as he carried the remains of his great friend Enrico Caruso three years earlier.

In 1925, yielding to popular requests, he sang two performances of *Hamlet* in his native Pisa. When a plaque commemorating the occasion was installed on the Teatro Verdi, it was destroyed by a band of Blackshirts. Outraged by this vandalism, Ruffo vowed never to sing again in fascist Italy—and he never did. Because of his political beliefs he became a target of the regime and the victim of pro-fascist demonstrations at home and abroad. He had to endure the humiliation of physical violence (in Marseille), denunciation by *agents provocateurs*, the revocation of his passport, and even temporary incarceration. Trapped and harassed in his own country, his days of glory all behind him, and having to endure the discomfort, deprivations and dangers of the war, the singer knew trying times during the years of fascist rule. A Captain Henry Pleasants of the advancing U.S. Army, a former music critic and future writer, published the following candid and none-too-flattering vignette in the December 11, 1944, issue of *Opera News*:

Ruffo is in Florence, very much the grand old man and finding plenty of nourishment for his vanity among the worshipful Florentines. I visited him only once and didn't enjoy the occasion especially. He insisted on behaving as if it were an interview and lectured me on the glories of the past, the iniquities of the present, the nature of art, etc., etc. As his observations were not especially profound I found this rather trying. He looks very well and speaks the most beautiful Italian I think I ever heard. Wants to do Boris at the Metropolitan. I told him Pinza was the Metropolitan's present Boris, and this prompted quite a long and not inaccurate critique on the art of Mr. Pinza. A fine voice and a fine figure, said Ruffo, but... *"Senza dolore."* He was remarkably unenthusiastic about de Luca's accomplishments in singing at his advanced age. All very well for the concert hall, he thought, but for the theatre you need—here he extended his fist in the traditional manner of Rigoletto advancing to the footlights to assault the Vendetta....

While this excerpt is incorporated here merely to add dimension to the image of Ruffo off stage as viewed by others, Pleasants' description of the "grand old man" must be taken with some reservation. It does not correspond with the perception of others, Italians and foreigners who met him during this period. Pleasants' statements can be ascribed to a personal bias and his loyalty to de Luca at whose house he spent the previous summer as "practically a member of the family. He sang for me and I sang for him, etc.," he writes in the same article, extolling the merits of the aging singer's voice; thus his resentment over Ruffo's remarks is all the more obvious.

The majority of biographical writings that deal with the artistic aspects of Ruffo's life are in a language other than English. Some of these have been translated for the first time specifically for inclusion in this anthology. The English version of *La mia parabola* that already exists in manuscript fell outside the scope and objective of the project that produced this book. The present volume aimed to assemble the sporadic and extremely elusive material that was available in English, at the same time trying to cover most aspects of his life. The editor is particularly grateful to the singer's son, Dr. Ruffo Titta, Jr., for his willingness to contribute an article as a tribute to the memory of his father. It is an honor to have been able to include his writing.

This book is offered to the many admirers of Titta Ruffo in the hope that it will satisfy, at least partially, their interest in a remarkable artist. At the same time, it should prompt other researchers to collect and publish additional material relating to his life and career, as much for the benefit of music scholars as for the enjoyment of operaphiles.

Notes

1. Titta Ruffo, *La mia parabola; memorie* (Rome: Staderini, 1977), p. 43.
2. Vincent Sheean, *First and Last Love* (New York: Random House, 1956), p. 42.
3. Eugenio Gara, *Cantarono alla Scala* (Milan: Electa, 1975), p. 12.

Titta Ruffo

AIDA FAVIA-ARTSAY

"Florence, July 23, 1953.... It seems impossible that the great Maestro is no more.... He passed away during the night of July 5, at 2:30 A.M., of angina pectoris. On the previous day he had a presentiment of his death. That morning, in spite of rain, he went to the *caffè* (in Italy the meeting place of men). There he saw his lawyer and immediately asked him to his house for the purpose of making out a will. The attorney expressed surprise at the rush. After dinner he called his doctor, who after a check-up found his heart and health in good condition. In taking leave from the physician he said: 'To think that some believe I am eternal; instead I must die, like all others, by law of nature.' And he added: 'How I wish I could die on the stage, while reciting Hamlet's monologue *To be or not to be....*'

"He spent the remainder of the day with these sad thoughts, and in the evening instead of retiring at 10 o'clock, as was his custom, he stayed up until midnight listening to Beethoven's 'Moonlight Sonata' and Chopin's 'Funeral March' and to a reading of the life of Baudelaire, for he loved suffering and always said that without pain no creativeness is possible. At midnight he fell asleep and around 2:00 A.M. he called, then angina pectoris did the rest. Despite all the affectionate care and the injections that the doctor gave him, the venerable Maestro soon expired....

"Titta Ruffo was buried on July 8, at the Monumentale of Milan. He

Courtesy of Aida Favia-Artsay. Originally published in *The Record Collector*, June 1951, and in *Hobbies* magazine, October 1953. Reprinted by permission of HOBBIES, the Magazine for Collectors from October 1953 issue. Courtesy of James F. Dennis, editor, *The Record Collector*.

is survived by his wife, Lea; a son, Ruffo, and daughter, Velia, both married; and sisters, Fosca, Settima and Nella, all with families."

The above are parts of a letter written to me by a close friend of Titta Ruffo, who assisted him in his last moments.

Two years ago I wrote Titta Ruffo, reminding him of our old acquaintance and asking him to give me some information on his life and career for an article. Shortly after, I received his reply which said in part: "I read with great interest your articles...and thank you very much for wanting to write an article about me....I am happy to be able to satisfy your desire to possess my autobiography, of which I was able to find a copy; and I'm sending it to you today so you may have the information you want.

"I am deeply moved at the remembrance of your father, and of you as a child...and from your writings I feel that you are a true artist and know thoroughly the art of singing, for only thus is it possible to write with so much knowledge and feeling."

This letter was followed by a beautifully autographed copy of Titta Ruffo's own book, *La mia parabola*.

After the article had appeared in England, in *The Record Collector* of June 1951, I sent the celebrated baritone a few copies of it and received the following answer: "...I thank you infinitely for the wonderful resume of my life which I read with much interest for its historical truthfulness...I hope some day to be able to personally express to you all my admiration."

Now that this unique artist whom I always revered is gone, all I can do to honor his memory is to give excerpts from the article he liked.

* * *

"Ma quella non era una voce, quella era un miracolo!"

So exclaimed Giuseppe de Luca when I asked him what he thought of Titta Ruffo's voice. "Even now," he added, "his terrific LA can bring down the roof!"

I played for De Luca some of Ruffo's recordings—those that best display his amazing upper range. "No," he said, shaking his head, "no matter how good, Ruffo's records fail to do him full justice." And he concluded: "His was the greatest baritone voice I ever heard!"

How right that great man was. As an artist of comparable stature he stated in a few words the essence of Ruffo's supremacy. That miracle of a voice—stunning in its wealth of throbbing opulence—when unrestrained, simply poured forth in torrents of dazzling tone. Even in its most lyrical moments it never lost that shimmering fullness. To me it suggests a chalice of massive gold brimming with heady *spumante*.

...Titta Ruffo has graciously sent me his book, *La mia parabola*.[1] In making use of this fascinating work, I had to limit myself—with regret—to the incidents that have direct bearing on his career and therefore are of paramount interest....

Ruffo Cafiero Titta was born in Pisa, on June 9, 1877. In a few years his family moved to Rome where his father Oreste Titta, a master-worker in wrought iron, became proprietor of a shop connected with an orphan asylum where boys were taught useful trades. His mother and five other little Tittas—Ettore, Fosca, Nella, Settima and Velia—completed the family. When on the way to fame, Ruffo Titta decided that his name was more euphonious when inverted and that is how he became known the world over as Titta Ruffo.

The family was not prosperous and Ruffo's childhood was not a happy one. This great artist whose beautiful Italian is one of the assets of his art, and who converses on academic subjects and quotes Dante, Carducci and Hugo—has never attended school! While his brother was being thoroughly educated, little Ruffo, at the tender age of eight, became a tiny factotum in a blacksmith's shop, in order to help the family budget with his fifty *centesimi* a day. Shortly he began working for his father until resentful of paternal abuses he ran away from home. He returned to his father for a while, but finally went on his own. His artistic ironworks are still greatly admired in Italy and abroad.

Meanwhile Ruffo heard his first opera at the Costanzi: *Cavalleria*, with Bellincioni and Stagno. Deeply moved, he discovered that night that he was a tenor. But due to the impurities inhaled at work his voice became raucous and aphonic, and the budding dream of becoming a singer was abandoned.

His eighteenth birthday brought his first love affair. However, he was soon cured of this widespread malaise. He also met Oreste Benedetti, then a student at the Santa Cecilia and later a famous baritone. Ruffo, impressed with his voice, was describing it at work with a phrase from *Belisario*, when lo and behold his own meek tenor turned into a thundering baritone. That was the birth of what De Luca termed "the miracle voice."

Then—Santa Cecilia. This is one incident I would like to elaborate upon. First, because the facts are usually distorted and second, to give a picture of the fabulous Persichini—teacher of Battistini, De Luca, Marconi and scores of other male luminaries of the opera—and the way he conducted his class at the Santa Cecilia. De Luca told me that Ruffo was not expelled, as it is often believed, but left of his own free will. And here is the story according to Titta Ruffo himself, which I am translating from his book. After he relates his successful examination with "Sei vendicata" from *Dinorah*, which led to his admission to the Conservatory;

the rejoicing of his family, and his father's chagrin at the son's prospective absence from work three times a week two hours each time, the great baritone continues:

"At the Conservatory the three classes of singing for men were held by the professors Ugolini and Persichini. I was assigned to the latter, who kept me during the first months simply as a listener. The lessons began at nine-thirty. Persichini always arrived on time. He was a handsome man, about sixty-five, tall, with wavy hair carefully parted in the middle; big white moustache, which he twisted continually, and a pointed beard *alla Napoleone III*. He usually wore a black coat and vest, striped pants pressed to look in the front like two razor blades, and shoes, also black, that announced his arrival beforehand. He was the prototype of a man of the *ottocento*. The pupils were very obsequious with him. They rose when he entered the classroom, and one took his gloves, another the high-hat, a third the cane.... Then he would ring the bell for his coffee. He would sip it slowly, often looking complacently at himself in the mirror and finally, would pull out a white handkerchief, wipe his mouth, gently parting his moustache, and return it into his pocket, with a little white triangle showing. For all this *messinscena* he would employ about twenty minutes. Then he would sit at the piano, pulling up his pants diligently to conserve the crease, limber his fingers with a dozen scales and call the first pupil.

"If I remember correctly, Persichini's class was then composed of seven pupils: three tenors and four baritones. It resulted that by beginning the lessons at about ten and ending them at noon, there was barely time for each to study a little over a quarter of an hour. The pupil that absorbed the Maestro's greatest care was Giuseppe de Luca, who, already having five years of study to his credit, was then going over the operas.

"Often his lesson alone would last three-quarters of an hour. So for the others there were left but ten minutes for a few vocalises; and sometimes it was so annoying to stay there all those hours without accomplishing anything that I would begin yawning and, at times, would even fall asleep. On the other hand my absence was felt in the shop and there were continual recriminations from my father over my not being at my place. Often at the conservatory I did not only feel annoyance, but anger and fury as well, against so much loss of time. And to top it all, the Maestro Persichini did not like me, and when he deigned sometimes— I was admitted, remember, just as a listener for the first months—to make me do a few vocalises, he would find my voice drowsy and would predict that I would never sing as a baritone. When I thought that, according to rules, I would have had to ripen for six years at this Purgatory rather than Conservatory, I felt depressed....

"When I began my regular lessons, one-quarter of an hour of vocalises every morning, the Maestro insisted that my voice was that of a bass and sought to educate it as such.... Thus rose between us the first dissentions. Meanwhile, my economic condition was becoming more and more distressing. At times I did not have with what to pay the modest monthly tuition. As a regular student I remained there about seven months. I did not even take the examination for the second course of singing."[2]

Here Titta Ruffo narrates about his studies of solfeggio and piano—obligatory at the Conservatory to all students of singing—and how his toil-hardened hands would not respond to the keyboard. He tells how much he liked and how well he did at the recitation class conducted by the well-known Virginia Marini, and concludes by saying that were it not for this bit of encouragement he would not have lasted at the Conservatory as long as he did.

In the period that followed Ruffo saved a little money by working extra hard, bought himself some clothes and set out for Milan, with a letter of introduction to Lelio Casini. The famous baritone had nothing but praise for the young Ruffo's voice and agreed to train it upon his return from an engagement. Meanwhile, our hero's funds were dwindling fast and he soon found himself going for days without food. So, to occupy himself, and also learn the artistic life, he would spend his time in the traditional *Galleria*—the refuge and meeting place of all the artists, from the most illustrious to the most obscure. There, sad and lonely, he would watch the strutting *divi* and listen to their "You should have heard me take that note" tales.

It was during this winter of 1897 that according to Titta Ruffo he made his first recordings...for Columbia! I confess that this bit of information astounded me. But let him tell the startling tale himself:

"...I went directly to the *Galleria*. By chance I met the Roman baritone Oreste Mieli, who, having remained without engagement in Milan, and in order to earn something, had employed himself with the newly rising Columbia Company, to find beginners with good voices. He proposed that I should sing some records, which would have served me as advertising and to show how my voice reproduced, as well. I accepted on the condition that I would be quickly given some money. Mieli did not lose time and leaving me said: 'Wait here for me, I'll be back in a quarter of an hour and will accomplish something.' In fact, after about twenty minutes he came back breathless, invited me to follow him and on the way explained to me that it was necessary to show my voice before talking about money. He convinced me by saying that other artists, already established, had begun gratuitously. I confessed to him that I did not have one *soldo* in my pocket, not even to buy a stamp for a letter to my mother, and I showed him the letter that I had in my pocket. We came, without my noticing it, to a side street of the Corso and entered a sort of a dark, first floor office. I was presented to the director. After a long preparation, having tried singing with the piano, here I was before some sort of a long iron funnel. I incised my voice several times. I saw that the thing was not easy as I had to continue singing for about two hours. 'It is a matter,' said the technician, 'of finding the right sound of the voice.' And so, in all, I sang seven or eight pieces. At the end I was very tired and asked for some recompense.

"After long discussion with Mieli, I, who ten years later signed a contract with the Gramophone Company and with the Victor Talking Machine Company of New York, for a goodly sum, had to content myself with twenty lire."[3]

And the next chapter begins: "The New Year's day of 1898 signalled the beginning of my career in the lyric theatre..." and continued: "I remained in the *Galleria* an hour. The incision of the records, which had succeeded magnificently, had procured me a certain popularity; some congratulated me upon the success."[4] The twenty lire earned from those recordings, by the way, was the first money earned by the voice that was later to prove a gold mine.

The time was coming for Ruffo to make his debut. He was signed up by the impresario Bolcioni—himself a baritone—for a company he was just forming. His teacher, Casini, would have preferred him to study a little longer, but rejoiced at the news, just the same. At the same time he got another contract with the impresario Cavallaro, through the help of his friend Emanuele Izquierdo, for a year's tour of the South of Italy and Sicily.

Titta Ruffo made his debut at the Costanzi of Rome, in the spring season of 1898, as the herald in *Lohengrin*—with Viñas, Di Benedetto, degli Abbati, Gnaccarini and Spangher; Mingardi conducting. And Ruffo, in his own words: "...represented amongst them the last wheel of the cart."

After the performance, all the singers congratulated the newcomer. Viñas said: "I've never heard a baritone voice like yours. If you study and conserve it you have much glory ahead of you."[5] That season Ruffo appeared in seventeen performances of *Lohengrin* and several of *Lucia*.

From then on it was smooth sailing. Arena of Livorno, in *Trovatore*, *Lucia* and *Rigoletto*; followed by the Politeama of Pisa, in *Trovatore* and *Lucia*. In October, 1898, the contract with the Cavallaro Company came into effect. First stop—the Comunale of Catanzaro, in *Forza del destino*, with Ester Adaberto and Emanuele Izquierdo; and *Bohème*. Then the Nazionale of Catania, in *Bohème, Ballo in maschera, Ruy Blas, Gioconda* and *Rigoletto*; and the Comunale of Acireale, in *Ballo in maschera*. Followed the Comunale of Salerno, the Brunetti of Bologna, the Garibaldi of Padova, the Regio of Parma, the Tosi Borghi of Ferrara and the Carlo Felice of Genova—at the latter in *Traviata*, with Angelica Pandolfini and Elvino Ventura. Ruffo was constantly adding more roles to his repertoire and more appearances to his credit.

al più eletto degli artisti: al buon Titta, offre
quale ricordo di quella data che nell'avaldo del Re
al courtanzi di Roma, regnava il primo passo
del suo glorioso camminio.

Il Lohengrin di quel giorno, l'amico di
sempre e ammiratore.

Francesco Vignas

Roma — marzo 1911

2. Francisco Viñas in the Title Role of *Lohengrin* (Lisbon)
   Photo: Vasquese
   Courtesy of Ruffo Titta, Jr.

Chile—Santiago and Valparaiso, the first of numerous engagements in South America. Italy, and a few appearances in *Otello* at the Verdi of Pisa, followed by *Ernani* at the Della Lizza of Siena.

1900, Massimo of Palermo, to substitute for Sammarco in *Rigoletto*, and Giraldoni in *Tosca*. Both these famous baritones proved very kind to their new colleague—Giraldoni even lending him his help for some stage business in the second act of Tosca. By then Ruffo's fee had mounted to one thousand lire for six performances. Next—Fenice of Venezia, as Conte di Luna and as Lucifero, in *Il Santo* by Ghin.

Covent Garden. There our hero's stay was, to say the least, an eventful one. He made his debut in *Lucia* and then sang his first Figaro, with Barrientos, Bonci and Antonio Pini-Corsi; conductor Mancinelli. Pini-Corsi helped a great deal with his knowledge of the traditions of the *Barbiere*. And then the unexpected happened. Ruffo was asked by the management to sing in a performance of *Rigoletto*, not stipulated in his contract, because Scotti, whose part it was, was taken ill. Ruffo accepted. The performance was to be in Melba's honour. Ruffo was presented to the diva, but at the orchestra rehearsal he had to sing the duets alone since, to Mancinelli's displeasure, Madame had refused to participate. The third act Ruffo sang *a voce spiegata*, and after "Miei Signori" the chorus joined the orchestra in what turned out to be an ovation. Next day, Ruffo, upon arriving at the theatre, saw that Scotti's name had replaced his in the programme. Resentful, he asked the reason for the change. The director, with the utmost calmness, informed him that Madame Melba did not intend to sing with Ruffo because he was too young to sustain such a part, and that she herself had asked Scotti to make an effort and sing as well as he could, to which Scotti, to please her, had agreed. Ruffo blew up! The director did not understand the epithets the baritone hurled at him in his best Italian, but had them translated and forthwith decided to sue. After the scene, Ruffo was joined at his hotel by Pini-Corsi, who told him of the director's decision and strongly advised him to leave London—the sooner the better. Pini-Corsi further explained to Ruffo that the reason for the hullabaloo was his mistake in using full voice at the rehearsal. He had paid for approval of the orchestra and chorus with the suppression of his name from the programme and the posters. Ruffo left London that very afternoon.

Several years later Ruffo was singing in *Africana*, at the San Carlo. Melba, who after a visit to Amalfi, Sorrento and Capri, was passing through Napoli enroute to her native Australia, attended the performance at the invitation of the director De Sanna. She expressed her enthusiasm for Ruffo's Nelusco and returned to hear his *Hamlet*. After the third act, De Sanna relayed to Ruffo, in his dressing room, Melba's request to sing Ophelia to his *Hamlet*. And Ruffo coldly replied: "Tell Melba that she is too old to sing with me."[6] Revenge is sweet, at times.

After the unfortunate incident in London, a very successful 1901-02 season in Egypt, in Cairo and Alexandria at the latter as the High Priest in *Samson*, with Virginia Guerrini; then Marcello, Iago, Telramund (no longer the Herald) and Kurwenal, with Borgatti as Tristan.

April, 1902—Buenos Aires, with Darclée, Garbin, Stehle, Borgatti, Cucini, Ancona and others of equal calibre. There, at the Colón, he appeared in *Aida, Trovatore, Africana* and *Zazà*. Then Egypt again, for the 1902-03 winter season.

One day in Milan, Ruffo was seated at the *Caffè Biffi*, when he was asked to audition for Toscanini, at La Scala, for the part of Rigoletto. That afternoon, with the accompanist Lorenzo Molaioli, he presented himself before Toscanini and Gatti-Casazza. He sang "Eri tu" and "Miei Signori." The result was a ten thousand lire contract for the La Scala 1903-04 season, to appear in *Rigoletto, Germania* and *Griselidis*. And to prepare for his debut at this major temple, a holiday at the Val di Ledro.

During the course of this story there were other holidays—by choice or otherwise—but I mention this one in particular as an illustration of Ruffo's keen powers of observation and deep grasp of human emotions, which made of his stage characters real beings, beautiful or ugly as they may be.

At a mountain crossway one night he met a man coming down with a bundle of wood tied with cords passed under his arms. His appearance struck Ruffo. Short of stature, with inflamed eyes, a nervous tic in the right shoulder, blisters on the lower lip, several front teeth missing, reddish hair, low forehead—the whole aspect and attitude was that of a mentally deficient. As he stopped to rest, Ruffo spoke to him and for an answer got a moronic toothless smile. Next day, Ruffo returned to the same spot hoping to see again the character that fascinated him so. The man came again, and stopped, smiling idiotically. Just then appeared a young peasant girl, also carrying wood. The poor miserable looked at her with an expression mixed with anguish and desire. He touched her, she repulsed him with disgust and walked away, leaving him gazing sadly after her. This was Ruffo's unsurpassed impersonation of Tonio—even to the last detail of the makeup.

To brush up before the great event—six performances of *Nabucco* at the Rossini of Venezia. Finally—La Scala, in *Rigoletto*. The critics disagreed in their opinions, nevertheless between *Germania, Griselidis* and *Rigoletto*, Ruffo gave thirty-two performances, of which seventeen were of the latter.

Firenze—four appearances as Rigoletto at the La Pergola; and in the autumn of 1904, in modern repertoire, at the Lirico of Milan.

Hardly a singer of merit missed Russia. So, in the winter of 1904, Ruffo arrived in the snow-covered Odessa. The success of the new baritone was such that he sang up to four performances a week, alternating

between *Rigoletto, Barbiere, Ballo in maschera, Trovatore, Zazà* and *Demon*—
the latter for the first time. Then St. Petersburg. Great success in *Rigoletto,
Trovatore, Otello, Barbiere, Demon* and *Linda di Chamounix*. There his fee
rose to six hundred rubles for each performance.

Paris—the fabulous Italian season of 1905, at the Sarah Bernhardt,
directed by Sonzogno. Came for the occasion Mascagni, Giordano and
Leoncavallo. In the roster, among others, were Lina Cavalieri, Regina
Pacini, Angelo Masini (then over sixty), Caruso, De Lucia, Garbin, Bassi,
Ruffo, Kaschmann and Sammarco. Ruffo, who was engaged mainly for
the part of Gleby in *Siberia*, sang it with such success that "La conobbi
quand'era fanciulla" had to be repeated. More glory in *Fedora*, with
Caruso; and *Barbiere*, with Masini.

Milan, and a visit from Victor Maurel, who told Ruffo that a more
prodigious human throat he never heard. *Le Jongleur de Notre Dame* at
the Lirico, and again St. Petersburg, in *Demon, Rigoletto, Trovatore, Pagliacci, Barbiere* and *Otello*; followed by a tour through Kharkov, Kiev,
Moscow, Tiflis and the Ukraine. His fee now reached one thousand
rubles for a performance (a small fortune in those days).

San Carlo of Lisbon, in his first *Hamlet*; and the Casino of Monte
Carlo, in *Ballo in maschera, Don Pasquale* and *Barbiere*.

Lirico, in *Zazà*, with Carelli and Schiavazzi. Then the Imperial of
Vienna—one performance of *Rigoletto* with Caruso. Russia again in 1906-
07, and back to Italy. Here Ruffo's life was obscured by a tragedy. A
famous prima donna, his devoted friend and guiding angel, died. Ruffo,
heartbroken, took to drinking and left the stage. One day, Sonzogno
called him over, reprimanded him for his behavior and bid him to return
to the strait and narrow path. And as an inducement promised to stage
Hamlet for him, at the Lirico. This began Ruffo's rehabilitation. He not
only took himself in hand and gave up drinking, but also realised the
necessity of a moral base for his life, and with that came a desire for a
family of his own. Shortly afterwards he was married and the union was
blessed with two children, Velia and Ruffo junior.

The last to sing *Hamlet* in Milan was Maurel, at the Dal Verme. Ruffo's
Hamlet at the Lirico was eagerly awaited. Leoncavallo assisted with the
messinscena. Liliana Grenville was the poetic Ophelia. In the theatre were
present all the singers of Milan, amongst them Renaud, Sammarco,
Giraldoni, Amato, and others from the pleiad of baritones. That night
Ruffo attained the height of his artistic achievement, and his popularity—its apex.

1907-08.—Bucharest, Warsaw, Lisbon. Real of Madrid—*Rigoletto*, with
Anselmi; with King Alfonso XIII and Queen Eugenia Victoria attending.
Ruffo returned to the Real for several consecutive years, appearing in
Trovatore, Linda, Don Carlos, Africana, Tristan, Aida, Barbiere, Falstaff, Bohème, Gioconda, Tosca, Andrea Chénier, Pagliacci, Hamlet and *Rigoletto*. He

sang repeatedly at court, receiving magnificent presents. King Alfonso, upon learning that Ruffo's hobby was stamp collecting, presented him with the first four stamps ever issued by the Spanish Kingdom. The famous torero Gallito killed a bull in Ruffo's honour and threw him his gold-embroidered mantels; and the great Mazzantini presented him with the rich costume he wore at his last *corrida*. On one of the performances in his honour, Ruffo was made a Commander of one of the four military orders of Spain.

Monte Carlo—*Linda, Cristoforo Colombo, Otello, Gioconda* and *Barbiere*. Buenos Aires—*Hamlet, Rigoletto* and *Barbiere*. Between 1908 and 1913 Ruffo appeared at the Colón in *Otello, Pagliacci, Paolo e Francesca, Gioconda, Africana, Aida, Don Giovanni, Don Carlos, Falstaff, Boris Godunov, Thaïs, Demon, Andrea Chénier, Cristoforo Colombo, Tristan, Tosca* and *Bohème*. Besides Buenos Aires—Montevideo, Rio de Janeiro, Santos and São Paulo.

In 1909, in Rome, while living in Mascagni's villa, Ruffo was asked by the Maestro to take part in a concert, in honour of the Tsar Nicholas II, at the Castle of Racconigi. Other participants were Farneti, Parsi-Pettinella and Grassi. In 1911, thirteen years after his debut at the Costanzi as the Herald, he returned there as Hamlet. 1912—Paris, *Hamlet* at the Opéra.

1912—North America. *Rigoletto* in Philadelphia, on November 4th, and immediately a contract with Victor. Then, a special performance of *Hamlet* at the Metropolitan, on November 19th. He was met with hostility by Gatti-Casazza and the singers but was saved by the huge attendance of the Italian element. Enormous success! Kolodin, in his book *The Story of the Metropolitan Opera*, writes: "On November 19th Titta Ruffo made his first appearance in the Metropolitan, the opera being Thomas' *Hamlet*, with Zeppilli (Ophelia), Huberdeau (Claudius) and Eleanore de Cisneros (Gertrude)...Ruffo's success was tremendous; and contrary to Campanini's practices, he repeated the Drinking Song at the close of the second act...."[7]

Chicago Opera Company, 1912-13, 1913-14 seasons; debut with *Rigoletto*, on November 29th. Edward C. Moore, the veteran music critic of the *Chicago Tribune*, writes in his book *Forty Years of Opera in Chicago*: "...But what a sensation he was when he first appeared! Apparently he had been born with a highly efficient knowledge of the stage as applied to several Italian roles, and his voice made his hearers weep tears of pure joy. Then and thereafter its most effective range was its upper octave, but that octave was almost enough to eclipse memories of Tetrazzini the season before. It had a B flat in it, and it could hold its own against any orchestral din that Campanini chose to invoke....

"So *Rigoletto* with Ruffo in it was suddenly converted from just another Italian opera into a shuddering masterpiece of tragedy. Then there was the curious mutilation of Shakespeare's masterpiece which Thomas chose to consider an opera, having cut out about half its plot and all its psychology, and Ruffo in spite of a greatly uneven performance as the prince of Denmark triumphed again. Finally, and most sensational, the Tonio of *Pagliacci*.

"No one else had ever done Tonio the same way. Ruffo's Tonio was mournful, tragic, imbecilic, trembling on the verge of epilepsy, a condition portrayed with almost the accuracy of a clinic. But it was a whirlwind of passion, and as far as the audience was concerned, it was a riot. They said that ushers gathered up split white gloves by the basketful after the performance was over."[8]

Moore mentions other operas in which Ruffo appeared—*Gioconda* (with Giorgini), *Cristoforo Colombo* (with Raisa), *Barbiere*, "in which Ruffo was immense," *Don Giovanni*, "a role which he should gently but firmly have been argued out of ever singing at all" and *Thaïs* (with Garden).

United States from 1913 to 1915, during which time he also organized two tours of operas in Louisiana, Virginia, Georgia, Colorado, California, Texas, Pennsylvania; and also Canada. He was elected honorary chief of a tribe of Colorado Indians.

1915—South America. Caruso and Ruffo in *Pagliacci*, first at the Colón[9] of Buenos Aires and then at the Solis of Montevideo. Those were sensational performances; the house was sold out in advance at fabulous prices. Two colossi outvieing one another—both conscious of the responsibility and both horribly nervous.

Meanwhile Italy had entered the war. In 1916 Ruffo went to his country and was assigned first to the 207 Reggimento Fanteria and, later, to the 33 Reggimento Artiglieria. The direction of the Paris Opéra requested the Ministry of War to release Ruffo for a performance of *Hamlet*, followed by *Pagliacci*.

War ended—Mexico. 1919-20 and 1920-21 seasons in Chicago, with visits to New York, in *Hamlet, Rigoletto, Otello, Pagliacci, Tosca* and *Edipo re*, Leoncavallo's last opera, which he wrote especially for Ruffo. During a performance of *Hamlet* at the Lexington of New York, in 1920, Ruffo, after the Brindisi, noticed in one of the boxes close to the stage, Victor Maurel. After acknowledging the applause he repeated the Song, directing his voice that time towards his illustrious predecessor. The two baritones were very devoted friends, and it was Ruffo's sad lot to sing at Maurel's funeral in New York, in 1923.

In New York, in 1920, Ruffo has a visit from Gatti-Casazza and an offer for the 1921-22 season, with the main purpose of producing *Otello* for him and Caruso. Finally the Metropolitan. Debut in *Barbiere*, on January, 19th, 1922. Besides Figaro, he was heard there, between 1922 and 1929, as Carlo V, Tonio, Amonasro, Carlo Gérard, Barnaba and Neri Chiaramantesi, in the first Metropolitan performance of Giordano's *La cena delle beffe*, on January 2nd, 1926. Ruffo tried to convince Gatti-

3. Titta Ruffo as Tonio in *Pagliacci* (Chicago)
   Photo: Matzene
   Courtesy of Horacio Sanguinetti

Casazza to produce *Edipo Re, Hamlet* or *Demon*, but in vain—the director was diffident. Ruffo's final performance at the Metropolitan was as Amonasro, in a matinee performance of *Aida*, on February 22nd, 1929.

Titta Ruffo sings in colours. He has created a palette—he calls it iridescent—of vocal sounds that bear the names of colours they most resemble. He explains it thus: "I strove to create, through my special technique, a real colour palette. With determined variations I made a white voice, then a dark and more intense one which I called blue. By enlarging and rounding the same sound I found the red. Then the black—the maximum of the dark....

"...What pleasure, when I noticed that I had succeeded in controlling my voice completely, and in perfecting the most difficult colours—blending the white and the blue with the red and the black, in a harmonious mixture....

"...I believe that a student of singing, after he has well implanted his voice in the fundamentals, from the lowest to the highest tones, always composed, free, supported; all gathered '*al disopra del palato,*' without muscular contractions, sustained only by the natural respiration—I believe, I say, that every student of singing, if gifted with feeling and imagination, that is, talent, can succeed with exercise in forming all colours of a sonorous palette, and thus express all the impulses of the soul, in all their shades and *chiaroscuri*. This, certainly, is neither easy nor quickly achieved. As Antonio Cotogni—one of the most genial and erudite artists—justly said: 'To perfect the human voice are needed two lives—one to study and the other to sing'."[10]

How well Ruffo's "*al disopra del palato*" agrees with Battistini's "*nella volta palatina*" and De Luca's succinct "*la sotto,*" pointing to the palate with his thumb. "At the top of the palate," "in the palatial roof," and "under there" (the palate) all mean the same thing—the starting point of the tone—under the tone height—against which beats the sound produced by the breath passing through the vocal cords and which, if unimpeded by unnecessary muscular contraction, acquires additional vibrations in the head chambers, resulting in a homogenous and perfectly balanced tone—a beautiful tone.

Of course, his powerful build and the singular structure of his head—an exceptionally high palate, wide cheek and nose bones and spacious head cavities—contributed immeasurably to the uncommon breadth of his stunning voice. Ruffo had the rare ability of producing a wide and, at the same time, well covered tone. His was the perfect example of singing forward and *nella maschera*. His tone was there before he attacked it; the vowel was formed before he articulated the consonant. Not the smallest part of his mighty resonators was left unfilled. Even in the softest passages—and he was past master of the pianissimi—he kept the position and never resorted to falsetto. As for his breath capacity and its conservation, they were marvelous. And his full-throated laugh, be it mirthful or mocking or sardonic, it was always as musical as his singing, and similarly produced.

Although equally at home in such unlike roles as Renato, Figaro and Gérard, Ruffo excelled in parts requiring interpretative dramatic singing and acting. He fused the music with the spoken word. His Tonio has never been approached, and as Iago and Hamlet he was supreme in his day. Ruffo was the Salvini of the lyric drama. His keen emotional perception and skill in modulating his voice; his sensitive nuances and consummate timing, united to give his embodiments a three dimensional aspect. And besides, his characters were all defined—he blocked them in definite forms and shaded them with contrasting values. This holds true for simple songs, also. One of my favorite records of Ruffo is his Victor "Non penso a lei." In the beginning he plays the nonchalant—why, the very idea, of course he does not think of the lady.... But in the end he does not leave the slightest doubt as to her whereabouts—and his—should he meet her with his rival. This 10-inch recording is so typical of Ruffo, and his voice in it is positively ravishing. A little misunderstanding with the orchestra in one spot disturbs the flow of the melodic line a bit, but such quibbles over the tempo are noticed in several of his recordings.

Titta Ruffo's Pathés present him at his not quite mature stage. More than anything, they are a promise of things to come. The gem is there but has not yet been polished or given an artistic setting.

Then came the 1907 G. & T.s, of which the best are "Miei signori," "Il balen"and "Dio possente." In the tumultuous and badly recorded trio from *Trovatore*, Ruffo has as partners his sister Fosca, and Izquierdo. The spectacular "Sì, vendetta," with Galvany, is just that, plus Ruffo's electrifying, blazing A flat. These early recordings display the advancing artistry that in 1908 Pre-Dogs reaches the peak of indisputable authoritativeness. Four of its worthiest examples—the *Hamlet* solos—reveal the reason for his superiority in that role. "Spettro infernal," Hamlet's invocation to the ghost of his father, is a sequence of imploring sentences—poignantly delivered—bidding him tell why he appeared. This in the score is followed by the murdered king's accusations, and then—"Spettro santo." Just a passage at the close of the first act but how much dramatic intensity this exulting promise of vengeance acquires through the outburst of Ruffo's vocal splendor and vibrating emotion. In the monologue, "Essere o non essere," Ruffo is the actor-singer par excellence. He is tired; he wonders, meditates—mostly in a bewitching mezza-voce. Through the pervading sense of weariness flows a never-ceasing undercurrent of emotion. "Come il romito fior" is a deep, eloquent expression of the unhappy prince's repentence, sorrow and love for his departed Ophelia.

The *Chatterton* is another superlative recording of that period. The role is that of a tenor and the pathetic "Tu sola a me rimani" is the swan song of the doomed poet who sees all his hopes of temporal happiness vanished. Ruffo sings it with lyric rapture to the ". . .*poesia, veste di Nesso ch'io non so strappar.*" Other excellent discs in this successful series are the magnificent "Cortigiani," "Per me ora fatale" and "Meriggiata." Of the two excerpts from *Malena*, by Ruffo's brother Ettore Titta, musically "Ma tu sfiorata" holds more interest. Ruffo evidently was fond of his brother for he often included his compositions in his concerts and recorded several of them. Of the duets incised at that time the best are "Dunque io son," with Galvany, which despite cuts and poor recording is one of the most exciting versions on records, "Nega, se puoi, la luce," also with Galvany, oozing with vocal grandeur—mostly on Ruffo's part, and the splendid "Lassù in cielo," with Pareto.

Amongst Ruffo's Gramophone Company discs released by Victor in 1912, in the United States, stands out his impeccable Prologo—two 12-inch sides. And on the Victors recorded in 1912, his voice was rapidly approaching its fantastic capacity, as heard in "Alla vita" and the two selections from *Zazà*: "Buona Zazà" and "Zazà, piccola zingara"—all arresting in their generous outpour of bubbling golden tone.

Ruffo reached the apex of his recorded vocal glory in 1914, when he made his thrilling *Dinorah*, the unique "Credo," the famous *Otello* duet with Caruso, the sensuous "Ecco, dunque, l'orribil città," the impressive "Aman lassù le stelle," the classical "Finch'han dal vino" and the astounding "Tremin gl'insani"—the latter as majestic and imposing as the temple Nabucco conquers. And it is not often one hears Ruffo sing a duet with himself as he does in this record. He begins with the recitative between Nabucodonosor—or Nabucco—the King of Babylon (baritone) and Zaccaria, the High Priest of Jehovah (bass). "Che tenti?" Ruffo thunders at Zaccaria, and as the bass continues: "Oh, trema insano! Questa e di Dio la Stanza!" "Di Dio, che parli?" he queries as Nabucco, in his best baritone. Then, again as the priest, he threatens: "Pria che tu profani il tempio della tua figlia scempio questo pungnal farà." And, finally, after Nabucco's aside, "Si finga e l'ora mia più forte scoppiera," he goes into his grandiloquent "Tremin gl'insani. . . ."

After making several records in 1915, amongst them Scarpia's Cantabile and the unaccompanied and difficult "All'erta, marinar"—two fine discs—Ruffo's recording career was temporarily halted because of the war. After his return to the United States he resumed his recording activities for Victor. By then his voice had become more mature and, at times, unsupported in the basses, but it still was a great and noble organ, resonant and free.

Between 1920 and 1923 he sang a number of praiseworthy records that included his one effort in Russian—the *Demon*. While the Italian language may sometimes be passable in a foreign born singer—especially one with other redeeming qualities—the Russian is Russian only by a Russian. Therefore, if a Russian piece is to be heard sung by an Italian voice—which is often desirable—it has to be accepted in its linguistic quaintness. Ruffo sings *"Nie plach ditia"* in the usual manner of an Italian singer singing Russian. That is the way my father sang it after living over twenty years in Russia, and so did all the other baritones who were there.

Among other records of this period were "Adamastor," "Pari siamo," "Nemico della patria?" "Son sessant'anni," "O casto fior," "Lo vedremo, o veglio audace," "Che fai tu qui?" and the two interesting recitations from *Hamlet*, released by Victor in 1924.

This group of the early twenties also boasted of a few extraordinary achievements worthy of special mention. Ruffo's insinuating "Era la notte" is devastatingly beautiful. His Iago is not bluntly brutal—he is a refined villain. He feels the ground, proceeds cautiously and carries out with unmatched finesse his suggestive narrative of Cassio's imaginary lust for Desdemona. He drops scented poison as he repeats the words of longing that Cassio supposedly uttered in his dream—soft, languorous, somnolent, charged with desire. There are no versions on records comparable to Ruffo's "Credo," "Era la notte" and its following "O mostruosa colpa," with Caruso.

Ruffo's Figaro—one of the best ever—is a gallant, rascally, lovable factotum; whilst his melancholy Dane's sorrow can't help but be drowned in the profuse flow of his tonal "liquore incantatore." From *Falstaff* Ruffo made two wonderful recordings. In his "Quand'ero paggio" he turns the clock back several years, so fresh is his voice. And in the mirror-like description he gives of Sir John's thinness when page of the Duke of Norfolk, words just fall off his lips, his diction is so clear. "L'onore! Ladri!" is again a tonal picture. Sir John's philosophising upon the usefulness of honour is skillfully portrayed by the baritone. Just listen how he changes the volume, texture and colour of his voice when describing parts of the anatomy, which—he strives to convince—the useless honour cannot replace. The last of his enumerations: "Nè un capello?" really acquires a hair-like thinness. And after commenting that the honour is not a surgeon but is merely "Una parola" (this, unfortunately for most baritones, ends in low A flat), he asks about the content of this word, and decides: "C'è dell 'aria che vola." No voice could portray better the lightness, clearness and motion of the air. In this soliloquy, as in Iago's narrative, are brought in use some of the subtlest shades from Ruffo's tonal colour palette.

Of his 1929 electrical *Africana* and *Andrea Chénier*, the latter is the better. Despite the spreading of tone and signs of wear, the voice is still beautiful.

Recently issued by the R.C.A. on L.P. and 45 r.p.m. the Ruffo-Gigli duet from *Gioconda* is indeed a welcome addition to the collection—it is finely sung and enacted. Let us hope that the other two duets with Gigli, from *Bohème* and *Forza del destino*, will also eventually see the light of day.

In every new crop of singers, there is bound to be a baritone with a healthy pair of lungs, and so we are excitedly informed of the appearance of "another Titta Ruffo." The same holds true for all the new Carusos and Chaliapins that sprout continually. This is amusing, but it may also prove tragic for the prodigy in question. Before long the "new discovery" begins to ape all the mannerisms of the singer he is supposed to resemble. But vocal characteristics fit only their possessors. And furthermore, anatomical structure of the vocal organs varies, and some natural peculiarities in voice production—effective and unpunished in one singer—may mean the ruin of another.

As time goes on, there will be other baritone voices—some different, some good and, no doubt, a few outstanding ones. But despite all the imitating in the world, there was and always will be—only one Titta Ruffo.

Notes

1. Titta Ruffo, *La mia parabola; memorie* (Milan: Treves, 1937).
2. Ibid., pp. 71-72.
3. Ibid., p. 87.
4. Ibid., p. 93.
5. Ibid., p. 103.
6. Ibid., p. 181.
7. Irving Kolodin, *The Story of the Metropolitan Opera* (New York: Alfred A. Knopf, 1953).
8. Edward C. Moore, *Forty Years of Opera in Chicago* (New York: Horace Liveright, 1930), pp. 105-106.
9. Only the first act of *Pagliacci* was given.
10. Titta Ruffo, *La mia parabola; memorie* (Rome: Staderini, 1977), p. 215.

The Incident in
Bogotá and Thereafter

RUFFO TITTA, JR.

Apart from a few references relating to later events, my father wished
to end his autobiographical narrative at June, 1924. There remained
thirteen years until the publication of the book and another sixteen up
to his death: in all a total of twenty-nine years. The readers of this re-
edition therefore expect some information on this ample segment of his
life.

I aim to satisfy this expectation as best I can with this new chapter by
returning to verified memories, letters, newspaper clippings, documents
found among his papers and elsewhere; but aware of its shortcomings
in comparison with the previous chapters [of *La mia parabola*] I beg the
reader to consider my modest contribution no more than a commentary,
necessarily less succinct than the rest.

* * *

For the completion of the picture of his artistic life I refer the reader
to the chronology of his career. From that it appears that the troubled
tour ended in the Colombian capital marking, in a certain sense, the
culmination of his parabola. As a matter of fact, his operatic appearances
became progressively less frequent and binding from then on, and in
the end virtually ceased, to be replaced almost exclusively by concerts
in his last years. I will therefore dwell chiefly on his personal life.

The reader of *La mia parabola* will not find explicit opinion of a political
nature, but has perhaps intuitively perceived on which side, as by some
atavistic force, were my father's heart and mind on this matter, already

Translated by George Nyklicek. Originally prepared for the 1977 edition of Titta Ruffo,
La mia parabola. Courtesy of Ruffo Titta, Jr.

prior to the assassination of his brother-in-law, Giacomo Matteotti. After that tragic event he wrapped himself in a pained and disdainful silence worthy of the immense respect to his departed relative.

The wave of indignation sweeping the country after the crime against Matteotti was so great as to end the days of fascism. It did not happen. Those who could have or should have seized the great historical opportunity to bring it down for once and for all did not want to or couldn't do it. The crisis resulted in a harsh strengthening of the chains of dictatorship. Returning to Italy to be close his sister, Velia, my father remained absent from the stage for about six months. In August of 1924, he took part in the funeral of his brother-in-law in the cemetery of Fratta Polesine.

He then resumed his artistic wanderings, with his spirit more hostile than ever toward those who had seized power at all levels and who had begun the systematic corruption of minds and moral principles, even defiling culture through the distortion of the arts. Yet he continued to believe in the sane principles hidden in the soul of the populace, so much so that in October of 1925, he did not refuse the public the service of his own art. After about a quarter of a century's absence he agreed to sing again in his own native city, appearing in two performances in the role of Hamlet, his favorite role. The audience gathered from everywhere, rewarding him with intense, warm enthusiasm, and his grateful admirers wanted to commemorate the event with a plaque in the Teatro Verdi. The "authorities" however, could not tolerate that an artist so well liked by the public should not allow himself to be linked to the "regime." Already in August 1926, a band of Blackshirts destroyed the plaque with hammer blows; I will describe this act of vandalism further on. That was the end. My father continued to reject attractive contracts from Italian theaters and repeated requests to sing at benefits, disgusted with the provocations and political compromises they involved.

From that time on his voice would be heard only outside of Italy, just as he lived most of the time outside Italy. He chose to live in France. When he was free of professional commitment, he would roam through Paris, where he always lived in hotels, in the Provence and the Côte d'Azur (Antibes, Cannes, Juan-le-Pins, etc.), and ended by taking up residence in Nice. In 1933 he allowed himself a long trip in Spain and a prolonged sojourn with friends in Great Britain, during which he gave a private concert and made his last recordings which remained unissued. But even his artistic activities abroad were bristling with pitfalls.

In August 1926, the Royal Italian Ambassador in Buenos Aires confidentially forwarded to the Ministries for Foreign and Internal Affairs in Rome numerous rumors, unsupported by any documentary evidence. These "confidential" rumors surfaced in the domestic-fascist papers. Titta Ruffo was denounced as a "distinguished scoundrel" and was accused of financing antifascist newspapers and having inspired some outrageous lampoon of the memory of the Queen Mother, Margherita of Savoia, that appeared in the Buenos Aires newspaper, *Italia del Popolo*. Reprisal came quickly: the aforementoned commemorative plaque flew to pieces. I remember how mortified my father was at the shabbiness and stupidity of the methods employed to injure him! Even some segments of the theatrical hangers-on conspired with the "regime" to prematurely eliminate from the marketplace those singers who were disturbing competitors.

On September 26, 1926, the Minister for Foreign Affairs, Dino Grandi, received a letter from the secretary general of the National Theater Guild, reading, in part: *". . . the Milanese atmosphere and especially our syndicate, are much aroused and have voted a strong Order of the Day. Because Ruffo, who recently returned from Argentina is to sail on the 6th to New York, I ask you officially to revoke his passport which would make it possible, here at home, to give him the lesson he deserves."*

The "regime" could not stifle expressions of dissent in the theaters abroad which were open to my father, but did not cease to use this form of molestation. Cries, such as "Down with Fascism! Viva Matteotti! Long Live Liberty!" uttered in the semi-darkness of a theater were countered by zealous signaling and intimidating actions by gangs around the villa in Rome, and by the revokement, effective or threatened, of his passport. The "regime" then exerted every possible pressure, at my father's expense, on his fellow countrymen who had any power in theaters abroad; these pressures were so effective that in 1929 they brought about the sudden cessation of every connection with the Metropolitan in New York, the theater dominated by the presence of Gatti-Casazza and the strong presence of Italians faithful to the "Roman salute."

The act of aggression in Marseille whose victim he was on February 18, 1931, should also be remembered. Its object was to prevent him from appearing in public in a city which had a large number of antifascists. But father did not let himself be intimidated by the anonymous letters and phone calls prior to the aggression, nor the blows and punches he received on the threshold of the theater as he was about to enter to prepare for the performance, not even by the faithless behavior of the impresario who was a party to the plot. Hiding the painful bruises on his head with hair and makeup, he wanted to face his audience. He was received with yells and insults by agents-provocateurs, blunted by the reaction of the numerous exiles present in the theater; but in spite of the considerable uproar instigated to silence his voice, he honored his contract and finished the performance of *The Barber of Seville* for which he was engaged.

1932 wasn't lacking in a macabre trick either: the announcement of his sudden death in Madrid, invented and spread by a branch office of the Italian press. The hatred for his dignified and immovable demeanor regarding the "regime" did not abate following his definite retirement from the stage. On the morning of October 16, 1937, in Rome, where he came for a family visit, he was taken from the house by two detectives; they seized his passport and after formalities at the police station he was sent to the Regina Coeli prison. There he was photographed and fingerprinted for the card-index of criminal records, they confiscated his money, cuff-links, collar buttons, suspenders and shoe-laces and threw him in a cell. "I found myself in a state of humiliating dismay," he later recalled, "forced to hold up my pants by hand, while my collar would stand open because of the missing button."

The arrest was due to two approximately identical denunciations: one from a certain Dr. Ubaldo Pera, dated October 10, on which could be read in Mussolini's handwriting: "Lock him up, M.," the other from the impresario Walter Mocchi, deposited on October 17. Here is the second one in its entirety.

In the year 1937 on the 17th day of the month of October in the Political Bureau of the Royal Police Station of Rome, before the undersigned official appeared Walter Mocchi, son of the late Luigi and Laura Nazzaro, born in Torino on September 27, 1871, residing here at 11 Piazza di Piscinula, who responded to questions as follows:

I have known the baritone Titta Ruffo for many years having had him under contract for various years at the Teatro Colón in Buenos Aires and other theaters of my concern. On the afternoon of October 7th I was on a train from Livorno to Rome, due to arrive in this city at 9:00 p.m. As I boarded the train and went through the corridors in search of a seat, I saw in one of the second class compartments the aforementioned Titta Ruffo in an animated discussion with passengers, unknown to me. I knocked on the window to greet him and he signaled me to wait. I then took a seat in the compartment of another carriage where I stayed for about an hour.

Around 7 p.m. stepping out in the corridor I met Titta Ruffo. After the usual greetings and after having spoken about the book he had just published I mentioned to him the formation of a motion picture company created under the presidency of Vittorio Mussolini, which proposed to produce operatic films. I stated moreover that production would begin with Rigoletto and therefore be a good opportunity for him to appear again.

To this he answered that he had already received a proposal from parties in Florence interested in the company to which he had given his firm refusal inasmuch as first of all he did not want to sing any more, and secondly and mainly because he did not want to have contact with the kind of people with whom he was incompatible. This circumstance gave Titta Ruffo the opportunity to show his political sentiments of pure aversion towards the Regime, which I had already noticed in conversations some years before in discussions of political matters in a hotel in Buenos Aires and again in Paris, on the occasion of a film which was to be made with him.

I thought it opportune at the time to point out the innumerable accomplishments of the Regime, the pre-eminent position in the world of the Fascist Government of Italy and other things, including education, both moral and physical, given to the Fascist youth. At this point Titta sprang up and censured the education of youth, and I can precisely quote his words as follows: "These youths are being raised as cannon fodder, ready for servility, without a sense of dignity, etc., etc." Then I pointed out to him that this youth, thus educated, in seven months had vindicated the disgrace of Adua [Abyssinia, now Ethiopia] and created an Empire; he brusquely interrupted the conversation and we parted practically without greetings.

I cannot state precisely whether on this occasion Titta Ruffo uttered the phrase "Country of abuses and insolence"; but the nature of the conversation as well as the tone in which Ruffo spoke of the Regime and the bitterness he had shown clearly implied that.

I do not recall if there were people in the corridor who could have overheard Titta Ruffo's discourse, except those passengers who passed through the corridor.

As soon as I finished my discussion with Titta Ruffo I returned to my own compartment and did not see him again. I do not know whether he had spoken to or met with other people.

Read, confirmed and signed by Walter Mocchi—Valente Donato, police commissioner.

The event became known to foreign journalists. The news provoked a sensation. Its effect wasn't slow in coming: after three days came the order of release, but, this time, the passport was not restored. Now he could no longer show that he had engagements outside Italy. Deprived of the status of an Italian living abroad and the liberty of not to live in a country dominated by a political regime he hated, he was forced to transplant bag and baggage from Nice to Italy. Rendering his existence more bitter, sad, disillusioning, an accumulation of the physical ailments of old age slowly set in, along with legal and fiscal problems inherent in the contracts drawn up in the United States, actions brought by malevolent persons, clouds of financial matters....

* * *

A review of the important events of my father's life cannot ignore a person linked to him with strong emotional bonds, and who comforted him in the solitude of his voluntary exile: a Rumanian immigrant to France, named Olga Isacescu. He had the good fortune to meet her in Nice. Olga was his faithful, devoted secretary, nurse and companion in the last eighteen years of his life, not far from the glories of triumphs and the adulation of his prosperous years. Discreet and unselfish, it was she who typed the manuscript of La mia parabola. After the death of my father she moved to Milan, although the climate of that city was not suitable for her precarious state of health, to stay near his mortal remains.

And there she lived in the worship of a memory until her death on March 2, 1981.

* * *

Deprived of his passport my father decided to move to the western part of the Ligurian Riviera. He eventually settled in Bordighera and in quiet concentration in that little town wrote the major portion of his autobiography. When the war between Italy and France seemed imminent—the border was closed—fearful of remaining isolated from his family and in order to be closer to Rome he did not hesitate to give up the quiet and the temperate climate of Bordighera so favorable to his health. With advancing years he suffered from an occupational disease, pulmonary emphysema and illness of the respiratory tract, and thus became sensitive to cold.

He then moved to Florence, never imagining that the vicissitudes of the war would make it difficult one day to maintain—and for awhile cut off completely—connections between Florence and Rome.

In Florence he bewailed the loss of the Riviera climate, but in recompense came out of the isolation in which he lived until then. In fact, he found the warmth of many friends, fellow artists and the comfort of a constant pilgrimage of visitors—Italian and foreign. It would be impossible for me to remember and cite them all. Confining myself to the world of opera I limit myself to naming only those about whom I am certain: the baritone Bechi, who was always close to him with affectionate devotion; the soprano Lina Cavalieri; the tenor Izquierdo; the baritones Mascherini, Montesanto, Silveri and Tagliabue; the tenors Lauri-Volpi and Di Stefano; the conductor Mugnone. During his years abroad, and after his definitive return to Italy, he never failed to rejoin the family he loved so tenderly. And when he was far away he always wrote many affectionate letters to my mother, to my sister and me; and complained if we did not repay him in equal measure.

On July 26, 1943, the news spread that Mussolini had been arrested; Titta Ruffo showed himself at a window and sang the "Marseillaise," to be joined immediately by a crescendo of voices thus celebrating liberty.

This was, indeed, the very last time that his voice resounded in public.

But the joy over freedom and the rebirth of peace was of short duration. On September 8 German troops invaded Italy, and on the 10th they occupied the capital and in a few days the entire country from the Alps to the so-called "Southern Kingdom."

Then began dark days for father and new great perils, the nazi-fascist "authorities" of Florence became arrogant. They began to torment him with invitations to sing in the radio and a refusal could cost him a high price indeed. There were grave moments of anxiety when he was advised to hide; he always found a safe refuge with trusted friends.

His first Florentine lodging was a bright little apartment, on the mezzanine floor of an old palazzo on the banks of the Arno. From the window he could enjoy the views of the nearby Ponte Vecchio. On the nights of August 3 and 4 the Eighth British Army penetrated the Oltrarno quarter of the city, the Germans retreated beyond the line of the river after having blown up all the bridges excepting the Ponte Vecchio. Passage was barred by the ruins of the surrounding palazzi which had been demolished by mines. The inhabitants had been given very short prior notice to evacuate their homes. After living for some time in precarious lodgings, he finally settled for good in an apartment in the Via del Campidoglio 4, near the Piazza della Repubblica.

* * *

The trivial—and only—experience with films in 1929 only strengthened my father's skepticism about the eventual success of cinematographic versions of opera sufficiently to refuse the most attractive offers of American producers determined to profit from the advent of sound-film, and wanting to exhibit on the screen complete operas such as *Carmen, Barber of Seville, Rigoletto*, and *Faust*.

Nevertheless, and especially after he left the operatic stage, he always longed to venture upon some nonoperatic film, as other famous singers have done, no more gifted than he in regard to photogeny and acting ability: Bechi, Gigli and Schipa, to mention only the Italians. There is evidence of discussions, preliminaries, and exchange of letters concerning numerous movie projects. I limit myself to mentioning a few promoters of such projects: Mario Bonnard, Pittaluga's director, for an eventual *Figaro* based on Beaumarchais' masterpiece, of a *Kean* by the elder Dumas; Jacques Prévert; Jean Renoir for a film based on *Les aventures du roi Pausole* of Louys; Arnoldo dello Sbarba, who was considering a production involving Roberto Rossellini; Vincenzo Tanlongo, who was thinking of a *Mastro Landi* with a screenplay by Giovacchino Forzano.*

Unfortunately the wish to appear on the screen also remained unfulfilled, for various reasons. The advent of the sound-film did not coincide with his vocal and physical prime. He was the first to be fully aware of it. His serious professionalism inhibited him from venturing into a cinematographic undertaking guaranteed by the prestige of his name more than by the intrinsic value of cinematic art.

* * *

*Librettist of Puccini's *Gianni Schicchi*.

My father had an infallible sense of intuition about history. Even when the fortunes of war seemed decided in the favor of the aggressors, he never doubted its final outcome. And when the "liberation" formally returned Italy to the rank of democracies he could not rejoice in it. He deplored the lack of profound, authentic renewal of laws and statesmen. "Cunning, servility, provincialism, superficiality, opportunism, subversion, in short, the old ailments of Italy are liable to be repeated, they are not vanquished. The Blackshirts moved about more insidiously than before, spread out and well camouflaged," he insisted.

He did propaganda work to gain voters for the Republic. A sympathizer of the partisans of the peace movement, he participated in the congress of this group held in Paris. In the beginning he followed with intense interest the main activities and manifestations of the progressive parties. He kept, however, within himself the spirit of complete freedom. He took no membership card. He did not solicit honors or an appointment for political merit. Disillusioned and embittered, he finally abandoned the political arena too.

On May 14, 1945, he had the great joy of an enthusiastic, warm reception in Pisa by his fellow citizens, on the occasion of the restoration of the commemorative plaque, destroyed by the Fascists, that was dedicated to him twenty years before.

* * *

Struck down by an attack of *angina pectoris*, Titta Ruffo died in Florence, in his own bed, at 2:30 a.m. on July 5, 1953. I was notified by phone in the middle of the night by Olga, her voice broken with grief. In the preceding days there were no warning signs of the possibility of a sudden end from such a cause. In observance of his wish, the body was transported to Milan, to the Monumentale Cemetery, where he rests alongside the remains of the beloved Benedetta.

* * *

After several years of absence, the news of his death suddenly brought back the name of Titta Ruffo to the front pages of the world press. His memory was accorded the most affectionate and universal recognition he could have received. Then began the long posthumous silence, broken every now and then by a radio broadcast of one of his records, by a short newspaper article, or some ceremony inspired by an anniversary date; it would be too long to enumerate all. Particularly warm, affectionate and consistent were those of his native city. On the anniversary of his death a street was named after him and a plaque was affixed to the facade of the house in which he was born. In 1961 a museum was opened in the Teatro Verdi which housed the greater part of his relics: costumes, operatic scores, gifts he received on his benefit nights, photographs, etc. And the tributes were repeated on the tenth anniversary of his death (orator Giorgio Gualerzi) and the twentieth (orator Gino Dell'Ira). I particularly cherish the commemorative ceremonies in Florence (orator Eugenio Gara), Moscow (orator Aleksandr Less) and Prague (orator Antonin Novotny).

In 1966 *La mia parabola* was published in Moscow; it was the first—and has remained until now the only—published translation of his autobiography. The Council of the Accademia di Santa Cecilia, on July 5, 1963, remembering the tenth anniversary of my father's death, proposed to the city of Rome that a street be named after him. The favorable decision of the City Council that followed on November 9, 1965 was fulfilled only a couple of years later. The tablet with the name of Titta Ruffo was placed—without any ceremony—in a new narrow street in the popular quarter of Primavalle, a zone whose thoroughfare the commission in charge of names, curiously enough, had reserved for the hierarchy of the Catholic church and personalities of Italian lyric art. Streets named for Popes, Cardinals, heads of religious orders, etc., are intermixed with streets commemorating singing celebrities of both sexes, Battistini, Caruso, Patti, and many others.

* * *

I feel obliged to mention at this point some of the most glaring inaccuracies, inventions, legends, etc., handed down either orally or actually in print, in regard to my father.

(a) The date of his birth is variously given as June 8 or June 10, 1876; this error in dates is particularly evident in the Anglo-Saxon literature and I cannot explain its origins. If my father's own assertions are not enough, I can guarantee that the exact date of his birth was June 9, 1877, as proven by unassailable documentary evidence. The date of his death is also variously given as the 6th as well as the 5th of July, 1953.

(b) It has been written, even in reference works (*A Concise Biographical Dictionary of Singers* by K. J. Kutsch and Leo Riemens, New York, 1969) that he thought of becoming an engineer and began course work towards that end at the University of Rome.

(c) According to an American journalist who visited him in Florence, at the end of his life Titta Ruffo was obliged to climb long flights of stairs to get to his apartment on the fourth floor, with the imaginable effect on his weakened heart. His last two residences in Florence were, however, on the mezzanine floors!

(d) Titta Ruffo never gave singing lessons; much less did he think of opening a "School of Singing." Neither did his brother Ettore, who taught for a long time in the United States, ever settle in Hollywood. When a journalist once asked him why he didn't give singing lessons, observing that he could have found plenty of affluent Americans willing to spend money to become his pupils, Titta Ruffo answered: "I never knew how to sing; that's why my voice didn't last beyond my fifties. I have no right to profit from my fame and try to teach something which I did not know how to do."

He always listened attentively and with sympathy to anyone wishing an audition and gave most generously of his time and counsel according to his own judgement, admonishing or dissuading the hopeful singer.

While on this subject, I think it would be of interest to cite part of a letter (dated November 8th, 1945) he sent to a young baritone on the eve of his debut in *Rigoletto*. He writes "Sing calmly! Pay heed to the cantabile passages with the soprano, seeking a mezza voce delivery, not too bright, as some baritones do at times; well accentuate the declamation in the 'Cortigiani' section; and put all paternal feeling into 'Miei signori' and the duet 'Piangi fanciulla', both of which epitomize the most painful and pathetic melodies in the opera; seek a soulful voice, all the secret is there, and also in the last act, accentuate the declamation in the recitatives and duet which precede Gilda's death. Sing! sing! and sing! with all human feelings. I will not come to the theater because it might make you nervous, but I will be there in my thoughts, with you. Remain calm, as if you were singing at home; your voice is an important one, and you will conquer. This is my wish. I embrace you like a son and God be with you. Titta Ruffo."

(e) Titta Ruffo never sang in *Pagliacci* with Caruso, exchanging roles! Neither did he sing music written for tenor (for example the "Siciliana" from *Cavalleria rusticana*) except as a boy. These are simply legends.

(f) An American journalist has written that Titta Ruffo finished his days reduced to misery, to the point that he had to sell piece by piece his costumes, swords, and objects which were souvenirs of his golden days. This touching on the subject of poverty is also repeated in the testimony of other visitors. The subject is always treated with dogmatic statements, at times seeking to paint an effective, emphatically dramatic picture. Yes, it is permissible to speak of a "financial parabola" in Titta Ruffo's life; it is enough to compare his sumptuous way of living during his golden period made possible by his large earnings with the forced parsimony, not without renunciation, of the postwar period. But from that to indigence there is a wide gulf! His costumes and theatrical memorabilia have always remained in the custody of the family. Most of them can be seen in the museum in the Teatro Verdi in Pisa. Some relics have been donated by his heirs to other theatrical museums, and some are still retained.

My father was not a shrewd, fortunate administrator of the fruits of his labors and art. He preferred to be paid in a lump sum for almost all of his recordings instead of a percentage. His savings, at one time considerable, were severely reduced by the 1929 Wall Street crash, by the drop of the Argentine peso in the last postwar period, and two great inflationary periods after the wars. In 1936 he sold the villa in Rome, investing the proceeds in real estate; even this new source of income dried up, owing to rent control regulations.

(g) To crown it all, in a book (*Tutti sulla mia barca* by Silvio Gigli, Milan, 1976) one can read that the author-interviewer was presented with the following string of pearls by Titta Ruffo: "I sang the Verdi *Requiem* and the one by Mozart like nobody else in the world. I knew Pope Pius X and his parents. In a concert on September 22nd, 1905 I sang, and encored, an "Ave Maria" before the Pontiff, who later received me in private audience...; I had cried out to his face 'down with the priests' and then discussed with him spiritual problems. The next day, in order to be pardoned, I sang a "Hymn of Praise" to the Madonna at St. Peter's which was recorded on discs."

It is superfluous to add any corrections. Moreover, the same engaging author warns the reader in his foreword to the book frankly, and not very subtly, that his story has a "pinch of fantasy" in it. In recounting his meetings with Titta Ruffo he was obviously carried away in his imagination.

And now, in conclusion, a last clarification to disperse any hopes fed by inaccurate information.

Some years after the publication of *La mia parabola* my father took up his pen again every now and then, for his own pleasure, to try his hand at some fiction. It was nothing more than an attempt to escape the sadnesss of the interminable hours filled only with memories. As he himself asserted in the preface to *La mia parabola* he did not nurture "literary ambitions," nor did he ever express to me the intention to release those pages. Therefore no one should expect anymore the posthumous publication of Titta Ruffo's writings.

4

Ruffo Titta—His Personality

CLARE P. PEELER

There is a story about a Polish emigrant who, not so long arrived on our shores, was required to fill out a census blank. He did so in his own peculiar way. Opposite "Name" he wrote "Rabinski"; opposite "Born" he wrote "Yes"; opposite "Business," "Rotten!"

If Titta Ruffo had to fill out such a blank he would have to write opposite "Name" "Ruffo Titta," for that is his proper designation. That is, "Titta" is actually his family name, but as it is also a familiar surname in Italy, the baritone turned his full name about so as to avoid confusion. Opposite "Born" he could unquestionably write "Yes"—no one in this world can be more full of the joy of living in it. As to "Business" almost every one has heard by this time about that $2,000 a night. Only two living artists have as good a financial return made them for their wonderful gifts to the world. Nothing about him is more amusing than his naive enjoyment of that fact.

When one first meets Signor Ruffo it is to be impressed just by that boyishness, that naivete. It does not seem possible that this medium-sized, powerful-looking young man, with his dark, curly hair, carefully divided above his broad forehead, who stands hesitatingly before one, could be the world-famous Italian baritone. He is so obviously uncertain what to do. But he sits obediently, as if to pose for a picture, and at intervals regards one sidewise out of long, clear blue eyes, then gets back into the proper pose for a world-wonder.

Suddenly, however, a chord is touched. New York, which has evidently appealed immensely to his imagination, is mentioned. "Ah, New York! I figure it to myself as one great man," he says, in rapid French. "It

Courtesy of *Musical America*. First published in *Musical America*, December 27, 1913. All rights reserved.

is like the Colossus of Rhodes, standing in the harbor with arms out-stretched in welcome!" His eyes brighten, enlarge; a smile of singular sweetness is displayed. He begins to talk quickly, with many gestures, and then it is you see the dramatic power of the man struggling to free itself. Presently he slips into a more natural position, in a seat nearer to you, and is no more Ruffo the baritone being interviewed—he is Ruffo the artist free to talk of what interests him, and a most charming person he becomes.

We touched on many subjects when we talked together at our first meeting—he with his friend, Mr. Younger. The facts of his birth in Pisa, thirty-five years ago; his early training in his father's Milan iron works, his leaving that decidedly unmusical employment at fourteen to study music, his failure at the Santa Cecilia Conservatory in Rome, his sub-sequent training under Signor Casini, and his marvelous successes af-terward in South America and in Europe—these were all known. That he had a wife and two children, to whom he is devoted, living in Rome, one also knew. But there were other topics of interest, his favorite roles, for instance.

Hamlet, it appears, he prefers above them all, with *Rigoletto* a close second. He is a most ardent student of Shakespeare, incidentally. But the very intensity of the demand which such roles make on him requires, so it seems, some comedy work as a reaction and this he finds in *The Barber of Seville*. Mr. Younger had related that Ruffo's animal spirits were the joy of all who came into contact with him; that his gaiety was so real and so charming that where he was no one could be dull. Looking at his laughing face, alit with the mere thought of the fun in *The Barber*, one could well believe it.

He was asked if he cared for the role of Escamillo in *Carmen*. "Not very much," he replied. "There is not enough for me to do. But I do like to sing it," he added boyishly, "because a great Spanish toreador once gave me such a beautiful bull-fighter's costume!"

His first real success was gained when he was twenty. At that time he sang the Herald in *Lohengrin* at Rome to the Lohengrin of Viñas, the great Spanish tenor. After the performance Viñas, himself applauded to the echo, had taken time to praise the green youth Ruffo and to prophesy for him a great future. Last year, when Ruffo, the idol of his audiences, sang at the Real, in Madrid, Viñas came to the baritone's dressing room. All the great tenor said was: "Did I not tell you so?"

As to Ruffo's musical ancestry he seemed to know nothing. His father had no singing voice, and no special interest in music. "But my mother," Ruffo said in Italian, "She had a voice magnificent." A brother, Ettore, who accompanies him this season on his American visit, adopted music teaching in Milan as a profession. He had indeed "practised" on his

4. Titta Ruffo as Escamillo in *Carmen*
   Courtesy of Kurt Binar

brother Ruffo to the extent of greatly assisting his musical development and has himself written an opera.

Just here Ruffo introduced a diversion quite his own. "Ecco, Signorina," he said, impressively holding up his hand. In perfectly correct English he said, laboriously: "Two br-r-others—four sisters," and then leaned back in his chair with a sigh of relief. He so evidently considered those four words of English an achievement beyond any triumph of bravura singing that all laughed outright. In spite of his American sojourn he has not added largely to this accomplishment, but his stock of English largely consists of "How do you do?" "I thank you very much," and "Good bye."

One was at loss to account for Ruffo's splendid physical development, seeing that he confessed his favorite diversion to be stamp collecting, which could scarcely be classed as violent exercise. It appeared, however, that his physique had been developed originally in his father's iron works, where he attained considerable skill. Of this skill the tomb of Sadi-Carnot, late French President, bears token in the shape of a crown of iron and copper wrought by Ruffo. All the iron work on his Roman villa was designed by him, but days of his handicraft have gone by. Since he has taken to creating golden tunes instead of iron crowns he keeps himself physically fit by long walks.

Tea was brought by his valet and served just as we began discussing opera houses. He had at that time not yet sung in North America, and his favorite house, acoustically, was the San Carlo in Naples. Of La Scala at Milan, the Colón at Buenos Aires, of the Real at Madrid and of the great Paris Opera House he spoke with admiration for their wonderful construction.

He had heard of the comparative coldness of North American audiences and seemed a little apprehensive. Yet two nights later one of the coldest audiences in the United States went mad over his Rigoletto, and the cries of "Bravo," "Encore, Ruffo," sounded over the storm of clapping.

5

Analysis of
Titta Ruffo's Handwriting

UMBERTO ELLERO

A curious item in Titta Ruffo's estate was a graphologist's analysis of his handwriting. Dr. Ruffo Titta, Jr., who was kind enough to place it at the editor's disposal along with his father's manuscript sample on which it was based, was unable to provide any information concerning its provenance. It is not known who Umberto Ellero was, where and when the analysis took place, or whether the graphologist knew the singer before he saw his handwriting.

Regardless of whether one believes in graphology or not, this document is not without interest. Dr. Titta is of the opinion that the graphologist was on the mark with his observations and agrees with his conclusions.

5.   A Sample of Titta Ruffo's Handwriting
     Courtesy of Ruffo Titta, Jr.

The handwriting with the frequent angular lines is indicative of a strong personality and an inflexibility concerning decisions. Furthermore, the harmony of the handwriting indicates that the strong personality is complemented by a sense of honesty that bears the stamp of his conscience and profound spiritual convictions.

The handwriting is rather large—a characteristic that reveals a strong awareness of his own worth almost bordering on pride which drives him to continuously improve himself. This characteristic does not bring harm to others; it is a noble ambition that also carries the likelihood of personal sacrifice rather than hurting someone else in its attainment.

These important disclosures of the handwriting, further emphasized by the thickness and weight of the strokes, indicate innocence, honesty, and credulity, accompanied by and confirming an enthusiasm that borders on the excessive.

The large and heavy handwriting also reveals by its evenness constancy and faithfulness, the sort that indicates highmindedness and a kind disposition.

The slight indication of the letters suggests sensitivity which, however, does not reach extreme passion or go beyond reason.

There is, finally, a gradual diminution of the letters within the words (the French call it *gladiolée*) which denotes sensitivity and a refinement of spirit.

(Signed)Umberto Ellero
Translated by Andrew Farkas

6

Titta Ruffo
Beyond the Limelight

RUFFO TITTA, JR.

Andrew Farkas, originator and enthusiastic editor of this collection of writings about my father, Titta Ruffo, has urged me to add the finishing touch to his work with a personal contribution from me. In yielding to his request, I first of all wish to express my appreciation and deepest gratitude for his arduous work accomplished to render homage to the memory of my father.

What could I add to this collection, I, who am neither a specialist on the subject, nor have inherited my father's literary gifts?

I will try, as sparingly as possible, to mention those things that should answer the questions of those interested in the life stories of the interpreters of the lyric stage, concentrating on the more intimate and human aspects of Titta Ruffo, the private person. However, I will not repeat anything I have said already in the Epilogue and notes I wrote for the new edition of my father's autobiography[1] which I published in celebration of the centenary of his birth, as this Epilogue, translated for the first time into English, is reproduced elsewhere in this volume.*

I will begin with his physical appearance and the distinctive characteristics of his personality. He had an average and well-proportioned build and measured gestures, yet he wouldn't pass unnoticed. He was a handsome man with a bright smile; he had a broad forehead, shiny dark chestnut hair, deep and pensive eyes. He was scrupulously clean about his person and about his clothing; he liked to dress with quiet elegance and fitting for the occasion. I never saw him unkempt. He spoke without the inflections of a dialect, with a clear and rhythmic diction. A brilliant conversationalist and blessed with the gift of mimicry, he could hold a listener spellbound, arousing emotions or hilarity by telling anecdotes

Courtesy of Ruffo Titta, Jr. Translated by Andrew Farkas.

*Chapter 3, pp. 29-39.

6. Dr. Ruffo Titta, Jr.

from his life, stories, jokes, or doing enormously successful imitations. Had he not been blessed by nature with an exceptional voice, my father probably would have become an actor.

Essentially extrovert by nature, he was subject to periods of deep depression however, and while it lasted he would isolate himself in profound silence. He loved his family with unwavering tenderness. Throughout his life he never failed to be near his loved ones with profuse letters full of feeling. He had passionate and emotional crises outside the family. He nurtured a particularly overpowering love for his chosen art, and this explains the dissatisfactions and existential anxieties that clouded the end of his career and the years that followed, up to his death.

Profoundly honest and free of malice, he behaved, until given evidence to the contrary, as if everyone were like him. Yet it wasn't easy to be on a first name basis with him and to gain his friendship because he considered it an extremely serious sentiment, but once granted, he became a faithful and steadfast friend. In support of this assertion it is sufficient to recall the proof of friendship given to Maestro Leoncavallo. The latter wanted to compose an opera suitable for Titta Ruffo's talents. My father promised to sing it for him. And he kept his promise, even though posthumously as far as Leoncavallo was concerned, and after having waited for the opera for years, at the cost of financial sacrifices on top of it, following Leoncavallo's caprices in regard to subject and librettist, having gone from a *Prometeo* by Colautti to a *Papa Lebonnard* of Illica, ending with *Edipo re* of Forzano. In short, Titta Ruffo was very patient and it must be said that he really felt a great affection for his friend to stand behind him throughout this erratic itinerary. In the end he had to struggle to have the opera accepted and performed, since apart from a few attractive pages of genuine merit it was devoid of inspiration and originality.

Titta Ruffo did not like to listen to his own recorded voice. After his death—keeping in mind that in 1953 78 rpm records were already rare and many of them deleted from the catalog—I found only very few records among his belongings. I discovered, with surprise, his lack of interest in their preservation; he had given away almost all of them. Prior to attaining the supreme splendor of vocal art, in a frustrating, perpetual strife to reach and perfect it he used them for self-criticism. Later, perhaps, he held some sort of subconscious grudge against them. Yes, they did make his voice known and popular throughout the world, but at the same time they represented heavy and indestructible touchstones whenever he had to confront his public, ready to judge him in a live performance. Finally, as he walked the long, descending path of his parabola—to borrow an image from the title he himself had chosen for his autobiography—those records began to awaken in his soul the con-suming reverberations of a past that could not be recaptured.

It will surprise the reader that I heard my father sing in the theater only once, and I will explain the reason for that. He practically stopped singing in Italy in 1914 when I was barely four years old, and when I grew up he would not allow me to interrupt, for any reason, my studies that kept me tied down, directly coinciding with his foreign engagements. He was not quite so demanding with my sister, and thus she had the good fortune to hear him in public more than once.

The only occasion when I heard him was in Pisa, in October 1925, in an evening performance of Thomas' *Hamlet*. My sister and I arrived in Pisa in the early afternoon of the performance, but could embrace him and talk to him in his dressing room only after the second act which has the famous "Brindisi"; only then had my father freed himself from the state of acute anxiety that gripped him for long hours before the per-formance. I attributed it to the exceptional circumstances surrounding the event. He was appearing on stage in front of the public of his native city after an absence of some twenty-five years, and he knew that I was about to hear him in public for the very first time. My mother, the only person he wanted at his side before the performance, and my sister too had assured me, that before facing the judgement of an audience Titta Ruffo was always stricken with a nervous panic, and the more he ago-nized awaiting the trial the greater his successful acquittal would be. Naturally, I heard him sing often in the intimacy of the home. I re-member him in particular immersed in the study of two roles new to him: Edipo, the title role of the aforementoned opera by Leoncavallo (1920), and Neri Chiaramantesi of *Cena delle beffe* by Giordano (1925). He would set himself with serious, total, I could say merciless dedication to the study of a role, the choice of makeup and appropriate costumes, immersing himself in the part and its interpretative problems. He would go over the music hour after hour, accompanying himself on the piano; he would seldom require the assistance of an accompanist.

Titta Ruffo grew up basically as an autodidact; self-taught, guided by intelligence, singular instinct and intuition. Self-taught was the superb singing-actor, the sincere autobiographer, the modest pianist accom-panying his *vocalises* and studies of scores. No school can boast having molded him as its pupil, nor, on the other hand, did he ever claim to be the student of any particular maestro, especially not in the field in which he excelled.

He was a loner in the theatrical world. Whenever he was engaged for some time in a city, he would prefer to rent a furnished apartment rather than stay in a hotel. Not in order to economize, but to feel more isolated and undisturbed. He never thought of cultivating "public relations," promoting interviews, or trying to gain favors or approval of the press, or visits to those in influential circles. He liked to entertain, but his invitations were never self-serving. For his professional needs he would always engage a simple assistant with the duties of secretary, interpreter, and general factotum.

As soon as he had the means, he wore costumes made to measure and accessories furnished by the best tailors. This reminds me of the long and laborious preparations under his personal supervision as enormous trunks and baskets, containing all the necessary things, were readied for shipping.

His retiring nature may, in part, explain why there are fewer books and articles about him than those devoted to other singers. My mother, for many years the valuable and prodigious helper and advisor during his career, often reproached him for his lack of concern about publicity, and she called my attention to the fact that the critiques were always significantly less warm than the reception of the public which filled the theaters, the scenes of his triumphs.

He was always an avid reader, preferring plays, poetry, novels and biographies of the classic authors. He liked to watch motion pictures and stage works performed by true actors from whom he could learn, and he regretted that he could seldom indulge in this diversion.

His autobiography clearly reveals that Titta Ruffo did not live through the experiences appropriate for one's youth. Still a boy, he went from the manual labor of the workshop to the boards of the theater; he never had the time to participate in sports with any regularity. He loved the sea; he liked to row and swim, but he did both with impetuous vigor and scant style. He was skilled at some games now obsolete, like the "tamburello" played outdoors, and Italian billiards. Poker was the only card game he played, or, rather, he amused himself with poker. He never ventured into a game with strangers, his partners were always friends or acquaintances, playing for modest stakes. He did have a driver's license but I don't recall ever seeing him at the wheel.

He enjoyed good food; in later years he had to renounce this pleasure for medical reasons and to avoid obesity. He was a moderate wine drinker but never touched hard liquor. I never saw him smoke. At the beginning of his career he was an enthusiastic stamp collector and eventually he owned a valuable collection, most of it given to him as gifts on the occasion of benefit performances. He lost interest in this hobby when he discovered that some of his rarest stamps had been stolen by a foreign maid who had suddenly disappeared and could not be found, and in the end he sold the collection. He liked to adorn his home with antiques carefully chosen with an eclectic taste: paintings, sculpure, furniture, tapestry and ceramics.

He wasn't very fluent in foreign languages. He could manage in Spanish and French, but he always had difficulty with non-romance languages.

He was reluctant to talk about the theater, especially at home; in his correspondence he would restrict himself strictly to the private side of his artistic activities. I don't remember a malevolent remark about a fellow-artist ever to leave his lips; his innocent parodies of some of them cannot be considered as such. Pettiness being alien to him, he would accept it as typical of his working ambience (jealousy, envy, gossip, and the like) and as human weaknesses not worth discussing.

One could ask me what was his relationship with his two great contemporaries, Caruso and Chaliapin. I know that he loved, respected and admired them. Their photographs were kept in a place of honor in his study. He owned their most noteworthy records and would listen or make others listen to those, rather than his own. I had the good fortune to meet Chaliapin; I met him when he came to Rome in April 1929 for two performances of *Boris Godunov*. Papa also happened to be in the capital in those days. The entire family attended both of those memorable performances. Papa and Chaliapin spent long hours together, at home and on excursions around Rome. In short, it seemed like a meeting between two old fraternal friends.

Hospitable by nature, my father welcomed all kinds of composers, musicians, writers, painters, sculptors and actors, but I recall only a few singers among them.

My father wanted to keep me alien to the theatrical world; the self-taught man was very severe, I must repeat, in demanding that I pursued my studies with seriousness and obtain a university diploma. "If my son had a voice," he used to joke, "I would scratch his vocal cords!" He maintained that a singing career demanded too high a price of renunciation and hard work from anyone who wanted to pursue it with a serious commitment. And he could not conceive of a life led without seriousness and commitment.

In the last years of his life if the subject came up, Titta Ruffo would willingly discuss the theater; not so much the personalities or his own experiences as its general problems, like the crisis of the development of opera, the scarcity of great voices, the brevity of careers as compared to the past; the importance in the modern economic world of opera production in regard to directing, scenic design, costumes and even orchestra; the decline of managements and the rise of opera societies. And he gave to all problems pertinent explanations, based on astute observations.

To those interested in the religious beliefs of Titta Ruffo I can readily say he was not an atheist. He respected and admired in a certain sense all the great religions. He considered them the greatest movers of human affairs, of the history of mankind, and he recognized their indubitable value of thought and ethics which they represent. At the same time he did not accept either the dogmas or the organized church, the source of power and wealth; he did not allow men to arrogate the mission of mediators and representatives of divinity. He believed in a superior, inscrutable transcendency. He prayed in solitude, in the depth of his own conscience, far from the churches.

In politics he held purely libertarian feelings; I think it was a paternal inheritance. Freedom, justice and brotherhood were not empty words for him but fundamental, inseparable values. At heart he always felt himself closer to the people, the defenseless and the poor than to the powerful.

I hope this panorama of recollections, although brief and sketched without too much organization, has succeeded in casting light on one truth: that Titta Ruffo deserves to be remembered and honored not only as a singer of historic significance, but as an above the ordinary human being as well. And, in giving this testimonial, I have done so with a clear conscience of having presented accurate recollections, with a mind yet undimmed by age and a heart unveiled by filial love.

Rome, December 4, 1980

Note

1. Titta Ruffo, *La mia parabola; memorie* (Roma: Staderini, 1977).

7. Titta Ruffo in 1919 (Chicago)
    Photo: Matzene
    From the collection of Andrew Farkas

Titta Ruffo

R.D.

On the exact stroke of 12:30, per appointment (this was some little while ago) a representative of the *Musical Courier* knocked at the door of 1808 Congress Hotel and was received by Paul Longone, representative of Titta Ruffo, the world renowned baritone. After renewing acquaintances with the distinguished artist and his wife, the four of us sat at a lunch table where the following interview was granted.

"Are you glad to be back in Chicago, Signor Ruffo?"

"Yes, very glad, especially after the royal reception your public accorded me when I made my reentree last night as Tonio in *Pagliacci.* Really such an ovation as the one given me, moved me to tears and it was with difficulty that I could proceed. I have received similar demonstrations elsewhere, but only after singing or doing a bit of acting that pleased my audience, but I believe it was the first time in my career that I had such a welcome on my appearance on the stage."

"Well, you see," ejaculated the representative of this paper, laughingly, "you are another 'T.R.' are you not?"

"Maybe, as my dear sir, I have often been called 'T.R.' and I was quite flattered, knowing that those two initials are also those of one of your greatest men, the late and lamented Theodore Roosevelt, for whom I have always had the greatest admiration, not only as a politician, but also as a man."

"How long have you been away from Chicago?"

"Six years, and many events have taken place since then. For quite a while, I was away from the stage completely, being a soldier under the Italian flag, and like an athlete, I found it hard to come back. You see, in everything in life you must be in training and when once you let go

First published in *Musical Courier*, March 11, 1920.

you find it a rather difficult task to train again. I am now in fine form but was not at my best when I first reappeared on the operatic stage. I was out of practice and had to get in shape again before being able to please myself, and as I am probably my most severe critic, I know what I can do and what I cannot do."

"What roles do you like the best?"

"Rigoletto, I prefer of all my parts. You see this is a very interesting character to portray. I have read Victor Hugo's *Le roi s'amuse*, and I have studied the part as would an actor. As a matter of fact, I always study my role first as to action and to words, leaving the music for a later period. Then after reading carefully the role, I memorize the words. No singer today can be a success on the operatic stage through his voice alone. The days are long gone by when an artist could win the continual favor of an audience through the sheer beauty of an organ. Today the public wants actor-singers and the public is always right."

"Did you study acting?"

"Certainly. I even played on the legitimate stage. With Gustav Salvini, the son of Tommaso, I appeared in Buenos Aires in *Amphion*, winning at the time a rather pronounced success in the drama."

"May I ask you to what, besides your voice, do you attribute your wonderful success?"

"An artist brings to the public the force that nature has given him, besides magnetism which is a wonderful quality for any public man to possess. You take two orators, for example, who will have to say the same words in a speech; both will say them differently. One will put it over, the other will not; yet both men will be capable, but one has magnetism and the other only force. One has a beautiful speaking voice, the other uncommon, but the one who has magnetism, the one who understands his public, will be the victorious one in that oratory contest. So really I attribute my success not so much to my voice, as to my general makeup."

"So you think strength one of the big assets for an operatic artist?"

"Surely, just as much as weakness is an asset."

"This is interesting, why weakness?"

"For contrast, my dear sir. If an actor singer would use, through an opera, only strength of speech as well as action, he could neither render the thought of the composer, nor of the librettist. His song would be monotonous and his action commonplace."

"I have heard that you were an enemy of conventionalism, Signor Ruffo, is that true?"

"Absolutely. I believe in individualism. To be a success on the stage, one must have a personality, but that personality must always be subdued by the role. To make myself clearer, I would say that when I played

Tonio in *Pagliacci*, I am no longer Ruffo, but Tonio a half wit, who has little to recommend him to the sympathy of the public. When I am Rigoletto, I am no longer Ruffo. I forget myself and the same exists when portraying any other role. I care not for what another artist has done in the role, though often I profit by others. For instance, before studying the role of Hamlet, I went and saw the best Hamlet of the day in Italy and in France on the legitimate stage in these countries and when I came to America, I made it my business to see Sothern in the same role, and by that visual study of the role without copying in any way their presentations, I found in them many touches well deserving exploiting when appearing in the same role in Ambroise Thomas' opera. As far as my costumes are concerned, I oversee their making. Speaking of *Hamlet*, for instance, the costume that I wear in the third act is an exact reproduction of a picture of Hamlet that I saw hanging in the Florence Museum."

"You surely are a student."

"Thanks. Yes, I study all the time. You see, today there are so many good artists that in order to be an exceptional one you have to be just a little bit better than the average, which is very high at the present time, and in order to obtain that enviable position in the artistic world, you have to study, and benefit by the study, for if you do not progress in your art, you are only wasting time. When studying you must have a goal in mind and when you reach that goal, you have to study more as no one can ever be perfect on the operatic stage. There is always a place for improvement."

"What new roles will you present to Chicagoans and New Yorkers, next season?"

"Following the promise of my dear and lamented friend, the late Maestro Campanini, I hope that Leoncavallo's last opera *Oedipe King* will be presented. Leoncavallo had nearly completed the work when death took him and only a few pages were left unfinished. But in no way will this interfere with the presentation of the opera which is a very powerful one."

"To sing *Oedipe* one has to be an actor, I am sure."

"You are right. I saw the play many times at the Comédie-Française in Paris when presented with the great Mounet-Sully in the title role, and I believe this will be of great benefit to me when I learn the part. As I will stay with you all next season, I expect also that the management will produce *Boris Godunov*, an opera that has had many hearings in New York at the Metropolitan, but which has not as yet been produced by the Chicago Opera Association. The part affords me splendid opportunities for histrionical display. Another role which I hope to appear in is Mephisto in Gounod's *Faust*. My Mephisto is so different from any other that I believe it will be of some interest to the American public. I sang the role at Budapest in Hungary meeting one of the greatest successes in my career."

Mr. Ruffo then went into a long discussion as to how he played the role and the distinguished artist greatly interested his visitor, being so kind as to sing part of the role and act it for his sole benefit. The performance was unique but the attraction would lose somewhat of its originality if it were here explained. His Mephisto must be a masterpiece which, when presented, will no doubt cause much discussion and criticism among those who believe in tradition. His Mephisto is far from conventional or traditional. It is just the opposite. Will it meet with great success? That is difficult to say, but that it will be one of the hits of the next season is a foreseen conclusion. Before leaving the charming couple and their astute representation, the latter clever enough to impress the late Campanini with the box office value of Ruffo, the great baritone, who receives the highest salary ever paid an operatic artist, the visitor bade farewell to his host, who showed him the picture of his boy, ten years, and of his girl, eleven years, stating "here is my boy and my girl," but gentle and amiable Signora Ruffo intercepted and stated "our boy and our girl."

"What is the name of the boy?"

"Ruffo."

"Yes, but his first name?"

"That's it—Ruffo—just like his father."

"That's funny, I thought your name was Titta Ruffo."

"Yes that's my name for the stage, but my real name is Ruffo Titta, but as Titta Ruffo is better, I reverse my name, taking for my Christian name my given name and vice versa."

"You certainly are unique, Mr. Ruffo, and are surely the most cordial and modest singer I have ever had the pleasure of interviewing."

"Come again. You will know me better next time."

8

The Real and the
Unreal Titta Ruffo

CHARLES HENRY MELTZER

It is safe to say that no one will replace Caruso at the Metropolitan. For there is none living who has just his value as a star of opera; and it is better that he should not be replaced. The greatest voice may do the greatest harm to art. If I am well informed, as I believe I am, the Metropolitan will, for some time to come, pay more attention than in recent years to opera, *qua* opera, than to stars. But there will always be some singers of the Metropolitan whose "personalities" no plan or rule will down. The Mary Gardens and Carusos of the stage cannot be leveled. They are outside the ranks because they are themselves. All are not equal on the operatic boards.

If all singers merely sang the notes set down for them we might lose something of the joy of lyric drama. The ideal company, I think, should be anonymous. It would be cruel, though, to rob the poor interpreters of Verdi or of Wagner of the ephemeral fame for which they strive and pray. Within bounds, they are entitled to their laurels. It is all a pretty question of proportion.

If any artist at the Metropolitan next season is brought into the lime-light on his merits the chances are it will be Titta Ruffo. He is a baritone, however, not a tenor. And it is hard to make an idol of a singer doomed by the tradition of the operatic stage to interpret characters which, as a rule, are wicked. Yet there have always been a few unusual baritones with whom the tenors of their day have had to count. Among them have been the admired Maurel, Antonio Scotti, and at last our Titta Ruffo.

It is Punch's secret that, for many years, the Metropolitan looked coldly on this artist. He was supposed to be a little bit too "personal." Perhaps Dame Rumor did the singer an injustice. He is much more modest than

First published in *The Independent and the Weekly Review*, October 8, 1921.

8. Titta Ruffo in 1921
   Courtesy of Kurt Binar

he has been painted. I have been seeing a good deal of him in Rome and he has talked about himself with charming frankness. Not like too many artists I have known. But with simplicity and, I believe, sincerity. He is immensely pleased at having been engaged by the stage manager of our chief lyric theatre. His one desire is to acquit himself with honor in all the roles which will be given him to interpret. He has, of course, a sense of his own worth. But he seems anxious to correct the false impression that he exaggerates his proper place in opera.

He spoke to me with deference of Maurel, to whom he bows as an interpreter and teacher. And he protested that he knew how brief and fleeting was the fame of every singer, compared with that of the composer and the poet.

This Titta Ruffo largely taught himself. At the beginning of his enviable career he had his ups and downs, rebuffs and snubs, like others. But he fought on until at last he made his mark.

"Once in Milan," said he, "I had been asked to sing, on trial, to a manager and an invited group of friends. To my consternation when I reached the theatre, I saw, among those who had come to judge my voice, two great composers—Boito and Franchetti. I protested that it would not be quite fair to let my engagement or rejection be decided by the opinion of such masters.

" 'I shall be called upon to sing before the public,' I objected to the manager. 'Boito and Franchetti are above the people who will make or mar me.'

"Boito and Franchetti thereupon rose and left the house, declaring that they understood my feelings. And, I am glad to say, I stood the test so well that I secured the engagement, which to me meant everything."

Titta Ruffo has since then become a favorite in Europe and in North and South America. His repertory is much more extended than one might suppose from his continual repetition in America, to suit his managers, of three or four great parts. Besides Hamlet, Rigoletto, and di Luna, he knows a dozen or more roles in which he hopes some day he may be heard. To give him a new chance of popularity he will appear next season in at least *Ernani*.

He has had a tendency, so far, in his interpretation of this role or that to give his temperamental qualities unbridled liberty at certain points. This has delighted, and will always thrill, the masses. But it has more than once not pleased judicious listeners. His Hamlet is exuberantly Italian. It is not Hamlet that Shakespearians can approve of. He has been hampered, to be sure, by Ambroise Thomas and an inept librettist. Yet it might help to some extent if he would check his fondness for excess in emphasis. The most popular, maybe, of all the songs he sings is Hamlet's noisy and preposterous "Brindisi." It is an insult to all Anglo-Saxon audiences. Yet Titta Ruffo somehow makes it irresistible.

Some day, who knows, we may hear Titta Ruffo in that too-long-neglected master work, *Don Giovanni*. But for a time he will go back to the old standbys, to well-worn *Rigoletto, Trovatore,* and *Don Carlos*.

Rome, September 1, 1921.

9

Titta Ruffo, Caruso, and Chaliapin

GEORGES CUNELLI

Titta Ruffo, Caruso and Chaliapin, the three giants of the operatic world, reigned supreme until the early twenties of this century. They achieved previously unknown heights of publicity, thanks to the propagation of their voices through the early magic channels of recording. Young people everywhere, especially in America, tried to learn singing from their records. For them the jungle noises of television, radio and the microphone were still unknown. The syncopated excitement of jazz was only just beginning to make its mark. These youthful fanatics of the operatic vogue declared war on the teaching studio and barricaded themselves in with their precious records. Some of them, who possessed good ear perception and a spontaneous imitative talent, rapidly succeeded in transforming the natural timbre of their singing voices into husky, metallic gramophonic voices. I remember many of my pupils in Rome, particularly those from America, coming to see me with these 'robot' voices. Thousands everywhere attempted to produce not only timbre but phrasing *à la* Caruso or Titta Ruffo. Unfortunately this short cut led to the vocal hospital, or 'vocal cemetery,' rather than the Metropolitan Opera House.

Like everybody else in those days, I was an enthusiastic admirer of Caruso, though I had experienced his singing only from his early gramophone records, which revealed the exceptionally brilliant quality of his voice. But the first time I heard him in the flesh, in 1909, at the Théâtre du Châtelet in Paris, I was profoundly disappointed. His voice struck me as dull, guttural and excessively forced. In the third act of *Aida* and the last act of *Manon Lescaut* it was husky, and in *Pagliacci* only his

Reprinted with permission of Stainer & Bell, Ltd., London. First published as Chapter 29 in Georges Cunelli, *Voice No Mystery* (London: Stainer & Bell, 1973). All rights reserved.

9. Portrait of Titta Ruffo, Enrico Caruso, and Fedor Chaliapin; Photograph
   of the Oil Painting by the Polish Painter Tade Styka (Paris, May 1912)
   From the collection of Andrew Farkas

overwhelming temperament and sense of character saved him. Later, in *Rigoletto*, at the Grand Opera, I heard him crack B natural, through pushing, in the Masini cadenza of "*La donna è mobile.*" Still later, in Milan, in 1916, in a charity season organised by Toscanini, his voice had deteriorated to such an extent that it was virtually indistinguishable from baritone in *Pagliacci*, and in the last act of *Manon Lescaut* it was little more than a raucous noise. To me this was a tragedy, because people who were fortunate enough to hear him at the beginning of his career, when he sang a much more lyrical repertoire, all agreed that his was the most glorious voice ever heard on the operatic stage.

However, although he was so greatly admired, he had his detractors, who formed themselves into rival groups and whose differences sometimes led to violent scenes. I well remember how, on the morning after his début in Milan, in 1916, the famous Gallery was transformed into a battlefield between his Neapolitan supporters, headed by the leader of the Milan *claque*, and the admirers of the baritone Montesanto*, who had scored an outstanding success in *Pagliacci*, which completely eclipsed Caruso. I added my own critical voice to the hubbub, and the storm became so intense that the police were called in to restore order. I managed to escape with a black eye, minus my hat and my music.

I heard Titta Ruffo for the first time when, at the age of eight or ten, I was taken to the beautiful Municipal Theatre in Odessa. I was very frightened. It was a most impressive, big voice for a childish ear to accept. The second time I heard him was in Paris, when I was already disillusioned and was hunting for an intelligent and competent teacher of singing. Ruffo was singing at the Opéra in Thomas's *Hamlet*. I shall never forget his vocalising in the formidable cadenza in the *brindisi* which sent a tingle down my spine—the quality of his voice, the duration of his breathing, the beauty of his high fifth, the projection and electricity of his production—it was like the final cascade in a display of vocal fireworks!

A year later he returned to the Opéra, where I had one of the outstanding experiences of my long life. It was just before the First World War, at the time of the terrible disaster to the French submarine *La Pluvoise*, which had sunk with all her crew on board. In response to an urgent call for financial aid for the bereaved families, the Government decided to give a charity performance at the Opéra. The brilliant *élite* of the day, covered with diamonds, transformed the Opera House into the Rue de la Paix (known as the 'street of diamonds'), making a fantastic show in the boxes. The French called it '*fer à cheval de diamants.*'†

---

*Later Montesanto became the teacher of Giuseppe di Stefano. In 1924, in Milan, I gave a few lessons and some advice to Montesanto.
† 'Diamond horseshoe.'

As for the performance, I did not believe it was possible to hear such quality and quantity of beautiful opera voices in one evening. The programme began with *The Barber of Seville*. Rosina was sung by Spain's best coloratura soprano, Elvira de Hildago. Count Almaviva was sung by the Russian tenor, Dmitri Smirnov, Don Basilio by Chaliapin, Figaro by Titta Ruffo and Don Bartolo by Pini-Corsi. There was also included, for the same high price, a performance of *Rigoletto*. The Duke of Mantua was sung by Caruso, Rigoletto by Titta Ruffo, Gilda by the Russian soprano Nezhdanova, Maddalena by Lapeyrette and Sparafucile by Journet. The conductor was Maestro Campanini.

The hero of this vocal Olympiad, for me, was Titta Ruffo, who impressed me immensely—and I had already heard a galaxy of baritones like Sammarco, Pandolfini, Scotti, De Luca, Note, Amato, Baklanov, Battistini, Cotogni and many others. For Chaliapin that evening I could only offer a consolation prize for acting and make-up. I did not admire him in Italian opera sung in that language, nor did I approve of his vocal technique. I did not like his disturbing mannerisms during singing, or the tight, suffocated top of his voice, and he often used falsetto instead of pianissimo.* On the other hand, I greatly admired the quality of his voice in Russian opera and his brilliant acting in his incomparable personal style of expression. He was a giant in characterisation, in make-up and in his imparting of meaning to words, which he always backed by magnificent miming. He was one of the finest exponents of the Stanislavsky method—almost independently of Stanislavsky himself.

One morning ten years later, in 1920, when I was teaching in Rome, I received a call from two laryngologists, Professors Bilancioni and Carli of the Rome Polyclinic. They informed me that they had a 'big fish' for me—the famous Titta Ruffo, who had kindly promised to put himself at our disposal for examination. Professor Bilancioni was at that time the leader of a devoted and enthusiastic group of young scientists who were studying the human voice in both its healthy and its pathological conditions, in the various fields of vocal expression in art and social communication. The basis of their experimental work was the study of voices and vocal machinery from the acoustical, anatomical and physiological points of view. At this time, of course, they had not the advantage of our present-day apparatus for objective observation.

I was not a scientist, but the professors appreciated my enthusiasm, my passionate desire to increase my understanding of vocal teaching and my search for the key to its innumerable problems in cooperation with them. It is difficult to describe how proud and thrilled I was when these two eminent men called on me to guide their experimental work in connection with the voice of this giant. Our main objective was to

*There are better bass voices than Chaliapin's in present-day Russia.

measure, by graphs, everything about his vocal apparatus and voice in action, with the exception of his breathing ability and his lung capacity, which were examined by a Verdun spirometer before his phonation. The rest—oscillation of tone produced by the movement of his diaphragm, reverberation recorded in his nasal cavity, control of air pressure through 'nasal olives'—all was inscribed on graphs. I suggested that we should make a visual examination of his larynx, measuring the length and width of his vocal cords, *ventricoli morgagni*, excursion of the soft palate and ear perception. In addition, the sinuses, frontal and maxillary, were examined by trans-illumination. Although our singer was hindered by 'olives' in his nostrils, and by an apparatus attached to his larynx and a special belt round his breathing zone connected by wire to a moving graph cylinder, his dynamic singing surpassed all our expectations. The surgery was empty except for a piano, and as a consequence the reverberations were enormously magnified. When, in the phrase *"alpari di voi"* from the Prologue to *Pagliacci*, he produced the A flat, the vibration was so powerful that both scientists ran from the room, screaming from pain in the teeth. Despite all my experience of noise, I too felt a little dizzy. In another aria, the *brindisi* from *Hamlet*, his holding of the cadenza in one breath for fourteen seconds was so fantastic that it left us open-mouthed with astonishment.

To complete our experiment I suggested inquiring into the extension of Titta Ruffo's baritone voice. On his own initiative he produced the tenor phrase from the "Cavatina" from *Faust*, *"Che la fanciulla mi revella,"* with the high C. I had rarely heard even a real tenor produce a high C of such volume and brilliance. Evidently only the tessitura of a tenor, not the extension, made Titta Ruffo feel vocally uncomfortable. Like Battistini, he had been advised from the very beginning of his studies to open the door to his future with a tenor key. Fortunately he had changed his vocal mind; he told me that his wife had been largely responsible for this correct decision. As a result, he held a unique position as the world's leading baritone. His vocal cords were very muscular and very large, but not too long for a baritone or too short for a tenor. He had a large pharynx and a vast nasal cavity. The well-known Roberts system of measurement revealed that the vital capacity of his lungs was one litre more than the athletic standard measure for his height. If one had not been aware of the details of his anatomical and physiological make-up, his voice could have been erroneously classified as a dramatic or Wagnerian tenor. The colour of his voice was produced by singing with an open throat, with the larynx in a low position and the soft palate automatically in a high one, the entrance to the nasal cavity never being closed. Being unable to resist in high *tessitura*, and having a clear timbre, he purposely changed his voice to dark colour and successfully adopted a new range, achieving a fantastic quality in volume and beauty of tone, especially in his remarkable high baritone fifth. The hypertrophic condition of his tongue tonsil explained the slightly guttural character of his glorious voice.* The operatic world accepted him, but his voice was really intermediate and not typical. Because of his achievements in re-education, the character of his baritone voice was never questioned by Italian ears, as it was in the case of Battistini. I explain this as being due to the special formation and disposal of the appropriate cavity of his resonance.

It was interesting, during the examination of Titta Ruffo's larynx, to see in a laryngo-mirror such a superb reflection of the aritonoidian cartilage and *santorini*. I have seen only a few cases of such truly operatic voices, as when, for instance, I examined the larynxes of leading operatic singers like Crimi, Grassi, Montesanto, de Muro, Besanzoni, Castelazzi, Maria Ranzow, Saltzmann-Stevens, Alice Miriam, Leliva and Journet. At this time it was impossible to examine the human voice in phonation. Rengenoscopy and Kinorengenoscopy did not exist.

Further details of this research work on Titta Ruffo were described by Professor Bilancioni in his book *La Voce parlata e cantate normale e pathologica*, which was published in Rome in 1923.

---

*Probably for the same reason, another 'giant,' the baritone Stracciari, also had this guttural character of voice.

Titta Ruffo in Opera
and Concert

ANDREW FARKAS

Some singers pursue a career for an extended period before they earn
their first critical notice which, more often than not, is a mere acknowledgment of their presence in the cast. Others, the fortunate few, are
singled out on the occasion of their debut, on the strength of their
performance of a role or due to some special circumstance surrounding
the event, sometimes both. There is an even smaller group whose every
appearance becomes a news item, whose mere presence in the cast makes
the performance newsworthy. Without a doubt, Titta Ruffo was such
an artist and remained so for the best part of his career.

Ruffo's appearances were international, yet the two most important
phases of his career, in terms of geography, are divided between North
and South America. Ruffo's Latin American engagements are detailed
in chapter 14 by Eduardo Arnosi; the present chapter attempts an ov-
erview of the rest of his activities with particular emphasis on his North
American performances.

Extensive research has yielded a large number of reviews which range
from straightforward journalistic reporting to competent music criticism.
In both cases these writings are revealing in several ways: They afford
us a secondhand assessment of the ascent, culmination, and initial decline
of a stellar career; a glimpse at Ruffo's maturation as an artist; the
contemporary opinions of his voice, acting, and interpretations; and the
audience response he enjoyed in his many roles.

It has often been maintained that printed reviews are not reliable indicators of the relative merits of a live performance. Yet it is difficult to deny that such observations are likely to have been based on facts when several critics identify the same faults or praise the same qualities of an artist. For this reason multiple reviews of selected performances have been presented. The concurrence or disagreement of the critics allows the reader to formulate a more accurate impression of the event and to better judge the validity of the critical opinions. Since casts can be ascertained from the Chronology appended to this volume (Appendix A), for the most part the cited passages all relate to Titta Ruffo alone.

It is only appropriate to begin the selection of reviews with the brief but positive notices commenting on Ruffo's debut role, that of the Herald in Wagner's *Lohengrin*. His debut took place at one of the major opera houses of turn-of-the-century Italy, the Teatro Costanzi of Rome, on April 9, 1898. The critic of *Il Trovatore* filed the following report, dated April 11: "Also noteworthy was Ruffo, a Herald like few others; enthusiastic applause greeted his beautiful voice and his singular attack in the execution of a role in which few had shone" (*Il Trovatore*, April 16, 1898).

More space is devoted to Ruffo by the enthusiastic reporter of another newspaper, *Il Mondo Artistico*. His critique is dated April 14; thus, conceivably, it may relate to the performance of the 12th. This critic calls the singer Tito Ruffo. Without access to the original program, it cannot be determined whether this was a mere spelling—or typographical—error, or if indeed Ruffo or his impresario decided to use "Tito" for his debut.

On other occasions I usually dispose of the rest of the cast with a few words; but now it would be an injustice not to say that signor Tito Ruffo brought out the full importance of his role as the Herald, singing excellently in his most beautiful [*bellissima*] voice of a perfect baritone. [R. C., *Il Mondo Artistico*, April 18, 1898]

Ruffo was fortunate in having made his debut in the company of first-rate artists. While the majority of the cast may be familiar today only to the specialist, those acquainted with historical voices will readily recognize at least the celebrated tenor in the title role. For the sake of record the cast is given in full. (Vittorio Mingardi conducted.)

Lohengrin	Francisco Viñas
Elsa	Lina di Benedetto
Telramund	Agostino Gnaccarini
Ortrud	Amanda Degli Abbati
King Henry	Francesco Spangher
Herald	Titta Ruffo

Ruffo spent the first couple of years of his career in the lesser theaters of Italy. Then followed two South American tours, in 1900 and 1902, with Cairo before and after the 1902 journey. Finally, he reached London on June 5, 1903, making his Covent Garden debut as Enrico in *Lucia di Lammermoor* opposite Bonci and Journet, with Wedekind in the title role. This performance was not reviewed in the *Times*, possibly because the paper had already reviewed the previous *Lucia* of June 1 with Scotti in the role of Enrico.

Harold Rosenthal in his *Two Centuries of Opera at Covent Garden* correctly places Ruffo's debut in *Lucia*, but without further reference to any other appearances goes on to narrate that he "was so successful at the dress rehearsal of *Rigoletto* which he was due to sing with Melba, that she protested that he was too young to play her father and he was removed from the cast. He never sang again at Covent Garden."[1]

Well, not quite. After his single Enrico, an apparently inconspicuous debut, he sang the first Figaro of his career a month later, on July 1, 1903. The *Times* carried the following notice in the July 2 issue:

Associated with the new Rosina [Maria Barrientos] was a new Figaro, Signor Titta Ruffo, also an actor of evident experience and a good deal of vivacity. It is true that his voice is not flexible enough to master thoroughly all the Rossinian roulades, but he played the part with courage and skill, and after all the singers of today who can execute all that Rossini asked of them are very few. The rest of the cast was excellent; and Signor Bonci deserves a word of praise for the admirable manner of his pious fraud as a pianist in the lesson scene....

In another review of the same event, the correspondent of the Milanese paper *Il Trovatore* had the following to say:

Titta Ruffo, who sang in *Barbiere* for the first time, following a performance by Pini-Corsi, a born Figaro, had a tremendous success. On his entrance [Largo al factotum] he shook the audience with his warm and powerful voice, and they erupted into an applause seldom heard in that theater. He was much admired throughout the opera which, it must be mentioned, he learned in just a few days. [*Il Trovatore*, July 5, 1903]

While Ruffo tells essentially the same story of the Melba incident in his autobiography,[2] his memory fails him in trying to recapture the details in the distance of thirty-four years and he reverses the sequence of events. He claims to have made his debut in London as Figaro, followed by Enrico which, in the light of documentary evidence, is incorrect.

The chronology appended to the centennial edition of *La mia parabola*[3] shows that he sang Figaro three times at Covent Garden, whereas he appeared in the role only once. The first two performances took place prior to Ruffo's debut with Pini-Corsi in the title role; the one with Ruffo was the last *Barbiere* of the season.

As for *Rigoletto*, two complete performances of the opera were given, on July 10 and 22, and "Act I, Scene 2" was part of a gala performance on July 7; on all three occasions Melba sang Gilda and the title role was taken by Renaud, rather than Scotti, as Ruffo erroneously remembers. Scotti sang the role only once, in the June 13 performance with Melba in the cast. In all likelihood the "incident" involved the performance that took place on July 10, 1903.

In pointing out the discrepancies of these important sourcebooks the objective is not to discredit these generally reliable works, but rather to illustrate with a classic example the dilemma of the researcher who, when confronted with contradictory evidence, must excavate the facts directly from the sources.

The next important step for Ruffo was his debut at Milan's famed Teatro alla Scala, a milestone in the career of every singer then as today. It took place on January 7, 1904, with Giulietta Wermez as Gilda, Giuseppe Anselmi as the Duke, Cleofonte Campanini conducting. It seems that in those days music critics were more honest than their counterparts in our time: They sat through the entire performance before they would set pen to paper and write their report. In consequence, they were forced to miss the deadline for the newspaper edition of the following day. Their review may have been a day late, but at least it was reliable, based on the entire performance which they witnessed from beginning to end. According to the reviews, the twenty-six-year-old baritone enjoyed a tremendous popular and critical success on the occasion of his La Scala debut.

Titta Ruffo not only fulfilled but greatly exceeded expectations.

It was known in Milan that he had a treasure of a voice, perhaps one of the most beautiful and powerful ever known, but it was much in doubt whether he could confront with honor the interpretative difficulties of a colossal role like Rigoletto with its indelible traditions. But he conquered the test with glory, and gave the unhappy jester a true, grief-stricken yet sober characterization that left everyone in awe. He had, if I am allowed to say so, especially in the monologue, the rare values of author and singer that showed him an artist of the highest order. It is unfortunate that in the second half of the third act the excitement he had successfully fought back until then got the better of him; but that won't happen on subsequent nights, and the success he had had will be greater and even more brilliantly assured. [*Il Trovatore*, January 9, 1904]

All singers of the period would sooner or later seek an engagement in Russia, as much for artistic prestige as for financial gain. Battistini, Tetrazzini, Caruso, and others sang for one or more seasons in St. Petersburg, Moscow, Odessa, and the lesser cultural centers of tzarist Russia, and were handsomely paid for their efforts. Ruffo, too, joined the ranks of other prominent Italian singers and traveled east for the first time in February 1905. The scene of his Russian debut was the Municipal Theater in Odessa, a major cultural center in prerevolutionary Russia. It took place on January 8, 1905, and the following telegram of the 10th conveys the excitement of the event.

Rigoletto debut Titta Ruffo colossal success; great artist surpassing expectations; extraordinary demonstration gave him opportunity to repeat monolog, prayer ["Miei signori"] vengeance duet with Gilda; recalled amidst of immense ovations. [*Rassegna Melodrammatica*, January 14, 1905]

His subsequent performances were no less successful. The February 22, 1905, letter of the Odessa correspondent of *Il Trovatore* also deserves to be quoted. It reports on the *Barbiere* performance that took place on February 17, 1905:

The baritone, Titta Ruffo, is an ideal interpreter of the role of Figaro, because he doesn't sing like the average baritone. His unusually beautiful voice, his splendid diction so essential for this role, his artistic taste, all unite in this role to give a true picture of the clever barber. His "Largo al factotum" had to be encored by general demand. [*Il Trovatore*, February 25, 1905]

Following his first season in Russia he returned to western Europe for his Parisian debut in Giordano's *Siberia. Fedora,* his second opera in the French capital, partnered him for the first time with Enrico Caruso. They each earned their well-deserved applause.

Titta Ruffo achieved a new success in *Fedora*. An elegant artist, he conquered everyone's affection and admiration. He was obliged to repeat the aria "La donna russa" which he sang exquisitely. The press hails the singing and perfect artistry of the celebrated singer. [*Rassegna Melodrammatica*]

Caruso and Ruffo were reunited a year later in a single performance of *Rigoletto* in Vienna, on October 6, 1906. Joined by Selma Kurz as Gilda, they gave what must have been one of those performances that remain in the annals of opera as an unsurpassable operatic event.

The *Rassegna Melodrammatica* carried not one but two telegrams, both dated October 7, 1906:

Last night at the Imperial Opera Caruso, Titta Ruffo, Kurz, maestro Spetrino, and other first rate German artists gave a thrilling performance of *Rigoletto*. It was attended by the Emperor and his entire court. Immense audience, endless demonstrations especially for Caruso and Titta, innumerable curtain calls, flowers and wreaths for the celebrated artists. The Emperor made Caruso a *Kammersänger*.

The second telegram makes a longer reference to Ruffo; in fact, it suggests that perhaps his success, or at least his audience appeal, was even greater than Caruso's.

Ruffo Titta in the title role was a true revelation. An unsurpassable singing actor, he was enthusiastically acclaimed. After the performance he was carried to his hotel; an impressive demonstration. A memorable evening, a triun/ph for the great baritone.

Ruffo was well received and well paid on his first visit to Russia, in 1905. Not surprisingly, his success resulted in further invitations, and he returned a year later for another extended engagement. It was followed by several shorter ones in 1906 and 1907. But between his winter (St. Petersburg) and spring (Moscow) engagements he spent about a month in Lisbon in January and February of 1907. It was an auspicious occasion for him, his first assumption of the role of Hamlet, the culmination of many months of serious preparation. The role became his favorite, and he performed it as often as the resources and repertory of a theater allowed. Taking into account Ruffo's exceptional dramatic gifts and his musical sensibilities, there can be no doubt that it was the "melancholy Dane" rather than Thomas' music that held such lasting appeal for him. The opera was savagely criticized and ridiculed by music critics from the time it left its native soil, particularly in countries where Shakespeare is standard theatrical fare. A telegram from Lisbon (reversing his name once in the same telegram, as would occur at times in reviews) dated January 25, 1907, speaks of Ruffo's triumph in the role:

Extraordinary performance of *Amleto*, great triumph for Ruffo Titta, ideal appearance, sublime voice, powerful artistry, evoking real delirium [of] difficult public; every phrase applauded, forced to repeat "Drinking Song" where he displayed the entire treasury of his vocal gifts, judicious phrasing, unique Hamlet, unsurpassable, a perfect original creation. Imposing performance attended by Court.... The press worships Titta Ruffo, proclaiming him the greatest baritone of our time.... *Amleto* is the greatest success of the season. [*Rivista Teatrale Melodrammatica*, January 28, 1907]

Ruffo introduced his Hamlet to Milan audiences in October of the same year in eight performances given at the Teatro Lirico. When he returned to Lisbon in 1908 it was *Hamlet* again, along with another work new to him, Mancinelli's now forgotten *Paolo e Francesca*.

1908 was an important year for Ruffo as it brought his debut on the second night of the inaugural season of the Teatro Colón in Buenos Aires. It signaled the beginning of a veritable love affair between the baritone and the Argentine public that lasted for more than two decades. Without a doubt the Argentines heard him in the best years of his career

10. Enrico Caruso
    Photo: Langfier, Ltd., London
    Courtesy of Ruffo Titta, Jr.

and more often than any other audiences. He gave his utmost and he was fully repaid for it in affection and *cachets*.

It was also in 1908 that the singer places the second incident that took place between Melba and himself, recounted by Favia-Artsay elsewhere in this book. Visiting Capri and Sorrento before embarking for Australia, Melba stopped in Naples. According to Ruffo, she went to hear him in *Africana* at the Teatro San Carlo and was so impressed with his singing that she returned for his next performance, *Hamlet*. However, Ruffo's recollection is faulty on this point; he sang *Africana* in April 1908 and *Hamlet* a year later, in April 1909. There is little doubt that Melba's offer to sing with him was indeed as Ophelia, but in the 1908 season the only other opera he sang was *Barbiere*. It is most likely that Ruffo is correct about the role but not the year.

Monday evening, on April 12, 1909, Thomas' opera, *Hamlet*, was presented for the first time this season at the San Carlo. Owing to the presence of the eminent Italian baritone, Titta Ruffo in the title role, the price of seats was considerably raised; however, the vast edifice was completely filled. The performance, on the whole, was most uneven. Interest, of course, centered in the visiting artist, Ruffo, who gave an admirable interpretation of the despondent Dane. The Neapolitans were aroused to the highest pitch of enthusiasm after the drinking song, which Ruffo was obliged to repeat. Graziella Pareto appeared to advantage as Ophelia, histrionically. However, at times, she sang in poor taste.... [*Musical Courier*]

During the years 1909 through 1912 Ruffo divided his time between South America and Europe almost equally. His European engagements centered around Monte Carlo, Madrid, and Naples, and it wasn't until 1912 that he ventured to a country he had not visited before. In the spring of 1912 he sang in Budapest for the first time. His arrival and debut were an unheralded event; thus, his phenomenal success came as a surprise for local opera goers. His "Largo al factotum" stopped the show with a five-minute ovation, his "Figaro was lovable, charming, without impairing the character's virility." One reviewer wrote:

Titta Ruffo's talent unites the best, most outstanding qualities in marvelous harmony. Handsome appearance; ringing, powerful voice of even strength through two octaves; exceptionally artistic singing; excellent *pianissimi*; nearly *coloratur* facility; forceful, even *fortes*; artistic perfection in the *recitatives*; and the artistic expression of an acting temperament. [*Magyar Nemzet*, March 27, 1912]

The *Pesti Hirlap* (March 27, 1912) called him a "veritable Caruso in baritone edition" and a "singing Zacconi: equally outstanding, almost perfect both as an actor and a singer." The *Pesti Napló* article of the same date said he was a "phenomenal actor, brilliant singer, great among the greatest."

11. Titta Ruffo as Figaro in *The Barber of Seville* (Paris, 1912)
     Courtesy of Ruffo Titta, Jr.

Because of the lack of advance publicity, his debut took place in front of a half-empty house. The unanimity of the reviews changed that overnight; the rest of his performances were sold out. His Rigoletto was a revelation, and the audience and critics could reconcile only with great difficulty the tragic jester and the jovial barber with the same artist. His third role, the inevitable Hamlet, was acclaimed as a Shakespearean characterization "barely weakened by Thomas' syrupy, sentimental music" (*Pesti Hirlap*, April 2, 1912). The reviewer of the *Magyar Nemzet* (April 2, 1912) judged him so thoroughly immersed in the character that "we nearly forgot that we were at the Opera and we seemed to be watching Shakespeare's tragedy. His delivery was more an ideal declamation than singing; the great monologue lost nothing of its conceptual magnificence despite the orchestral accompaniment."

Paris was once again the city that reunited Ruffo with Caruso, first in a performance of *Rigoletto*, then on the occasion of the French premiere of Puccini's new opera, *La fanciulla del West*. The following telegram sent on May 17 from Paris describes the festive event.

In front of a most imposing audience *La fanciulla del West* was performed last night at the Grand Opera. Maestro Puccini was present; he was much fêted and recalled several times in front of the curtain. The principals were greatly appreciated, La Melis, the tenor Caruso, great in the role of Johnson and Titta Ruffo, a superb singer and actor in the part of Sheriff Rance. [*Rassegna Melodrammatica*, May 21, 1912]

Ruffo's North American debut took place in Philadelphia, in the title role of *Rigoletto*, on November 4, 1912. The predictable success surpassed expectations. According to the brief report of the Philadelphia *Morning Telegraph*, "Ruffo's voice lived up to its reputation. His success was assured from the moment he appeared on stage.... At the end of the third act he was applauded for nearly ten minutes and had to respond to numerous curtain calls."

Following the hastily wrought report of the morning paper, a full-length review of the event appeared in the evening paper.

Titta Ruffo made his first appearance in an opera house of North America last evening in our own Metropolitan as the thwarted, anguished Jester of *Rigoletto*.

Through the advance heralding of his reputation, the effective records he had prepared for the phonographic machines and the adventitious assistance given to his coming by the fact that the Maecenas of the local grand opera had guaranteed $2,000 per night, a salary enormous for any singer to say nothing of a baritone, he had created an anticipation so large and curious that only a consummate artist could have fulfilled the expectation, raised in the minds of music lovers and could have satisfied the critical instinct.

All anticipations, all expectations, all possible criticisms were satisfied by the

12. Titta Ruffo as Jack Rance in *La fanciulla del West* (Paris, 1912)
Courtesy of Ruffo Titta, Jr.

event and the personality. Mr. Ruffo proved himself a truly great artist. He demonstrated this not only by the technical processes of vocalization, by the possession of a suave, rounded, swelling, proportioned, emotionally expressive voice, by accomplished and convincing methods of acting, by impregnation of his own personage with the characteristics of the tragic figure he was impersonating, but by a union of all these external faculties of and internal essential qualities in the singer's art. Further and best of all he demonstrated his standing and standards by that rare, wonderful, adroit achievement—the art which makes its product seem natural by the concealment of the outward and mechanical means of expressing art.

Not only is Mr. Ruffo a baritone of great price, but he seems worth every dollar or lira of his emolument, or however he reckons it. He disappointed few if any of his hearers, only those possible few who expected a prima donna vocalist whose tones would soar to the chandeliers with a chance of smashing the crystals or might retreat profoundly into the below-stage recesses with a rumble.

This is not to say that Mr. Ruffo's voice is not of proper register; as a matter of fact it is extended enough to enter at either end of the gamut into the tenor and bass registers. Its chief asset is its even graduation of tone, its uniformity of "scale," its chief charm is its sweetness, lucidity and varied color.

As an actor Mr. Ruffo, on last evening's evidence, might fairly compete with most of the tragedians of our stage. He is not ranting or grotesque; he leaves the scenery intact during his progress even in crises and moments of stress. He gets into the psychology of his role and his impartment of it is not merely the illusion of "makeup" and costume, but the convincing aspect of human nature. In Rigoletto he had the most "grateful" part in opera for the baritone, with the exception, perhaps, of Athanael in *Thaïs*, but certainly Rigoletto is the major role for the display of the register in Italian opera. Like Mr. Renaud in the French lyric-drama, Mr. Ruffo distinguished himself as the Fool of the Mantuan court. He revealed the human being under the misshapen form of the Duke's entertainer. As the play proceeded he exposed the anguished father with breaking heart under the Jester's cap and bells. It was all-poignant. Seemingly, too, this performance was music-drama of closely connected voice and action, not merely Italian opera with its artificial succession of solos, duos, and choruses.

This general level of excellence was due to the influence of the star, that is to his powers of repression, of reserve force, of holding in strength for climaxes instead of spending it, and later losing emphasis in "big" moments. While main attention belongs to the appearance of Mr. Ruffo, pleasant words must be written concerning the advent of Alma Gluck as Gilda. She was a slender Gilda of lovely looks, and barring a tendency to pose in Pre-Raphaelite style, her stage presence was good. After the first act she sang very well, rendering the "Caro Nome" with fine feeling. [Philadelphia *Telegraph*, November 5, 1912]

The other reviews were no less enthusiastic. Reviewing the same event, *Musical America* headlined it as "Signal Triumph for Titta Ruffo in Philadelphia."

The debut in America of Titta Ruffo, the famous Italian baritone, with the Philadelphia-Chicago Company at the local Metropolitan Opera House last evening, proved an event which, notwithstanding the high expectations caused by the glowing accounts of the singer's wonderful ability, left no sense of disappointment. At first hearing Ruffo appears to be all that the sometimes overzealous press agent had said he is, and it may unhesitatingly be recorded that, in the title role of *Rigoletto* last night his triumph was complete.

Still a young man, and possessed of all the fire and enthusiasm of youth, this famous Italian, whose salary, said to be $2,000 a performance, was guaranteed by the public-spirited Mr. Stotesbury, of this city, combines with his wonderful voice the forceful and sympathetic talent as an actor that seems to leave nothing wanting in his artistic equipment.

In his make-up as the deformed jester last night, Ruffo disguised whatever good looks he may possess presenting Rigoletto as an elderly man with gray hair and white chin beard, somewhat infirm and, in the more tragic episodes of the opera, pathetically swayed by great emotion.

The tragic moments, notably in the third and fourth acts, were realized with an immense power that, added to the effect of the marvelous voice, literally thrilled the audience.

Ruffo's voice, which is used with the utmost ease and naturalness, his vocal method appearing to be simply that of one who sings without effort and with the guidance of brain, is of tremendous power and resonance, and of remarkable range and flexibility. It fairly rolls out, in ringing volumes of sound, but has also the charm of warmth and richness, being of an appealing quality in the middle register and in tender passages capable of great pathos, while Ruffo knows how to produce startling effects without being unduly sensational.

One of his greatest moments last night was in the third act, when he took a high note in full voice and held it for a surprisingly long time, letting it diminuendo into the softest of tones. It was after this act that the audience gave full vent to its enthusiasm, up to this point having been a bit restrained in its bestowal of applause, and Mr. Ruffo and Alma Gluck, who was Gilda, after being recalled again and again, finally repeated their scene before the curtain. Miss Gluck was a girlish and appealing Gilda, and while her forte is not that of the coloratura soprano, the "Caro Nome" aria being well sung but without dazzling brilliance of effect, her pure, sweet and vibrant tones gave delight and she was cordially received. Orville Harrold, "loaned" by Oscar Hammerstein for the occasion, while not in the best of voice, was a handsome and vocally pleasing Duke, and Margaret Keyes, singing admirably in rich and sympathetic contralto tones, as Maddelena, scored a success. Henri Scott, as Sparafucile; Constantin Nicolay, as Monterone, and Louise Berat, as Giovanna, also won deserved favor, with Campanini as conductor.

A.L.T.
[*Musical America*, November 9, 1912]

The baritone's success was firmly established by the time he introduced his Di Luna to Philadelphia audiences. It was favorably reviewed by Arthur L. Tubbs in *Musical America*, and even though it appeared in the November 30, 1912, issue, there can be little doubt that the performance predated his New York debut.

That Philadelphia seems almost literally to have "gone mad" over Ruffo was again demonstrated on Thursday evening when the baritone appeared as the Count di Luna in *Trovatore* before an audience that filled the house with all the available standing room crowded. Ruffo was undoubtedly the "magnet", not the opera, popular as it is.... As the Count, Ruffo made use of all his limited opportunities in his usual sensational manner, dwelling long upon high notes and lavishly pouring forth the resonant tones of his voluminous voice. His principal aria, "Il balen" was superbly sung and the audience clamored for a repetition, Ruffo, however, declining. In marked contrast to his character delineations in *Rigoletto* and *Pagliacci* the baritone looked handsome and courtly as the Count and showed dignity and grace in his acting.

When Ruffo first stepped to the footlights on the stage of the Metropolitan Opera House in New York, it was not as a member of that illustrious ensemble, but as the star of the Philadelphia-Chicago Company. He sang the title role in Thomas' *Hamlet* on November 19, 1912. Richard Aldrich, music critic of the *New York Times*, devoted not one but two articles to the event, both of which impress the reader by their intelligent analysis and sober objectivity. Both articles are reproduced in this volume.

In the early decades of this century, New York City had several newspapers, thus allowing for a diversity of opinions on the same subject. Since Titta Ruffo's New York debut was such a significant operatic event, it seems that every music critic wanted to be present and have his verdict preserved for posterity. Considering that in all likelihood the distinguished gentlemen of the press worked simultaneously with and independently from each other, it is remarkable on how many points their reports agree.

Considering Titta Ruffo's performance with more temperate deliberation than many in the audience seemed disposed to accord it, it will have to be acknowledged that his sensational heralding has not served him to best artistic purpose. That he possesses the secret of arousing the frenetic acclamations of the multitude is absolutely undeniable. But that he satisfies the fastidious is open to grave question. Whatever his brilliant record in the past, whatever great achievements he may be destined to put to his credit in the future, Mr. Ruffo quite failed last Tuesday to impress one as a great, serious, convincingly sincere artist....

His voice is large of volume, agile and of wide range. It is of a distinct tenor quality at the top, in which register it has much hard brilliancy, vibrancy and resonance, and it is true to the pitch. The lower tones on the other hand are wooden, hollow and deficient in resonant qualities. The texture of the voice is not of the finest; and it failed to disclose last Tuesday that melting lusciousness of quality that had been ascribed to it. Moreover, it is distinctly tremulous, especially on loud, sustained high tones. It lacks warmth. And it is to be regretted that Mr. Ruffo finds so little need for attention to subtleties of shading. He discloses questionable taste, moreover, in his manner of emitting high notes blatantly and in prolonging them far beyond their written value. But as he has abundant breath supply he is tempted to the abuse of his resources in this manner. His delivery of the "Drinking Song" was madly acclaimed on the strength of such effects, but it was not artistic.

As an actor Mr. Ruffo impressed one as conventionally operatic, as wanting repose, distinction and refinement.

H.F.P.
[*Musical America*, November 23, 1912]

H. E. Krehbiel, the famous critic of *The Tribune,* had a totally different view of what he had seen and heard:

He is unquestionably an extraordinary singer, extraordinary in the volume and range of his voice, in his command of the technics of singing, especially in his breath-control, in the vitality and vibrancy of his tones, his ability to give them dramatically expressive color, his finished diction. He is extraordinary, too, in his dramatic action—extraordinary from the viewpoint provided by the opera.

Writing in *The American*, Charles Henry Meltzer, another distinguished music critic, was in accord with Krehbiel:

Titta Ruffo held his audience by the supremacy of his art, the nobility of his voice and the excellence of his virtuosity. He never strained. He was never meretricious. His art was flawless. The limpid purity and suavity with which Titta Ruffo produced his tones led many to declare he was really not a great baritone but a great tenor.

Pierre V. R. Key, critic of *The World* and the future biographer of Caruso and McCormack, was less enthusiastic, even though he begrudgingly recognized the baritone's special gifts.

While there can be no question as to Ruffo's rank as a great artist, in some respects he was not fully up to expectations in the role he sang and acted last night. And there are a number of New York musicians, competent to speak, who today feel a sense of disappointment over the voice and the art of Ruffo as revealed on this occasion.

W. J. Henderson, whose collected writings about music and opera are a lasting document of his life devoted to music, was also highly critical in his review published in *The Sun*:

This Italian baritone has certain gifts which will insure him popular favor while time spares him. His voice is a high baritone, and like most voices of its kind is hollow and cold in the low register. But in the middle and upper range it is a voice of magnificent power. It is not warm in quality, but it has vitality and

dramatic value. Mr. Ruffo sings with great freedom and without forcing. He
has enormous breath support and his control is perfect.

And finally, a puzzling, confused, self-contradictory unsigned article
from *The Herald*:

...But in the legitimate tones where other baritones glory, Mr. Ruffo's voice
can scarcely be called beautiful. He has a "vibrato" most pronounced, and the
lowest notes he sang last night were without "color" or resonance. Nor is his
voice huge in volume. Stripped of its top notes—but that would be another story.
The fact remains that his is a sensational voice and Mr. Ruffo is a sensational
singer. His acting is crude.

The negative observations about his singing were obviously not shared
by all, particularly not by his listeners who gave him an ovation every
time he sang in public. But there was at least one irate reader who took
the trouble to write a letter to the editor of *Musical America*. Mr. W.
Warren Shaw of Philadelphia, in a letter dated November 29, 1912,
roundly rebuts, in impassioned tones that somewhat distract from his
message, all the criticisms leveled at the baritone.

What none of the critics bothered to take into consideration was the
peculiarity of the circumstances. The fact that he was the highest paid
baritone in the world and about to make his New York debut on the
stage of the great Metropolitan Opera Company (he was not a member
of that company but aspired to become one) must have had an effect
on his delivery, and not necessarily for the better. Since Arthur L. Tubbs
was the only reviewer who had seen Ruffo's Philadelphia performance,
it is worth quoting his report also of the New York *Hamlet*.

The operatic event of the past week was the first appearance of Titta Ruffo in
Hamlet on Wednesday evening, when the great baritone even surpassed his
former notable achievements at the local [Philadelphia] Metropolitan Opera
House as Rigoletto and as Renato in *The Masked Ball*. While in his previous roles
Ruffo has fully come up to all the high expectations formed by what had been
heard of him, and triumphed completely, he gave, before the largest, most
brilliant and most enthusiastic audience of the season, in the title role of Ambroise
Thomas' Shakespearean opera a new and even more remarkable revelation of
his powers, both as singer and actor. [*Musical America*, November 23, 1912]

The carping of the critics notwithstanding, Ruffo's public success was
of such magnitude that a "concert debut" was hastily arranged at Carnegie Hall on November 25, to be followed by another in the Hippodrome on December 15. Ruffo shared the concert platform with soprano
Helen Stanley, and he was supported by an orchestra under the baton
of Ettore Perosio. Ruffo sang four opera excerpts and three Italian songs,

one of them by his brother who was shown in the program as Ettore Titta Ruffo. "Ruffo" not being a part of his name, Ettore was obviously trying to capitalize then, as later as vocal coach in Chicago, on his brother's fame.

H.F.P., the tradition-bound critic of *Musical America*, again found fault with Ruffo's concert work.

That Mr. Ruffo's methods and style would be obviously unsuited to the concert platform was a foregone conclusion. His motions, gesticulations and perambulations are precisely things to be expected of the singer whose province does not extend beyond the operatic stage. Naturally enough, they offend finer tastes. A practical knowledge of concert platform etiquette is not altogether to be despised by the opera singer whose ambitions rise to the concert pitch if he really wishes to be taken seriously in his new sphere. Mr. Ruffo will eventually feel the indispensability of this.

Vocally the baritone did nothing that necessitates a material readjustment of the verdict pronounced a week earlier. He can certainly not be said to have stood the test of the Mozart "Serenade" [from *Don Giovanni*]. He did demonstrate in the three short Italian songs that his voice is capable of warmth and that the expression of sentiment is not altogether a sealed book to him. On the other hand, his singing showed little more subtlety or regard for artistic refinement of effects than it did in *Hamlet*. His tremolo stands forth most pronouncedly and he lapses frequently into the use of the "white voice." On this as on previous occasions, the loud high tones, long drawn out, did the trick and the audience shouted itself hoarse over his performance of the close of the *Pagliacci* Prologue, vulgarized as it was. [*Musical America*, November 30, 1912]

Another reviewer, while no less critical, was more considerate in manner and tone. His article essentially agrees with the opinion of his colleague regarding Ruffo's mannerisms; however, at the same time he concedes the irresistible appeal of his voice.

Last Monday night Sig. Titta Ruffo gave a concert in Carnegie Hall, New York City, and scored a complete success. A New York critic says: "There was a large audience, made up to a very considerable extent of the contigent which ordinarily worships at the feet of Signor Caruso. A large spirit of freedom and familiarity prevailed in this contingent and manifested itself in appeals to the singer for music of the kind dear to its soul, and Signor Perosio, and Miss Helen Stanley, a recent accession to Mr. Dippel's forces, also took part, the lady contributing far and away the most enjoyable part of the entertainment from an artistic point of view. Signor Ruffo, however, provided all the elements of the sensational order. He sang with all the excellences of which mention was made in the review of his Hamlet, electrifying his hearers with his brilliant high tones, and the next moment causing the judicious to marvel and grieve at the persistency of his mannerisms—of voice color and rubato especially—and a moment later to rejoice in the admirable distinctness of his diction. It was characteristic of the audience that there was not a sign of recognition when the orchestra began the prelude to the serenade from Mozart's *Don Giovanni*, which he sang in response to a recall after the buffo air from *Il Barbiere di Siviglia*. He took his hearers completely into his confidence—willing prisoners they were, too—with his songs with pianoforte accompaniment, and doubled the number originally set down in the list. [*The Opera News*, December 2, 1912]

The next operatic center on the baritone's agenda to conquer was Chicago, the future scene of many of his great North American successes. The Chicago audience, just like the Philadelphia public before, took him to its heart and even when some of his interpretations fell short of expectations, he was criticized with kindness, without the high-handed orneriness of the know-it-all New York critics.

Edward C. Moore gives a vivid description of the baritone's first Chicago engagement in his *Forty Years of Opera in Chicago*.[4] He claims that the initial successful presentations of the season were

... promptly overshadowed by the approach of an artist whose advance publicity made even Miss Garden look to her laurels. This was the "greatest of all baritones," Titta Ruffo. An unbridled imagination had worked for months preparing his advent. Ruffo, if you will believe what got into the papers, had come out of the ranks of the iron workers of Rome, had been turned down by his singing teacher for incompetence—how many dozens of singers like to have their patrons believe this—was the recipient of the largest fee on record ($2,000 a performance was admitted) and spent all his spare time between working ornamental iron candlesticks and reading Shakespeare. The last touch was a bit unfortunate, for Ruffo in the course of his Chicago season appeared in Ambroise Thomas' version of *Hamlet*.[5]

Moore goes on to describe Ruffo's spectacular debut in *Rigoletto* and the sensation he created with his original interpretation of the role of Tonio—a passage already quoted in full by Aida Favia-Artsay. Moore found Ruffo a superb artist, both vocally and histrionically—a judgment firmly supported by Nicholas de Vore. Reporting on the progress of the Chicago season, de Vore wrote that the *Pagliacci* Prologue as sung by Ruffo

... marked the greatest enthusiasm yet aroused in the present season of opera in the Auditorium. Perhaps the fact that so wonderful a portrayal was hardly expected accounts in part for the tremendous outburst of more than applause by which he was compelled to repeat a part of his unhackneyed presentation of one of the most hackneyed of operatic arias.

A consideration of the art of Titta Ruffo from a point permitting of sufficient perspective reveals characteristics which justifiably account for the tremendous success with which he has been everywhere received. Vocally, he may have his equals; even in musicianship he is hardly supreme, but the overpowering sincerity with which he enters into his role, the histrionic perception and repression with which he brings out the psychological essence of the character he would typify, and the versatility with which each characterization of his limited repertoire is made to stand out as utterly unlike any other of his portrayals, constitutes an ensemble of operatic equipment which has seldom been equalled in the ranks of the contemporary stars. There is no denying but that his conception of Tonio not only differs from every existing tradition of the role, but exercises an influence throughout the whole work which makes the plot for the first time tangible and consistent,—psychologically speaking. The impulses of Tonio become elemental and instinctive, without becoming depraved or even wilfully malicious. [*Musical America*, December 14, 1912]

At the conclusion of his first North American season, Ruffo returned to Europe to fulfill engagements on the continent. Budapest was the locale of his excursion into the bass repertory. Giving up his customary role of Valentin, he sang Mephisto in Gounod's *Faust*. The role had greatly intrigued him and he meant to sing it again, but as far as it can be ascertained from the chronology of his performances he never did. Years later he recalled his Budapest Mephisto as one of the great successes of his career, yet the recorded excerpts he left behind do not suggest particular originality or even suitability for the role. Even though the *tessitura* is relatively high, calling more for a bass-baritone than a true bass, Ruffo's voice was taxed by the range of the role. Both in the "Serenade" and the brief excerpt from the Church Scene he takes unwritten higher options, deliberately avoiding troublesome low notes that did not lie comfortably for his voice. Let it be remembered however, that this occurred in an epoch when liberties taken with the printed score were more common, going so far as the purposeful alteration of scores to accommodate a certain singer, like Massenet's re-writing of the tenor role of Werther for the baritone range of Battistini, or Leoncavallo doing the same for Ruffo with the title role of *Chatterton*. Apart from the relatively few low notes in the role of Mephisto, Ruffo must have been able to cope with the music. His stentorian voice undoubtedly created a formidable impression by its sheer volume. In any case he enjoyed a great popular success.

As it was foreseen—an easy prediction!—the appearance of Titta Ruffo in *Faust* at the Népopera of Budapest was a huge success. The creation—true, absolute, impressive—of the role of Mephistopheles by the great baritone surprised the audience who, with frenetic screams, demanded an *encore* of "Le veau d'or"— on which the *divo* lavished the full richness of his phenomenal voice—and the inimitably delineated "Serenade." Creating stunning effects, the *divo* was absolutely marvelous in the Church Scene. [*Rivista Teatrale Melodrammatica*, April 30, 1913]

The Hungarian reviews (all published on April 23, 1913) were equally complimentary but uncharacteristically short, even though it was known

13.   Titta Ruffo as Mephisto in Gounod's *Faust* (Budapest, 1913)
      Courtesy of Ruffo Titta, Jr.

that this was his first assumption of the role. The *Pesti Hirlap* called him "a veritable *chevalier infernal*, elegant and cynical...his singing and acting equally masterful." According to the *Magyar Nemzet*, "Ruffo sang this definitely bass role whose depths could not suit his ringing baritone. Yet his marvelous vocal artistry conquered these difficulties and his winning characterization duly impressed the audience." The *Pesti Napló* wrote that the hero of the opera was not Faust but Mephisto, whose voice "boomed with tremendous force."

One also gains a glimpse at an undocumented side of the singer from an article in the *Pesti Napló*. By the time he arrived in Budapest, the theater's first *Hamlet* performance was fully prepared. Ruffo, however,

...re-rehearsed all of his scenes and almost re-directed the entire piece. He took the director's chair at the rehearsal and explained *Hamlet* to the cast in great detail. Concerning some scenes he delivered a veritable literary discourse, quoting Shakespeare authorities, dazzling the artists of the Népopera. They listened in amazement to Titta Ruffo who left after four hours of work. In four hours he redirected *Hamlet*. [*Pesti Napló*, April 13, 1913]

The reviews acknowledged his directorial contribution which was evidenced in the performance, as much on account of its merits as by "the sharp contrast of the last scene which Ruffo left untouched." His personal success was great as always, but he insisted on sharing the applause with his colleagues. "He literally dragged conductor Fritz Reiner in front of the curtain" (*Pesti Napló*, April 16, 1913).

When Ruffo returned to the United States in late 1913, he introduced to his Philadelphia and Chicago audiences several roles in his repertory he had not sung before in the United States. As the reviews attest, his portrayals ranged from complete success to near failure.

The first of these relates to the Philadelphia premiere of *Cristoforo Colombo* by Franchetti. Arthur L. Tubbs' review of the performance contains the following notice about Ruffo's delivery of the title role:

The role of Columbus gives Ruffo many opportunities to disclose still further his distinguished ability both as actor and singer. In no other part has his voice had more of the sympathetic quality, and last evening his expression of varied emotions, from poignant grief to passionate intensity was a demonstration of remarkable versatility. The death scene was accomplished with so much realism that it would have been thrilling, even had Ruffo not sung a note. As it was, the combination of histrionic skill and vocal beauty attained an achievement that is unusual on the operatic stage. [*Musical America*, November 29, 1913]

Ruffo also sang Rigoletto, Tonio, and Barnaba in *La Gioconda* in Philadelphia. He performed the same roles in Chicago, adding Figaro, Don

14. Titta Ruffo in the Title Role of Franchetti's *Cristoforo Colombo* (Buenos Aires? 1909)
Photo: Matzene Studio
Courtesy of Kurt Binar

Giovanni, and Athanael in *Thaïs*. The reviews, as already suggested, were mixed.

Don Giovanni had not been given in Chicago for several years (fourteen according to one reviewer, five according to another). While Ruffo was not competing with the recent memory of another outstanding artist in the role, he had to measure up to the experience of at least one music critic, whose observations are amply borne out by Ruffo's recordings of two arias and a duet from the opera. He sang the role in Chicago twice; the following review pertains to the first performance which took place on December 18.

Titta Ruffo was the Don Giovanni, a role this reviewer has heard sung by such artists as Renaud, Maurel and Scotti. Though comparisons are odious, it may be said that Mr. Ruffo's conception of the part, vocally as well as histrionically, was far below the high standard of perfection expected from such a wonderful artist. The role of Don Giovanni requires physical as well as vocal refinement and in the former Signor Ruffo is lacking. The role also lies too low for his voice, which, after all, is an unusual voice, being neither a baritone nor a tenor, and in the Mozart score the lack of medium register in Ruffo's voice was at times disconcerting. The "Serenade," which generally is encored, was heartily applauded, even though Signor Ruffo wanted to improve on the music of Mozart by interpolating some variations of his own. [*Musical Courier*, December 24, 1913]

Edward C. Moore agrees with this verdict and does not hesitate to point out the same shortcomings in Ruffo's impersonation of the title role.

Ruffo came to the front again in the name part of Mozart's *Don Giovanni*, a role which he should gently but firmly have been argued out of ever singing at all. For the Mozart opera contained few high notes for him to trumpet forth and his audience to get hysterical over, and it was about as far from his manner dramatically as vocally.[6]

But Maurice Rosenfeld was less harsh in his judgment. He claimed that the opera was given

...principally for the purpose of giving Titta Ruffo, the baritone, another opportunity to show his versatility. That he was less convincing in the title role of this opera than in any of his other characterizations does not detract particularly from his remarkable achievements. He sang the music with his accustomed skill and played the part in as artistic a manner as usual, but he did not create that sensation which he has made in other roles. [*Musical America*, December 27, 1913]

The same reviewer was well pleased with his "boyish and exuberant" Figaro and found him vocally "one of the most satisfying singers we have heard in the role." Moore wrote "Ruffo was immense as Figaro."

Ruffo's work in *Thaïs* had the critics divided. Some praised him for his obvious qualities; others felt his shortcomings for the role weighed more heavily in the balance. In all likelihood, the criticisms must have been objective and on target. Ruffo was an Italian singer with an Italianate voice, singing style, and temperament. In the role of Hamlet his interpretation transcended the national characteristics of the music: Thomas' Hamlet need not be interpreted, even vocally, as a Frenchman any more than Shakespeare's as an Englishman. But Massenet's quintessentially French opera, based on the equally French writing of Anatole France and in the stylistically accurate company of Mary Garden and Charles Dalmorès, Ruffo's robust vocal presence must have been incongruous in the extreme. *Musical Courier* reviewed the December 26 performance, the first of two given:

Titta Ruffo as Athanael did a powerful piece of acting, which made a lifelike figure of the sentimental priest. Endowed by nature with a voice of colossal dimensions, Ruffo's fortissimo passages were tremendous and his sonorous tones rang out thrillingly, while the lyrical episodes were done with equal art and effect. [December 31, 1913]

Reviewer M. R. of *Musical America*, however, found his interpretation substandard, certainly in light of what the Chicago audience had come to expect of him.

A great disappointment was in store for the assembled multitude in the performance of Titta Ruffo, the distinguished Italian baritone. He could not get into the spirit either of the dramatic or musical opportunities of the character of Athanael in this opera and was quite out of the picture throughout the entire evening. Not that his singing was less artistic than we have heard it in other operas, but the music lies somewhat too low for him and his Italian in juxtaposition to the other principals' French was one distracting element, and as the Cenobite Monk, he really could not live the part. [*Musical America*, January 3, 1914]

Edward C. Moore presents a different, blatantly gossipy side to the story of Ruffo's failure in the part. He claims that

Ruffo had told some of his friends that the star part of this performance was going to be Athanael, and that Miss Garden had been told of the remark. In any event, it developed into a highly diverting artistic battle between the two.
It was a tactical error on Ruffo's part for two reasons: one that here was another part written too low for his effective register, another that he was confronting an extremely adroit and resourceful artist who considered that the star part of the opera was Thaïs herself. Ruffo had all the first scene and half the second in which to register himself. He did his best, but then Miss Garden appeared, letting out a few extra convolutions in her pantomime and personality,

and the rest of the opera was a complete rout for the baritone. He had enough. Never again was the Italian evangelist to busy himself with the wiles of the French-Scotch-American charmer.[7]

He reaped his usual share of accolades in his other roles, particularly for his Tonio which was rapidly becoming a classic interpretation, and for his Cristoforo Colombo, of which the reviewer of *Musical America* wrote (December 13) that he "accomplished colossal things with his portraiture of the noted navigator."

It was around this time that the Chicago Musical College announced that Signor Ettore Titta Ruffo had joined the faculty of its voice department. By this time Ettore had permanently added "Ruffo" to his name for American use, undoubtedly to enhance his own marketability. The baritone, the rightful owner of the celebrated name, did all he could to promote his elder brother's career. In the same article that announced the elder Titta's appointment, *Musical America* published a letter by Titta Ruffo that deserves to be quoted in full. Since the singer had not fully mastered English (in fact he never did), the letter must have been composed in Italian and translated. However, there can be no doubt about it that these are Ruffo's words, and as the publisher indicated, the letter carried his signature.

In view of the fact that numerous vocal instructors have endeavored to claim the credit of having been my "teacher" I desire to state emphatically that my brother Ettore is the one to whom practically all such distinction is due. I studied four months at the Santa Cecilia Conservatory in Rome under Signor Persichini and was told that I possessed neither voice nor musical talent. Afterward I received instruction from Signor Sparapani for two months and from Signor Casini for four months, but as this was not sufficient tuition for an operatic career I placed myself under the tutelage of my brother. I remained his faithful pupil for six years and am the living proof of his scientific method of voice production. All those asserting that they have been my "teachers" and therefore responsible for my success arrogate to themselves false and mendacious prerogatives.

Very sincerely yours,
(signed) Titta Ruffo
[*Musical America*, December 27, 1913, p. 41]

From Chicago the baritone returned to New York for a concert at the Hippodrome on January 4, 1914. The *New York Times'* critic was unimpressed and voiced a complaint about his singing that had not been encountered before.

The greatest defect of Mr. Ruffo's singing is his rhythmic sense which often was insecure. There were several differences with the orchestra as to rhythm, and on the evidence offered the verdict must be returned in favor of [conductor] Nahan Franko.... If it were not necessary to appraise this singer in the light of the extravagant viewpoint on which his sponsors continually insist, it would be easier to praise him for his voice is of unusually fine quality and his style of singing generally pleasing.

Musical America's reporter, A.W.K., while condemning the "undignified behavior" of his "ardent admirers," conceded that "...his singing is the kind that arouses noisy enthusiasm, that lifts many otherwise sensible persons from their normal condition into a sort of frenzy."

This was followed by an entire concert tour which included a joint recital in Chicago with Luisa Tetrazzini, another darling of local audiences that always doted on coloratura sopranos. M. R. of *Musical America* (February 28, 1914) dedicated most of the space to her and, after listing the baritone's numbers, devoted only one sentence to his singing: "Ruffo, too, was in good condition and his voice had warmth, power and temperamental qualities."

Ruffo then returned to Philadelphia for another series of performances. Recalling the humiliation Ruffo endured from Melba in London, and the baritone's justified—if ungallant—repartée he dealt the diva in Naples several years later, it is all the more surprising and intriguing that they were cast to sing in *Rigoletto* together in the City of Brotherly Love, on February 18, 1914. It is difficult to conjecture how this casting came about and one can only guess that the participants' disposition toward each other was influenced by mutual respect: The aging Melba even in her years of decline was still Melba, and Ruffo had attained such preeminence among singers that now it was Melba's turn to be honored by his presence in the cast. The performance went well even though *Musical America*'s critic faulted Melba for her growing inability to cope with the high notes and *fioritura* of the role. Ruffo, as always in this role, did his best.

He also sang Don Giovanni just once more, on February 21, 1914. Although the critical reception seems to have been kinder than in Chicago, the chronology of his performances shows that he never attempted the role again.

...Mozart's opera was given a very creditable presentation, the appearance of Ruffo in the title role being an event of especial importance. He makes the perfidious *Don* a man of courtly manner and attractive mien, whose easy conquest of many feminine hearts is not incongruous, and acts it with buoyant ease and masculine grace. The music enables him to show the flexibility and the beautiful lyric quality of his voice, as well as some of its tremendous power.... Both the drinking song and the serenade...were repeated. [*Musical America*, February 28, 1914]

In addition to the roles already mentioned he also sang one performance of *Hamlet* in Philadelphia, on February 28, 1914. As on most occasions, it was well received.

Since it was a Ruffo farewell the house was crowded, many standing, and the
baritone was at his best. From his appearance at the rear of the stage, arms
akimbo, black clothed and immersed in thought, to the last scene of the soliloquy,
he was dominant; and this vehement Italian portrayed the meditative Dane with
keen perception of values. His fine delivery of the "Drinking song" was repeated
and his tenderness for Ophelia was marveously simulated in one usually so robust
emotionally. [*Musical Courier*]

After the conclusion of the return engagement in Philadelphia, the
Chicago Opera Company toured the country. Ruffo sang Tonio and
Rigoletto with them in such distant locations as Los Angeles, Portland,
and Seattle. When he finally returned to the east coast he gave one joint
recital with Anna Fitziu in New York on April 27, 1914. Because of the
outbreak of World War I, this was the last time he appeared on this
continent until 1920. His return in that year was welcomed with predictable enthusiasm.

The opening of the eighth week of opera last Monday evening was full of
enthusiasm and musical interest. After some six years Titta Ruffo, the famous
Italian baritone, reappeared in Chicago in his individual characterization of
Tonio, in *Pagliacci*. It was the occasion of one of the most riotous demonstrations
ever witnessed at the Auditorium. Greeted by an audience which taxed the
theater to its utmost limits, the eminent baritone received an ovation rarely
accorded any other singer on our operatic stage.
Ruffo has changed but slightly since he last visited this city, apparently having
taken on weight. He still sings with that ringing power, that round, full-throated
tone and that clear diction which were his most prominent operatic accomplishments formerly.
He had scarcely reached the end of the Prologue before the audience broke
into vociferous cheers, stamping, whistling, so that he had to repeat the last part
of this introduction. Throughout the performance he made his role stand forth
conspicuously, and scored a big success.…
For Titta Ruffo's second appearance he chose the most grateful of all his roles,
that of the name part in Verdi's classic, *Rigoletto*. Of this tragic role Ruffo has
made a personal characterization, thrilling in its absorbingly dramatic action. Of
the Vendetta scene at the close of the third act he made a veritable whirlwind
of passion and intense feeling. [*Musical America*, January 17, 1920]

Ruffo sang only three performances in Chicago, followed by a concert.
He shared the concert platform, as had been his habit, with a soprano.
On this occasion it was Yvonne Gall, the French soprano, whose nation-
alistic feelings created an incident that must have been embarrassing

15. Titta Ruffo in the Title Role of Thomas' *Hamlet*
     Photo: Ermini, Milano
     From the collection of Andrew Farkas

when it occurred, but is amusing in retrospect. Margie McLeod told the story, tongue in cheek.

The artists of the Chicago Opera, with the exception of Yvonne Gall and Titta Ruffo, left Chicago Saturday night at midnight for New York. Mme. Gall and Ruffo were delayed because they were scheduled for a joint recital at the Auditorium Sunday afternoon, which was to be the final note in the successful ten weeks' season of opera. They gave the recital and the program, vocally and artistically, was all that could be desired. The most interesting part in the program, however, was not billed. After all, perhaps the blame for an exceptionally fine display of temperament on the part of the artists is to be placed on Mr. Ruffo's accompanist. He evidently forgot the last and most important phrase in the Prologue, "Ring Up the Curtain," or else had a premonition of trouble descending, and decided not to raise the curtain. At any rate, Mr. Ruffo called him back to the stage. Then, apparently to make up for the disappointment on faces of those who know what he can do with the Prologue, Ruffo put over his big note with even more sustained power than usual. Then the audience settled back to enjoy the rest of the program, the duet from *Don Giovanni*, but there was no "rest" as far as they were permitted to hear. Things were coming fast and furious behind the "drop." France and Italy were in the throes of battle. "Eet shall be in Français," said Yvonne Gall. "Never," shouted back Ruffo. "Vive l'Italia." And there were a lot of other things said that those who find expression only in English could not fully appreciate. Then a gentle person sidled from the wings and in a meek voice announced that there would be no last number on the program. [*Musical America*, February 7, 1920]

The two artists must have come to terms after the recital, since they repeated the concert the following Sunday at the Hippodrome, without an incident. Then followed a series of performances by the Chicago Opera forces at the Lexington Theater. Ruffo sang his three best roles: Tonio, Hamlet, and Rigoletto. His success in his first *Pagliacci* on January 28, 1920, was so overwhelming that the following day it reverberated in the New York press, as if every paper had a reviewer planted in the audience to witness the "event." Their unanimity suggests that at age 42 Titta Ruffo had reached his vocal and artistic zenith, the apex of his parabola.

Katherine Lane, *The Evening Mail*:

Pagliacci began with a tremendous ovation to Titta Ruffo, who sang the Prologue with something so big and human and thrilling in his beautiful voice that the audience forgot its opera manners and shouted. Even people with no Latin temperament cried "Bis" and "Bravo," and at last Mr. Ruffo repeated a part of his aria.

The Globe:

Titta Ruffo got the most tremendous explosion of applause that the season has brought. The audience went frantic when he finished the *Pagliacci* prologue, and the tumult did not abate until he repeated the latter part. He is a personality, his acting is packed with expansive power; there is not another singer so dynamic before the public.

Max Smith, *New York American*:

As a matter of fact the triumph of the day was Titta Ruffo's. It was for him that most music lovers flocked to the Lexington last night. And when he had given expansive utterance to the Prologue, proclaiming the top notes with a force and effusiveness bordering on the phenomenal, the crowd burst into a tumult of vociferous applause such as had not yet been heard east of Broadway this season. Of course, there was an encore; there always is when Ruffo sings the Prologue.

Richard Aldrich, *New York Times*:

In *Pagliacci* Mr. Titta Ruffo dislocated the usual order of things somewhat by making the baritone part of Tonio the center of attraction, instead of Canio. The enthusiasm was ready to take fire on the mere appearance of Mr. Ruffo before the curtain in the Prologue; and did so. So great was the excitement after it that he finally repeated the last part.

Mr. Ruffo's voice, which seems finer than it did on his former appearance in New York, is one of immense power and sonority. It is still young, fresh and vibrant. It is a voice of bronze till it is forced to its extreme power in the upper tones, when it is as a brazen clarion.

And, finally the *New York Herald*:

It was good to see a New York operatic audience really wake up and shout its approval. There is too much polite applause and too little real enthusiasm. But such an ovation as Mr. Ruffo received is almost unparalleled in the history of baritones in New York. He had to repeat part of the Prologue. His voice is the most vital, the most thrilling among operatic baritones. His idea of the Prologue dramatically is different from that of other singers. He is original as well as thrilling, and his singing was more artistic and less theatrical than when heard here before. There were reports that Titta Ruffo lost his voice during the war, for he did not sing when his country was in the fighting on account of his military duties, but his singing is now better, if anything, than before.

His success notwithstanding, his decade-old nemesis (or so it seems), H.F.P., still on the *Musical America* staff, found *Hamlet* a convenient excuse for another "dig" at the singer.

16.   Titta Ruffo as Tonio in *Pagliacci* (Chicago, 1919)
Photo: Matzene
Courtesy of Ruffo Titta, Jr.

With Tonio behind him and Rigoletto before, Mr. Ruffo sported the trappings and the suite of woe of the Prince of Denmark Friday evening of last week. In this selfsame contemptible travesty of Shakespeare the singer first unloosed upon New York back in November, 1912, the fullness of his noisy glory....

The performance last week naturally proceeded from and revolved about Titta Ruffo. A horde of Italians made the night hideous with their shrieks and ravings over the stalwart vocal tours-de-force of their countryman. The drinking song was repeated—there was no way out of it. Ruffo's Hamlet is no new matter. Some like it, others do not. The former defend it on the ground that Barbier and Carré are not Shakespeare. So be it! In the present case issues of characterization are of no importance. Mr. Ruffo gave free rein to his voluminous, brazen voice. There was nothing refined and little musical about the display. The nearest approach to distinction might have been discerned in the pinchbeck perversion of the "To be or not to be" soliloquy. But since nine-tenths of the audience were stupendously pleased the rest may be silent. [*Musical America*, February 21, 1920]

Yet this reviewer's colleague at the same magazine, identifying himself with the initials O.T. (Oscar Thompson?), gives an entirely different appraisal of the singer in the next issue.

When Titta Ruffo sings, there is bedlam. In Ruffo is found the living exception to the rule that only a great tenor, among men singers, ever can create a furore. Baritone though he is, he presents a box office lure comparable to Caruso. The tempest of enthusiasm he stirs whenever he hurls forth his prodigious high tones would have brought exultation to the heart of any tenor who ever trod the boards of opera.

New York has really been hearing Ruffo for the first time, in the notable engagement of the Chicago Opera forces at the Lexington Theater, now at its close. His lone operatic appearance in *Hamlet* and a concert program seven years ago scarcely revealed his unusual attributes to New York's worshippers of song. During the Lexington season he has been heard six times, twice in *Pagliacci*, twice in *Hamlet* and twice in *Rigoletto*, with the result that his vocal powers now are fully known and he has established himself in Gotham, as elsewhere, as one of the most sensational singers of the day.

Tremendous vitality, clarion top tones, a resonance through the upper and middle voice that suggests the vibration of a great gong, the whole effect being that of an organ of bronze, and ability to clothe the characters he presents with an original and compelling personality—even though a repellent one, as in his half-wit conception of Tonio—these are qualities that stamp Ruffo as one of the towering operatic figures of the day. He has, in addition, a voice of amazing flexibility. He sings for his audiences, not for the critics. Ask those audiences who is the mighty baritone of today. Back will come a roaring response—"Titta Ruffo!" [*Musical America*, February 28, 1920]

On his triumphant reconquest of the scenes of his former great successes, Ruffo finally returned to Philadelphia. He gave a recital on March

1, 1920, and his reception was as warm and enthusiastic as could be expected.

Titta Ruffo gave his first Philadelphia recital and made his first appearance here since his sensational successes with the Philadelphia-Chicago Opera Company a decade ago, before an audience that took up the stage as well as the auditorium of the Metropolitan Opera House....

Mr. Ruffo's voice in the intervening years seems to have gained in power, resonancy and artistic capacity, and in the communication of feeling, especially in the field of folk and popular songs. He sang many of these to the manifest approval of his countrymen present, and sang them with real feeling and fine simplicity. The inclusion of such pieces gave the program a novelty of aspect that would have been missing had Mr. Ruffo specialized in the operatic arias for which he is best known. [*Musical America*, March 6, 1920]

An even more successful concert took place in the Hippodrome. Ruffo was joined by a former concert partner, Anna Fitziu, and pianist Arthur Rubinstein. If Rubinstein placed this concert in correct chronological sequence in the second volume of his autobiography,[8] that is, subsequent to Chaliapin's return to New York, then the following review does not pertain to the concert described in this book. If, however, the two artists appeared together at the Hippodrome only once, then Rubinstein's recollection of Ruffo being in poor voice is obviously erroneous.

Titta Ruffo's admirers, 7,000 strong crammed the Hippodrome last Sunday night and almost lifted the roof off that structure with their shouts, stamping and clapping. New York has witnessed only a few such clamorous demonstrations within the past few years.

The great organ tones of the baritone in the "Eri tu" aria from Verdi's *Ballo in maschera*, the Mozart *Don Giovanni* "Serenade," Costa's "Sei morta nella vita mia" and his other offerings stirred the audience to a frenzy of excitement. Men and women on the stage rushed to clasp his hand; agitated compatriots in the high heavens roared out long vowels of ecstasy. Caruso himself has not received a stronger tribute. Of course the encores were many. Another fact should be recorded to the credit of Mr. Ruffo: he insisted that the musicianly accompanist of the evening share in the applause. [*Musical America*, May 1, 1920]

Ruffo also sang a concert in Springfield, Massachusetts, in May. "In Ruffo's singing there may be the excesses due to a vehement temperament, but it will always be wonderful singing. His voice is one of the finest of our day and he uses it with marvelous power and ease; what Caruso is among tenors he is among baritones," wrote the reviewer of the *Springfield Republican*.

Upon his return to Chicago in the fall of 1920 he sang Rigoletto, performed two roles new to Chicago—Carlo Gérard and Iago—and created the title role in the world premiere of Leoncavallo's posthumous work, *Edipo Re*, on December 13, 1920. Margery Max reviewed the performance for *Musical America*:

Even for Ruffo's vocalism the music was too much, in at least two instances, where his voice changed to a roar in swooping from some fortissimo high notes to a lower range. But, on the whole, despite the tremendous volume of sound required by the score, and poured out without stint from Ruffo's powerful lungs, his voice sounded more beautiful, more touched with pathos, than in any other role. It swept through all the tragic moods—anger, despair, hate, pathos; and Ruffo became, for the time, Oedipus Rex. In none of his roles has he so thoroughly sunk Titta Ruffo into the character he was enacting. [December 25, 1920]

The singer closed (almost) his local engagement with a performance of *Otello*. René Devries reviewed the December 29, 1920, performance.

Ruffo was the Iago. This is sufficient to assure a careful study of one of the most interesting portraits in the baritone repertory. His Iago lacked slyness and adroitness, but for that very reason it was more powerful. His [Iago] is a brute, a ruffian, a master scoundrel, a most unsympathetic creature, a white gloved villain. A very clever study, well worth seeing. In glorious fettle he poured tones of such magnitude as to astound the tympanum.... This performance was billed as his farewell but the marvelous success of the production prompted the management to secure Ruffo for another appearance in Chicago in the same opera, this on January 16. [*Musical Courier*, January 6, 1921]

On April 24, 1921, he gave a joint recital with Tetrazzini in the Hippodrome. According to the reviewer of the *Musical Courier* (April 28, 1921), "there never has been quite such a a multitude as applauded and cheered the two famous artists." Needless to say, the concert was a success.

The 1921-22 season finally brought Ruffo's long-awaited debut with the Metropolitan Opera Company of New York. It will be recalled that he did sing Hamlet on the stage of the Met in 1912, but not as a member of the company. There were rumors of a new production of *Otello* for Caruso and Ruffo in the 1921-22 season, but tragically, because of Caruso's extended illness and his death on August 2, 1921, this plan never materialized.

When Ruffo finally did join the company his services were not utilized to the fullest. Reportedly there was a cordial dislike between Ruffo and Casazza-Gatti, the Met's morose general manager. This may explain why Gatti made no efforts to please the singer. Between 1922 and 1929 he sang only forty-six performances in the house and eight more on tour— not a busy schedule by any standard. He never appeared in some of his celebrated roles, most notably as Rigoletto. During Ruffo's tenure the role was a De Luca property, but as Danise and Millo Picco were allowed to sing it once and Basiola twice, Ruffo too could have given a perform-

17. Titta Ruffo in the Title Role of Leoncavallo's *Edipo Re* (Chicago, 1920)
Photo: H. A. Atwell
Courtesy of Ruffo Titta, Jr.

ance. He sang only seven roles at the Met, the baritone lead in *Ernani*, *Pagliacci*, *Aida*, *Andrea Chénier*, *Gioconda*, *Cena delle beffe*, and his debut role, Figaro, in the *Barber of Seville* on January 19, 1922. His partners on this occasion were Cora Chase, Mario Chamlee, Mardones, and Didur, under the baton of Papi.

The opera had been given earlier in the season, but last night's performance had special interest. Titta Ruffo, the distinguished baritone, made his first appearance at the Metropolitan, singing the role of Figaro. He was to have made his Metropolitan debut in *Ernani*, on December 8, but a severe cold prevented his appearance. It was a great delight to his admirers to welcome him last evening. The house was packed and when Mr. Ruffo made his appearance to sing "Largo al factotum" in the first scene he was received with tremendous applause and cheers. Mr. Ruffo's Figaro was undoubtedly a surprise to those who had heard him only in tragic roles. It was many miles away from his Hamlet and Edipo Re. For instance, the *recitativo secco* as it is technically called—the rapid Italian dialogue patter—he sang with great facility, with elasticity, with unction, and with color. This *recitativo* plays an important part in the comedy of Rossini's opera and it was a significant element in Mr. Ruffo's gay and infectious impersonation. He sang some of the vocal numbers well and some more than well, though the temptation to use the full volume of his great voice in questionable places was irresistible. The florid passages in the first scene, too, were hardly in his line, but he showed cunning in turning them to humorous uses. On the whole, then, it can be recorded that Mr. Ruffo's Figaro was pleasing in its glee, its vivacity, its genuine humor, and its touches of a hitherto unrevealed skill. [W. J. Henderson, *New York Sun*, January 20, 1922]

An article in *Musical America* signed with the initials C. F. confirms the previous judgment.

The latest recruit to join the merry band of Figaros, who have frolicked with the pattering vocables of Rossini's *Barber of Seville* at the Metropolitan, Titta Ruffo vaulted into his place as one of Giulio Gatti-Casazza's stellar baritones on Thursday evening. Four times previously he had been announced to appear, but laryngitis interfered. He was given a heart-warming welcome, with the greatest heat manifesting itself from behind the rail and in the far balconies.

The big-voiced Tuscan had some difficulty beginning the "Largo al factotum" because of the applause which greeted him as he entered, and was manifestly nervous as he sang it. The fun of subsequent scenes restored his normal poise and he delivered the rapid *secco* with much skill and not a few touches of effective comedy, coloring his phrases drolly and not infrequently propelling forth tones as vital as they were powerful. [January 28, 1922]

As the review states, Ruffo's debut was repeatedly postponed because of a stubborn case of laryngitis that refused to clear up. The notices of his subsequent performances clearly indicate that he was not yet fully recovered when he resumed his activities. One wonders whether his illness and his premature return to the stage had caused some lasting damage to his voice. In any case, with the wisdom of hindsight, it appears that the descending trajectory of his parabolic career can be dated from the ultimate endorsement of his art: his Metropolitan Opera debut. He finally sang in *Ernani* for the first time on January 28, nine days after his debut, opposite Ponselle, Martinelli, and Mardones. Oscar Thompson reviewed the performance:

When the greatest possible number of standees had been admitted to the Metropolitan Saturday afternoon, attendants cleared the lobby of hundreds of disappointed ones. The reason for the crush was the first appearance of Titta Ruffo in *Ernani*, the Verdi opera which General Manager Gatti-Casazza revived especially for Ruffo, but which was given without him at its first two representations because of the baritone's stubborn indisposition. The throng about the rail was as vociferous as it was dense and piled demonstration on demonstration in behalf of the big-voiced Tuscan.

Regally costumed and of kingly bearing, Ruffo made something more, dramatically, of the role of Don Carlos than his predecessor [Danise] did, but, in truth to tell, he did not sing it as well. There were indications that he was not in his best voice; per example, his failure to seize upon the opportunity to sing the optional high A-natural in "O sommo Carlo," an opportunity seldom overlooked by baritones who have this note in their compass—as Ruffo proved he had, a year ago, when he sang it in Iago's "Brindisi" in *Otello*. Of more concern, however, than this omission, was his rhythmic uncertainty, his savage dismemberment of "Lo vedremo," and his lack of fluent lyricism in "Vieni meco, sol di rose." [*Musical America*, February 4, 1922]

His February 2 Tonio was also marred by vocal problems, according to J.A.H. of *Musical America* (February 11, 1922): "In *Pagliacci*, Titta Ruffo made his first appearance as Tonio at the Metropolitan. He was not in good voice and struggled with hoarseness throughout."

At his joint recital with Frieda Hempel on February 19 at the Hippodrome he was still struggling with vocal difficulties. Reviewer H. J., after pointing out the presence of Rosa Raisa, Giacomo Rimini, and Joseph Schwarz and his bride in the audience, went on to say:

Mr. Ruffo's first number was the "Drinking Song" from Thomas' *Hamlet*, which he did not sing with quite his usual gusto, but subsequently he offered a lavish outpouring of his voice in the "Toreador Song" from *Carmen*, which evoked tumultuous demonstrations of enthusiasm. His extraordinary breath control and the richness of some of his higher tones when he sang full voice were of exhilarating effect, while on the other hand, his mezza-voce lacked carrying quality and his phrasing was by no means finely polished. [*Musical America*, February 25, 1922]

His vocal troubles continued to disrupt his activities during the rest of the spring of 1922. He was scheduled to sing a joint recital with soprano Graziella Pareto at the Hippodrome on April 2, but he canceled in the last minute and John Charles Thomas appeared in his stead. Three days later, on April 5, he canceled a *Barbiere* at the Metropolitan and Giuseppe de Luca took over the role of Figaro. Finally, following the close of the Met season, he sailed for Europe on April 23.

Ruffo had not been heard in London since 1903. Why the Covent Garden management did not find it their artistic duty to invite back one of the foremost baritones in the world remains a mystery. It is highly unlikely that Ruffo held a grudge against the theater, especially if one considers that he had forgiven even Melba, the perpetrator of his unglorious premature exit from Covent Garden, and had sung a *Rigoletto* with her in Philadelphia in 1914.

When Ruffo returned to London in 1922, it was only as a recitalist. He sang at both the Albert Hall and the Queen's Hall. He had a huge popular success, just as in every other country where he appeared, but the British critics looked for more restraint and more refinement than the baritone, after years of yielding to South and North American demands for volume and grand effects, was prepared to give. As careful analysis of his notices reveals, he misjudged—or, perhaps, was insensitive to—the difference in national tastes. His celebrated high notes and the volume of his powerful voice—often likened to a clarion and described as bronze—invariably enthralled his listeners and ensured his success. He made the lifelong assumption that a big sound was expected of him beyond all the other attributes his artistry had to offer. It would appear in retrospect that he felt he had to choose between pleasing his audience and pleasing the critics. The choice he made is reflected in the objective report of the London critic who demanded more besides volume from the "world's greatest operatic baritone," and rightly so, especially on the concert stage.

Titta Ruffo, who followed Battistini at Queen's Hall (May 5) is a singer of quite different type. From the depth of a colossal chest poured out tone with cheerful abandon. For the most part he was astonishingly effective in a flamboyant style; but he had some very indifferent moments, musically, and cannot be said to have been ever inspired. Of course it is difficult to rise to the promise of the new sonorous advertising. To be heralded as "the world's greatest operatic baritone" is a handicap. After that, comparisons are inevitable, and the claims for Signor Ruffo can then hardly be allowed.

He may have been affected by the extreme boisterousness of his audience, and perhaps did not know of the sort of behaviour expected on our concert-platforms; anyway, he played into the hands of his noisy admirers in a way rather below our standard for a great artist, and carried on as though in full operatic trappings, innocent of restraint and repose. His exaggerations were least out of place in "Largo al factotum," from Rossini's *Barber*, where the appeal must be theatrical—for the voice is wonderful, the high notes commanding, and he careered the difficulties of the old music with the utmost ease. Indeed, it is difficult to imagine it better sung. In the bluff bravura style he is eminent, and also a few contemplative moments were sung with beauty of tone.

But it seemed characteristic that his two chief songs were a drinking song and a buffo air. Either Signor Ruffo is not so much a master of variety as he might be, or else he did not give us of his best. The quality of the voice is bass baritone. We did not find its lack of the lyric baritone's legato quite compensated for by its various exceptional powers. Miss Yvonne d'Arle assisted at this concert.

H.J.K.

[The Musical Times, June 1, 1922]

The article makes no reference to any vocal troubles; thus, his condition must have markedly improved by the time of the London concerts. Still, upon his return to America in the fall, reading between the lines of many subsequent reviews one has the feeling that he never fully regained his former control over his voice. The reviewer of his October 22, 1922, recital at Boston's Symphony Hall, again with Yvonnne d'Arle, only mentions his singing being "characterized by a robustness of voice and graphic projection which have become typical of his performances."

In late fall of 1922, *Musical America* columnist of "Mephisto's Musings" fame had an opportunity to meet Ruffo socially when he was invited to lunch with him at his apartment. Although his observations are brief and his report mere vignettes, they are revealing regarding the baritone's personality and the lasting impression he could create on others. The reporter's comments and the selective quotations of Ruffo's replies add some valuable details to the artistic image.

With all the artists, foreign and domestic, did you ever realize how very few of them are what might be called "personalities," those who do not alone impress you by their compelling presence, their authority, their artistic power, but who would be conspicuous, even great, if they had never sung or played a note? . . .

You are not more than five minutes with Ruffo before you realize that you are face to face with a man of tremendous magnetic power. The very way in which he straightens himself out, fixes his attention on you, the courteous yet intense manner in which he listens, the remarkable clarity and incisiveness in which he discusses any matter, are all characteristic. You will find as you converse with him that he is not alone a past grand master as an artist in opera, in concerts, but that he is a philosopher, a widely read and highly cultured man, a man who even today finds time to read works of history, philosophy, a man who is interested in something more than the mere role he plays.

When I complimented him that he was singing with more reserve and, therefore, with greater charm than ever, he said that of late he had been more reticent with regard to the volume of tone that he used, but had endeavored to put greater power into the interpretation of the role. This led to a discussion of the difference between artists and singers, as well as the difference between actors and artists....

Ruffo said with regard to operatic artists that he thought the difference lay between those who thought of nothing but their voice and how they could make it effective and those who made this subordinate to the presentation of the role in which they appeared. He admitted, however, that there were certain passages in operas where the public demanded a grand volume of tone, and that this was particularly true of southern European nations and those in South America.

On one matter we thoroughly agreed, namely, that the claque, particularly as it is today at the Metropolitan, is a nuisance. Ruffo appeared to think that a claque, with which he asserted he had never had any relation whatever, was able to injure an artist, not so much by abstaining from applause, but by applauding when it should be silent. [*Musical America*, December 30, 1922]

When he sang his first *Ernani* of the season on December 16, 1922, it was again Oscar Thompson who wrote the review, just as on the occasion of his first assumption of the role at the Met in the previous January. Although he praises the baritone's performance, he points out that Ruffo is now singing with more reserve.

Ernani, one of the early Verdi operas which refuses to stayed buried, asserted its still considerable vitality Saturday afternoon, when its performance this season served to bring back to Metropolitan audiences Titta Ruffo and Rosa Ponselle. The former, for whom *Ernani* was revived last season, but who appeared in it but once sang his music with more of freedom than when he last essayed it, and made many moments of it effective through the use of his unique and powerful voice. That he did not dispense high tones with his wonted lavishness of a few seasons ago (the optional high A natural in the "O sommo Carlo" ensemble failed to tempt him) was of small consequence, and clamorous enthusiasm reigned behind the rail where the standees were foregathered to shout their bravos. [*Musical America*, December 23, 1922]

Ruffo's association with the late Rosa Ponselle dates from the Met *Ernani* performances. They sang together nineteen times at the Met during the decade that witnessed his accelerating decline. Yet if one is to trust Ponselle's judgment as well as her memory, "...there was *nobody* like Titta Ruffo. He could sing it all, high notes and low notes, *piano* as well as *forte*."[9] In fact, he was one of the three miracles in singing that Tullio Serafin had claimed to have known, the other two being Caruso and Ponselle. She also mentions that, "sadly, the sheer volume of his voice often overshadowed its intrinsic beauty and the exquisite *mezza voce* possibilities it afforded. One of his longstanding complaints was that the public never accepted his *mezza voce* singing; they expected him to sing at full volume, especially in the familiar arias."[10]

Oscar Thompson also gave a good notice of the Amonasro Ruffo sang a month later at the Met, on January 18, 1923. Considering that it was the first time he undertook the role in this country, perhaps it deserved more detailed treatment than it was given..

Thursday afternoon's special *Aida*, another of the many benefit performances of the season at the Metropolitan, was given a new element of interest in the appearance of Titta Ruffo as Amonasro, his first assumption of this part in America. The big-voiced baritone made the role highly impressive both in vocal power and in its dramatic and pictorial aspects. The frustrated attempt at assassination in the Nile scene, usually an obscure incident, was lifted to high relief by Mr. Ruffo's intensity. [*Musical America*, January 27, 1923]

After two years' absence Ruffo returned to Chicago, but only for a concert. Partnered by Yvonne d'Arle again, with violinist Fritz Renk also on the program, he was

vociferously received by an audience predominantly Italian. He was in excellent voice. He produced the same prodigious volume of tone without apparent effort as in former seasons, except that an occasional high note sounded forced. This, however, was forgotten in listening to the beauty and richness of the lower and middle registers. He sang with more restraint than when he last appeared here, but this only added to the artistic worth of his interpretations. His listed numbers included "O casto fior," from Massenet's *Re di Lahore*, the "Toreador Song" from *Carmen*, "Adamastor" from Meyerbeer's *L'Africaine* and a group of Italian, French, and Spanish songs, but had to add many extras. [*Musical America*, February 17, 1923]

His joining the Met set a pattern for his activities for the rest of the decade. He would fulfill engagements in Europe and South America, but would return to the United States for the fall and spring, and would also travel throughout the country. His appearances, though well received, would no longer create the sensation as before. For example, J.A.H. of *Musical America* (December 26, 1923) devotes only one sentence to his Gérard in *Chénier* on December 17: "Mr. Ruffo was clapped and cheered after everything he sang, and 'Nemico della patria' interrupted the performance for several minutes." Oscar Thompson treats his December 11, 1925, Barnaba in *La Gioconda* the same way, even though it was his first appearance with the company that season: "Mr. Ruffo's singing was excellent as he was in his best voice and the role of the Venetian spy is one of his best" (*Musical America*, December 19, 1925).

His return to Budapest in the early spring of 1925 commanded a great deal more attention. Even though his reappearance after a twelve-year absence was a festive occasion, the reviewers did not hesitate to record, with benign regret, the passage of time that showed in the voice of their onetime favorite. His musicianship and stagecraft were recognized and acknowledged without reservations, but his voice was "worn," according to the critics, having lost much of its former brilliance. Yet Ruffo was compared with the aging Battistini who sang Figaro in Budapest only two days earlier: Ruffo's high G was likened to the "radiant southern sun" compared with Battistini's "tame moonlight."

His Hamlet, on the other hand, earned the usual accolades. The critic of *Pesti Napló* (Aladár Tóth?) wrote that "Titta Ruffo's Hamlet is such a grandiose creation that it cannot be criticized, only analyzed" (April 9, 1925). Izor Béldi of *Pesti Hirlap* complained that "this Hamlet is a characterization equally magnificent in vocal and histrionic terms; it is a pity that only the voice part can be preserved on records and his superb acting is lost the instant the curtain falls. It should also be captured to let actors learn from it" (April 9, 1925).

The interviews he gave in Budapest contain several passages that reflect on his complex personality and the variety of his interests. Asked about theatrical life in Italy, he referred to "the ruler of the stage: Luigi Pirandello. In my opinion however, Pirandello's success is ephemeral, his is the theater of the moment. He never could and never will be able to create anything as grandiose as Gabriele D'Annunzio. Because Pirandello only thinks, D'Annunzio feels too" (*Pesti Napló*, April 1, 1925).

János Fóthy quotes Ruffo speaking of his daughter and son ("who has a beautiful baritone voice") that "they hopefully will not become singers. God forbid! They should never know, and the public doesn't know it either, what superhuman struggle it is for an artist to solve the secret of art. What terrible self-torment!...Let my son live a beautiful, calm free life...in fresh air under God's blue sky." There is also a trace of sadness as the singer meditates why people struggle for grand goals.

Glory? Fame? It passes. Everything passes, life, memory, everything in the world. Often I feel like shouting at people that nothing is important, only life itself. One should live without striving for the unattainable or for things that can be reached only after much suffering, to live for the beautiful moment that often gives the very most to a person. Live as the ancient Greeks lived in Hellas, my favorite epoch, the most beautiful people, the people of the greatest artists. Lots of sunshine, air, gorgeous green meadows, gaiety. [*Pesti Hirlap*, April 1, 1925]

If Ruffo's routine appearances at the Metropolitan ceased to be an extraordinary event, he still made news once more in the American premiere of Giordano's *La Cena delle beffe* at the Met, on January 2, 1926. The opera, based on Sem Benelli's play *The Jest*, belongs in the verismo school and gave ample opportunity to Ruffo to give his best. An unsigned review (Thompson?) in *Musical America* gives qualified praise to his performance:

Ruffo as Neri had opportunity to expend the full volume and sonority of his extraordinarily powerful voice. That boastful bully had need of some such voluminous organ though he might have been more patrician in his use of it. In appearance, too, the baritone admirably bodied forth the muscular braggart, and when he struggled with his captors there was more than the usual semblance of a fight. His simulation of madness had effective details, which were partly nullified, however, by others that bordered on the comic.

The entire characterization was one of large, roughhewn lines, as vehement physically as it was vocally, and hammering home its points with the blows of a sledge....

Some of the baritone's big tones were of noble beauty. Others were driven so hard that their resonance lost focus. In all, it was an operatic impersonation of much power, but of curiously conflicting virtues and defects. [January 9, 1926]

After fulfilling his Met obligations Ruffo went on tour with the Chicago Civic Opera Company. One critic wrote of his Boston performance of *Un ballo in maschera* (January 29, 1926): "Mr. Ruffo's stentorian singing as René was the best feature of the Verdi opera." In Baltimore, Giacomo Rimini had to substitute for him in *Tosca*, but soon after, in Cleveland (February 19, 1926), "Titta Ruffo sang Iago in splendid style." He also sang three *Traviatas*, in Birmingham, Memphis, and Miami, which is all the more surprising as he had not sung the role of the elder Germont for nearly two decades. Unfortunately, no review could be located of any of these performances which must have been quite spectacular with Muzio in the cast, and Charles Hackett alternating the role of Alfredo with Antonio Cortis.

In early 1927 Ruffo was engaged by the La Scala Grand Opera Company of Philadelphia to sing five performances in the company's home town and two in Pittsburgh. Because of the company's severe financial problems Ruffo sang only one of the scheduled performances. He appeared as Iago in *Otello* on January 29, 1927. W. R. Murphy praised his delivery of the role.

An outstanding dramatic performance of *Otello* marked the reappearance of Titta Ruffo as an operatic artist in the Metropolitan Opera House [of Philadelphia], the scene of his first American triumphs....As Iago, Mr. Ruffo gave a masterly characterization of the part, and was rewarded with almost countless curtain calls and excited cries of "Bravo" and "Bis." [*Musical America*, February 5, 1925]

Unfortunately for the singer, Ruffo reaped the rewards of his singing onstage only, not off of it. As the *New York Times* reported on March 2 and again on March 20, 1927, he was suing the company for his $2,500 fee, extraordinary for a baritone. "He alleged that a check for this amount tendered for his performance in Verdi's *Otello* had been returned to him by a bank with the explanation that it could not be honored."

Between Philadelphia and his return to the Met in the fall he had only

a handful of engagements in Europe. In the absence of other explanations, one must attribute this to a greatly diminished demand for his
services. His obligations at the Met and in Philadelphia were relatively
few and he was back in Europe early in the spring of 1928. He returned
for the last time to Budapest and, as it became his custom, he first gave
a series of interviews. Some of his statements deserve to be quoted in
full. In an interview with János Fóthy he speaks of American culture.

America has a soul, a special soul, different from ours. One shouldn't think that
American life is as mechanical as it is said to be. Take the negroes, for instance.... I love the race which is full of soul, full of intellect. They have singers
now who could be the envy of any European opera house. You should see how
cultivated the negroes are in Pennsylvania! A piano in every home, they play
Bach and Wagner. I recently read a volume of poetry by a negro poet—it has
marvelous lyric depth! Here, in Europe, they know nothing of this, they only
know the negroes of the jazz band. They aren't curious about the true, intellectual
Black world. [*Pesti Hirlap*, April 25, 1928]

In another interview he was asked about the "greatest artists" with
whom he sang. "Greatest artists? I know famous artists but there is only
one greatest artist: Chaliapin. He is the greatest, unique, glowing talent.
A genius! Chaliapin, only him! I have no opinion of other artists" (*Pesti
Napló*, April 25, 1928).

He sang two performances during his final Budapest engagement. He
first appeared as Scarpia in *Tosca* at the Városi Szinház, and by some
curious quirk of bookings Marcel Journet sang the same role at the Opera
House on the previous night! Comparisons were inevitable and they
turned in favor of Journet, ten years his senior. Ruffo was heavily criticized for his interpretation, presenting Scarpia as a senile, old, crotchety,
mean lecher. It is worth noting that this was the same interpretation he
gave to the role at the Colón fully two decades earlier, as early as 1908.
It met with disfavor on the part of the Argentine critics, although he
was then in his prime. His diminished vocal resources in 1928 only
seemed to accentuate the character's fragility, making his violent out-
bursts in the second act incongruous and objectionable. The friendly
Fóthy only hinted at his poor vocal estate, but Kovács of the *Pesti Napló*
was more explicit. "The Maestro's appearance tonight must have been
painful for his followers, friends and fans. The King of the Baritones'
voice is broken, what is left of this once brilliant and glorious organ only
survives because of his ingenious musicianship" (April 28, 1928). The
implication was that Ruffo at fifty, a relatively young age for a baritone,
could no longer live up to the vocal demands of his repertory.

Prior to the performance, a concert of Italian songs and arias was
advertised to follow *Tosca*. Presumably this oddity was devised to "top"
the Journet performance. In the absence of any reference to this concert

in three reviews of the evening, one must assume it did not take place despite the newspaper announcements.

Figaro, his second and last appearance, came off somewhat better. One critic kindly wrote that in this role "he had but one rival: his former self" (*Pesti Napló*, May 1, 1928). He sang "Quand'ero paggio" from *Falstaff* in the lesson scene poorly, and several Italian songs well. But the reviews left no doubt about it: This was the twilight of a magnificent career. He had been singing for thirty years at that time, never holding back, always giving his utmost in every performance. It is a matter of speculation whether longer years of study would have benefited his vocal longevity; pushing his voice to its limits for three decades took its toll, in terms of his age, prematurely.

Nonetheless, Ruffo was somehow still holding his place in the operatic world as the decade was nearing its end. He enjoyed a popular success with his faithful audiences, but the critical notices, though essentially friendly, grew increasingly brief and politely evasive. The baritone was only fifty-one years old when he sang Amonasro in *Aida* on February 22, 1929, his last appearance at the Met. It passed without fanfare; presumably neither the singer nor his admirers realized that this was destined to be his last operatic performance not only in New York, but in the rest of the United States as well.

Then came the public announcement about his plans to make "talking pictures," or "talkies" as they were called then. Unfortunately for him, but even more regrettably for future generations, his high hopes for motion picture work did not materialize.

Titta Ruffo, baritone, announced last night before sailing for Italy on the liner Augustus that he had severed his connection with the Metropolitan Opera Company and would devote most of his time in the future to singing for sound movies. Mr. Ruffo said he had contracts for ten short subjects and two long pictures, which would bring him a total of $350,000.

Mr. Ruffo said he had already completed four of the ten short subjects for Metro-Goldwyn-Mayer Corporation, and that the first of these was to be released in April. His pay for the ten short subjects, he said was $100,000. The four he has completed are arias from *The Barber of Seville, Otello, Africana* and a a group of Italian folk songs.

One of the two long pictures for which he has signed will be based on his life, the singer said. It will tell the story of a painter who became famous on the opera stage as he did.

There is a great future for all artists in the talking pictures, the singer said. "I felt that this new medium gives the artist a better chance to put himself across if he has heart and soul in his subject," he declared. "I believe it gives him a chance to make his work far more effective and it enables him at the same time to reach far greater audiences.

"Another advantage which this new medium offers is the permanency of record. The work of a great artist will never die."

Mr. Ruffo said he had heard and seen the four short subjects which are completed. "They have convinced me that the new medium excels the phonograph record in recording the artist's voice," he said, "and in addition it gives him an opportunity to record for all time his excellence in histrionics. The new medium gives adequate volume to the voice and produces a far better range."

It is not Mr. Ruffo's intention to forsake the opera stage completely, he said. While abroad he will sing in Paris and later in Italy, and before his return to the United States will appear in Rio de Janeiro. Mr. Ruffo intimated that other leading members of the Metropolitan Opera Company might follow his example and work for the sound films. This gained support when it was learned from an authoritative source last night that other stars had received offers of lucrative contracts from talking picture promoters. Fedor Chaliapin, the Russian basso, who sailed on the Aquitania last night, is understood to have offers amounting to $200,000, but so far has not accepted any. He is reported to have told friends that he is not anxious to work with the new medium because he is not certain that he would find the work satisfactory. [*New York Times*, March 23, 1929]

The sound recording of two of the four short subjects Ruffo is quoted to have completed survived. "Largo al factotum" and the *Otello* "Credo" circulated privately in the early 1960s on LP (The Golden Age of Opera, EJS 142-A). Only the first of these two selections could be traced as having been shown: the *Barbiere* aria was screened as a Metro Movietone short in New York on April 24, 1929. Without a critical comment of any sort, *New York Times* film critic Mordaunt Hall merely records that the film was shown in his review of the main feature (April 25, 1929): "Before the screening of *Madame X* there were presented Titta Ruffo in a short audible film singing the 'Figaro' aria from the *Barber of Seville*, and also a talking and singing Technicolor production 'Climbing the Golden Stairs,' a revue produced by Gus Edwards." The phrasing suggests that the Ruffo film was shot in black and white; its whereabouts is unknown.

As detailed by Ruffo Titta, Jr., elsewhere in this book, the baritone's plans for a film career never materialized on either side of the Atlantic. But within a year of this tentative test of audience response to filmed operatic fare, MGM signed up another baritone, the first and thus far the only one to successfully combine a full-scale operatic and film career: Lawrence Tibbett. Curiously and coincidentally, MGM's next star male vocalist was also a baritone: Nelson Eddy. Although he was trained for opera and put in some apprentice years in Dresden under Fritz Busch, his excursions into live opera were sporadic once he had established his film career.

Following his departure from the Met, Ruffo tried to remain moderately active in other parts of the world, although the remaining years of his career were not without problems. There is a puzzling news item, for instance, in the July 8, 1931, issue of the *New York Times*, headed "Ruffo Quits Engagement":

Buenos Aires, July 7. Titta Ruffo, Italian baritone, terminated his engagement at the Colón Theatre today without explanation and left for Genoa tonight on the steamer Conte Verde. He had completed the sixth of a proposed series of twenty appearances.

Although Ruffo sang six more concerts during 1933-35 and a staged *Hamlet*—Act I, Scene 2 and Act III, only—in 1934, his last New York engagement signaled the end of his career. Coincidentally, it was also his last visit to the Americas. He was invited to participate in the variety show that opened the Radio City Music Hall on December 27, 1932. *Musical America* (January 10, 1933) shows him costarring with Coe Glade and Arnoldo Lindi "in a condensed version of *Carmen*." Considering the length of the festive program and the role of Escamillo, this must have meant the "Toreador Song" and only that. Curiously, both *Musical America* and the *New York Times* (December 28, 1932) mention him only as one of the star attractions among many performers, but without adding a word of commentary about his singing.

He was engaged for a series of performances but he withdrew from the program following opening night. His reasons can best be assessed from a letter to his son, dated December 31, 1932:[11]

My dear Ruffo,
Today is the last day of the year and the only joy is having your letters which made me feel so good. The news I am sending you *is not happy*. To come here was a great mistake on my part. I committed it with the thought of not wanting to spend the winter without anything to do, a thing that is deadly for someone with my nature, however, it would have been better. Roxy[12] made a tremendous fiasco; the entire press is against him for having spent tens of millions on that ugly, senseless theater. The show is pure *vaudeville*, with magicians, ballet dancers, Chinamen, trained dogs, and similar useless stupidities. I have never seen a similar Babel: suffice it to say that at the rehearsal I was made up and dressed as the Toreador for several hours, waiting for my entrance, my number of Carmen, with mediocre artists; at the performance they made me go to the theater at 8 p.m. and I sang at midnight. The following day, as you can imagine, I withdrew. The gesture was approved by the entire musical community. Thus I have spent a lot of money, I will have worries, and this time again I have deprived myself from spending Christmas and the New Year with you.

> To you, with all my heart,
> your Papà

RADIO - KEITH - ORPHEUM

PROUDLY PRESENTS

THE INAUGURAL PROGRAM

OF THE

RADIO CITY MUSIC HALL

UNDER THE PERSONAL DIRECTION OF

RADIO CITY

IN ROCKEFELLER CENTER

18. Inaugural Program of the Radio City Music Hall

THE PROGRAM

•

The Entire Performance Conceived and Supervised by "ROXY,"
Director-General of the Radio City Music Hall and the RKO Roxy Theatre

1. SYMPHONY OF THE CURTAINS

CAROLINE ANDREWS, *Soloist*
"Hymn to the Sun," from Rimsky-Korsakoff's "Le Coq d'Or"
The great "Contour Curtain," first of its kind in the world, was constructed under the Ted Weidhaas patents by Peter Clark, Inc. Operated by thirteen motors, its flexible contours open new vistas in the field of stage decoration.

2. DEDICATION . . . *By* MARTHA WILCHINSKI

ROBERT T. HAINES
Musical setting by DESIDIR D'ANTALFFY
*Organists—*DICK LEIBERT *and* ARTHUR GUTOW

3. "SEPT. 13, 1814" . . *Arranged by* FERDE GROFE

Francis Scott Key . . . TAYLOR HOLMES
THE RADIO CITY MUSIC HALL MALE ENSEMBLE
On the night of Sept. 13, 1814, a young American, Francis Scott Key, was a prisoner-of-war on a British frigate during the bombardment of Fort McHenry. During the action, pictured in this scene, young Key received the inspiration for that noble poem that later became our National Anthem.

4. ORCHESTRAL INTERLUDE

RADIO CITY OVERTURE . . . . . FERDE GROFE
HAROLD VAN DUZEE, *Soloist*
THE RADIO CITY MUSIC HALL SYMPHONY ORCHESTRA
*Conductors—*ERNO RAPEE, MACKLIN MARROW, CHARLES PREVIN, JOSEPH LITTAU.
Prologue by Desidir D'Antalffy *Lyrics by* Irving Caesar

5. IMPRESSIONS OF A MUSIC HALL

(A) THE WALLENDAS, *Continental Aerialists*
(B) THE KIKUTAS, *Oriental Risley Act*

6. IN THE SPOTLIGHT

EDDIE AND RALPH (*Sisters of the Skillet*) in "The Pulling Scene" from "The Dentist of Seville"
Choral Ensemble

7. THE RADIO CITY MUSIC HALL BALLET

PATRICIA BOWMAN, *Premiere Danseuse*
Choreography by Florence Rogge. Music by Maurice Baron.

8. FRAULEIN VERA SCHWARZ *of the Staats-Oper, Berlin*

Who is making her first appearance in America at the invitation of "Roxy"
"LIEBESWALZER," from "Wiener Blut," *Johann Strauss*
Specially arranged by Leo Blech

9. KIRKWHITE AND ADDISON, *London Music Hall Dancers*

10. THE TUSKEGEE CHOIR . WILLIAM L. DAWSON, *Director*

(A) "BEAUTIFUL CITY" . . . *William L. Dawson*
(B) "GOOD NEWS" (traditional) *Arr. by William L. Dawson*
(C) "TRAMPIN' " (traditional) *Arr. by William L. Dawson*
This is the first appearance of this celebrated choral organization in New York, who come from Tuskegee Institute specially for this engagement.

11. RAY BOLGER, *outstanding young American Dancing Comedian*

12. HARALD KREUTZBERG

Assisted by Margaret Sande, The Radio City Ballet Corps and Male Dancers, presenting, for the first time anywhere "THE ANGEL OF FATE," *A Dramatic Dance Scene*
Choreography by Harald Kreutzberg. Music by Friedrich Wilckens
The Angel of Fate, descending from Heaven to perform his work on earth, visits a royal feast. Displeased at the orgy, he places the Mask of Death upon the King's face. Later, meeting an innocent maiden, the Angel finds, to his sorrow, that she becomes sophisticated through his teaching, and too becomes a victim of the Death Mask. On a battlefield the Angel dances with a mask symbolic of modern warfare. The soldiers, following the Angel's example, lift their masks to their faces, and die. In the final scene, the Angel, his tasks on earth completed, ascends once more to Heaven.

117

13. THE RADIO CITY MUSIC HALL ROXYETTES
Directed by RUSSELL MARKERT
"WITH A FEATHER IN YOUR CAP"
Music by Jimmy McHugh   Lyric by Dorothy Fields
JEANNIE LANG, *Soloist*

14. DOCTOR ROCKWELL

15. NIGHT CLUB REVELS
RAY BOLGER, PATRICIA BOWMAN, OTTO FASSELL,
BERRY BROTHERS, JOSIE AND JULES WALTON, JOAN
ABBOTT, DOROTHY FIELDS, AND JIMMY McHUGH
(Miss Fields, daughter of Lew Fields, is making her first stage appearance)
THE RADIO CITY MUSIC HALL ROXYETTES, BALLET CORPS, CHORUS
"HEY, YOUNG FELLA!" by Dorothy Fields and Jimmy McHugh
"MAD MOMENTS" . . . by Harry Revel and Mack Gordon
"RIDING HIGH" . . . by Harry Revel and Mack Gordon

INTERMISSION

16. EXCERPTS FROM "CARMEN" . . . *Bizet*
Carmen . . . . COE GLADE
Escamillo . . . . TITTA RUFFO
Don Jose . . . . ARNOLDO LINDI
The Dancer . . . . PATRICIA BOWMAN
The Radio City Music Hall Chorus, Ballet, Roxyettes, soldiers,
matadors, cigarette girls, etc.
ACT I.   Scene 1. Street Scene
          Scene 2. The Cigarette Factory
          Scene 3. Flower Song, Don Jose
ACT II. In the Tavern
ACT III. At the Mountain Pass
ACT IV. Plaza del Toro
Directed by Desiré Defrere, formerly stage director of the Chicago
Civic Opera.   Choreography by Florence Rogge.

17. DOCTOR ROCKWELL

18. MARTHA GRAHAM *and her Dance Group*
Choric Dance for an Antique Greek Tragedy
Music by Louis Horst.

19. MINSTRELSY
DE WOLF HOPPER, RAY BOLGER, THE TUSKEGEE CHOIR,
TAYLOR HOLMES, GLENN AND JENKINS, JOAN ABBOTT,
DR. ROCKWELL, SISTERS OF THE SKILLET, JOHN PIERCE,
BERRY BROTHERS, THE RADIO CITY MUSIC HALL
ROXYETTES, BALLET CORPS, CHORUS and
WEBER AND FIELDS
"HAPPY TIMES" . . by Dorothy Fields and Jimmy McHugh
"JOURNEY'S END" . . by Dorothy Fields and Jimmy McHugh

CURTAIN
(NOTE: Every effort will be made to adhere to the program outlined above, but due to its magnitude it is
necessarily subject to alteration or change of routine.)

THE RADIO CITY THEATRES
PRODUCTION STAFF
Production Director . . . . Leon Leonidoff
Art Director . . . . Robert Edmond Jones
Musical Director . . . . Erno Rapee
Associate Conductors—Charles Previn, Joseph Littau, Macklin Marrow
Staff Composers and Arrangers—Ferde Grofe, Maurice Baron, Desidir
          D'Antalffy, Earle Moss, Otto Cesana
Staff Organists—Dick Leibert, Arthur Gutow, O. A. J. Parmentier,
          Betty Gould
Associate Art Director . . . . James Reynolds
Ballet Director . . . . Florence Rogge
Director of Opera . . . . Desiré Defrere
Associate Ballet-Master . . . . Lasar Galpern
Director of Roxyettes . . . . Russell Markert
Director of Chorus . . . . Leon Rosebrook
Director of Radio Programs . . . . Leo Russotto
Stage Manager . . . . William Stern
Electrical Engineer . . . . Eugene Braun
Chief Sound Engineer . . . . Harry Hiller
Chief Projectionist . . . . Arthur Smith
In Charge of Costumes . . . . Hattie Rogge

ADMINISTRATIVE STAFF
Chief of Administration . . . . James H. Turner
Manager of Theatres . . . . Charles W. Griswold
Assistant to "Roxy" . . . . S. Jay Kaufman
Director of Publicity . . . . . . Martha L. Wilchinski
Secretary to "Roxy" . . . . Leah Klar
In Charge of Maintenance . . . . . . David P. Canavan
Supervisor of Hospitals . . . . . . Anne Beckerle, R. N.

Musical instruments in the Night Club scene supplied through
the courtesy of The Conn Musical Instrument Company. Motion
picture scenic effects in Technicolor by Robert Bruce.

Next Sunday, Jan. 1st, 1933, 12:15 p.m.
FIRST POPULAR SYMPHONY CONCERT
LEOPOLD STOKOWSKI
Guest Conductor
Augmented Radio City Theatres Orchestra of 225
For Benefit of Unemployed Musicians.   Admission $1.00

RADIO
CITY
MUSIC
HALL

FIFTIETH STREET
AND SIXTH AVE.
NEW YORK
•
TWO PERFORMANCES
DAILY..2:15..8:15 P. M.
•
BEGINNING
DECEMBER 27, 1932
•

Notes

1. Harold Rosenthal, *Two Centuries of Opera at Covent Garden* (London: Putnam, 1958), pp. 299-300.

2. Titta Ruffo, *La mia parabola; memorie* (Milan: Fratelli Treves, 1937), pp. 215-218.

3. Titta Ruffo, *La mia parabola; memorie* (Rome: Staderini, 1977), p. 365.

4. Edward C. Moore, *Forty Years of Opera in Chicago* (New York: Horace Liveright, 1930).

5. Ibid., pp. 105-106.

6. Ibid., p. 130.

7. Ibid., p. 132.

8. Arthur Rubinstein, *My Many Years* (New York: Knopf, 1980), pp. 147-148

9. Rosa Ponselle and James A. Drake, *Ponselle: A Singer's Life* (Garden City: Doubleday, 1982), p. xxiii.

10. Ibid., p. 92.

11. Letter from Titta Ruffo to his son, Dr. Ruffo Titta, Jr., December 31, 1932.

12. Samuel L. ("Roxy") Rothafel, a radio and motion picture entrepreneur and the first manager of Radio City Music Hall.

Titta Ruffo Appears in Thomas' *Hamlet*

RICHARD ALDRICH

Hamlet	Titta Ruffo
Claudius	Gustave Huberdeau
The Ghost	Henri Scott
Polonius	Frank Freisch
Laertes	Emilio Venturini
Marcellus	Edward Warnery
Horatio	Constantin Nicolay
Gertrude	Eleanora de Cisneros
Ophelia	Alice Zeppilli
General musical director	Cleofonte Campanini

Expectation had been laid in trains of gunpowder all through the Metropolitan Opera House last evening—especially in the upper and rear portions of the house—and was ready to take fire and blaze up when the spark was applied. It was all, of course, for Mr. Titta Ruffo, the very expensive Italian baritone who is at present the chief ornament of the Philadelphia-Chicago Opera Company. That company began its series of representations at the Metropolitan last evening, and presented Ambroise Thomas' opera of *Hamlet*, with Mr. Ruffo as Hamlet, it being his first and, as has been announced, his only appearance in opera here this Winter.

Probably for no other reason than the coming of a much-heralded baritone would Ambroise Thomas' *Hamlet*—or, as it was sung in Italian,

Reprinted from Richard Aldrich; *Concert Life in New York, 1902-1923*. (New York: Putnam & Sons, 1941). First published in the *New York Times*, November 20, 1912. Copyright © 1912 by The New York Times Company. Reprinted by permission.

perhaps it should be *Amleto*—have made its reappearance at the Metropolitan Opera House. It had not been heard there before last night in sixteen years—its last previous performance was in that season when Mme. Calvé and Jean Lassalle found it congenial opportunity for their remarkable art. For some seasons before that it had had only a few scattered performances, and the mists of oblivion were already slowly gathering about it.

The opera, in fact, scarcely maintains any vitality in the operatic world outside of Paris, and it is known by the rising generation of music lovers in New York chiefly as being the source of that florid song with a waltz rhythm and a Norse ballad sung by the mad Ophelia bringing flowers, and perhaps to a lesser number of a bacchanalian song by Hamlet in praise of liquor, unknown to students of the English drama, but considered necessary by the French librettists. Nor is it likely that *Hamlet* will gain anything more than a transitory flicker of renewed life even from the popularity of Mr. Titta Ruffo.

There was an enormous audience present, and it flamed into enthusiasm all the opportunities given it by Mr. Ruffo, which were many. It is not often that an operatic baritone can create so speedy an excitement as he created here and is reported to have done in Philadelphia. He was uproariously applauded after every solo number that he sang; and after the drinking song at the end of the second act, in which Messrs. Carré and Barbier, the librettists, made so great an improvement upon Shakespeare, he was recalled many times, and in response to calls of "bis," which came from his countrymen deployed through the house, he repeated it to their even greater approval. Whatever may be said of anything else, it is clear that Mr. Ruffo achieved a great success last evening.

He has, in fact, many qualities that make an immediate popular appeal. His voice is of immense power and sonority. It is still young, fresh and vibrant, and its youthfulness is still one of its chief charms. It is a voice of rather metallic quality; a voice of bronze, until it is forced to its extreme power in its upper tones, when it is as a brazen clarion. And these tones are the sensational feature of his singing. Mr. Ruffo's vocal style allows of little variety of color and of little variety of emotional or dramatic expression, such as a greater musical endowment and vocal skill might find even in Thomas' music. He undertakes very few "covered" tones, and in a tenor such an organ would be recognized as a "white" voice. Mr. Ruffo's stentorian upper tones are of the sort that easily arouse such excitement as prevailed last evening; but it is a voice that soon exhausts its variety of effect.

As an actor he has been extravagantly praised. Now, Thomas' *Hamlet* is a wretched perversion of a masterpiece; but it still retains some dim outlines of Shakespeare's conception, and in this opera he invites some dangerous comparisons, that he does not meet with invariable success.

His style is tense and vivacious, restless and uneasy. He made certain strongly marked and obvious points; but for subtlety or suggestiveness or consistently and definitely conceived and skillfully executed delineation of character his impersonation was not notable. It is an impersonation whose traits and outlines are chiefly melodramatic.

In the later scenes of the opera, where there is less temptation to extravagance of voice or action, Mr. Ruffo was more satisfactory, even though provocative of less tumultuous enthusiasm. . . .

19.   Titta Ruffo in the Title Role of Thomas' *Hamlet* (Buenos Aires, 1916)
       Photo: Frans van Riel
       Courtesy of Ruffo Titta, Jr.

12

Some Further Remarks About Mr. Titta Ruffo, His Singing, His Acting, and Ambroise Thomas' Opera of *Hamlet*

RICHARD ALDRICH

It was not surprising that Mr. Titta Ruffo created a deal of excitement at the Metropolitan Opera House at his first appearance there last Tuesday evening—his only one in opera—in Ambroise Thomas' *Hamlet*. Nor was the excitement wholly confined to those of his countrymen who are usually most demonstrative and energetic in applauding Italian singers with high notes, great lung power, and other claims to immediate popular approval. These merits seemed to gain approval in all parts of the house, and the applause was well distributed, until there began that sort of long-distance applause like the cheering that is done at political conventions when it is necessary to make a record. It was not difficult to place most of this.

Mr. Ruffo is a conspicuous example of the kind of vocal art that is at present most successful and prevalent in Italy; he has a powerful voice, great breath capacity, brilliant and telling high notes; but little of the finer qualities of vocal art. The beauty, finesse, and subtle effectiveness that come from the skillful and assiduous cultivation of those finer qualities are becoming scarcer. Fortunately there are still other kinds of Italian singing in which art is considered as well as voice; and, also fortunately, America has secured some of the notable representatives of it.

Mr. Ruffo's voice is indeed wonderful in its high tones. These are remarkable for a baritone; and he does not fail to make the most of them. But its middle and lower tones, which should also be precious possessions of a baritone, are of inconsiderable value. They have much

Reprinted from Richard Aldrich, *Concert Life in New York, 1902-1923* (New York: Putnam's Sons, 1941). First published in the *New York Times*, November 24, 1912. Copyright © 1912 by The New York Times Company. Reprinted by permission.

less power; they have little of the clarion brightness and brilliancy of the upper ones. Nor is the voice of the same excellence when it is used at a lesser power. Then the metallic quality gives place to something of hollowness and dullness.

One of Mr. Ruffo's most extraordinary excellences is his immense power and control of breath, which not only gives his voice its vigor, but also enables him to sing phrases of great length and involved cadenzas with apparent ease and spontaneity, and with as much power at their end as there was at the beginning. Thus, the final phrase of the drinking song, of which he makes a brilliant cadenza, is an extraordinary piece of vocalization, and caps the climax of a song that has extraordinary power to stir the audience. Of the lack of varied tone quality and the use of any but "open" tones in Mr. Ruffo's method of singing mention was made in these columns before. What they mean to lovers of artistic singing need not be stated. The immense bravura and gusto of Mr. Ruffo's singing of such music as lends itself to brilliant treatment are enough to take many an audience off its feet. But for the expression of emotion, tenderness, pathos, and sentiment he has few resources, vocally or temperamentally. And herein lay one of the causes of Mr. Ruffo's failure to justify the high expectations that had been aroused of him as a dramatic singer. With such a singer variety of purely tonal expression, dramatic and emotional color of the voice supply and enhance the effects that an actor obtains from his reading of the lines—the significance that he puts into the words and phrases through emphasis, inflection, tone, pitch, and the innumerable shades of expression that the spoken word permits. In one way the singing actor is more limited, in another less. He is limited by the outline, compass, and character of the musical phrases that the composer requires him to interpret; but he is provided with the higher emotional potency of music—into which he can put innumerable beauties if he has them at his command.

Some may say, to excuse Mr. Ruffo's failure in justifying the high expectation raised as to his ability as an actor, that *Hamlet* is too poor a lyric drama to enable an actor to exert his full powers in it. Perhaps so; but poor as it is, it enabled Mme. Emma Calvé sixteen years ago at the Metropolitan Opera House to create a profound impression upon many fastidious critics of acting, purely by her histrionic interpretation, when she appeared as Ophelia. It was an impersonation of fragile and tender beauty, suffused with the poetry that even Carré and Barbier could not eliminate from Shakespeare. And only less was the impression made by Jean Lasalle, the French baritone, with his subtle delineation of the traits of Hamlet that still persist in the opera, dimmed as they are in outline. There have been many very fine dramatic effects made in very poor operas, even in some of the worst travesties of Shakespeare. There are, perhaps, not many who can remember what the great baritone Faure and the great soprano, Christine Nilsson, did with the parts of Hamlet and Ophelia when they "created" them at the first performances of Thomas' opera in Paris in 1868. But that they must have done much with such opportunities as the opera afforded them is clear from contemporary testimony and from the long-continued success they had in it.

The Italian baritone noted certain passages with discrimination and unforced effect, notably the scene with the ghost, in what the French librettists have made the second scene of the first act; there were good bits in his scenes with Ophelia later in the opera. Of course, his tour de force was the drinking song, not only vocally, but dramatically. In general it seemed, however, that this method was restless and uneasy; and that with this restlessness he commanded a comparatively small range of gesture, pose and, particularly, facial expression. He often ran into melodramatic exaggeration; as for instance at the close of the pantomimic play at the end of the second act. Though the librettists have exaggerated and misdirected Shakespeare in their conduct of the action, Mr. Ruffo's violent assault on the King and Queen seated on their thrones seemed beyond reason and justification.

There was a great deal of "parlando" in Mr. Ruffo's singing of the recitatives in which *Hamlet* abounds. But parlando in these recitatives is unnecessary. They are what Thomas has done best in the opera; and in the form in which he wrote them they have at least a plausible accent and expression as being suitable for carrying the text. They should be sung and not spoken. When Thomas leaves declamation and undertakes to write melody he falls to the lowest levels. The melody is Meyerbeerian melody at its worst, of most poverty-stricken and superficial substance— melody without strength or character, composed of weak little fragments pieced together, with an equal insignificance in the harmonic and orchestral texture of the accompaniment; never by any chance aught but commonplace. With what relief does the listener hear, after all this pretentious and hollow commonplace, that Norse folksong that forms part of Ophelia's song when she comes in mad, bringing flowers. Here, at least, is something natural and strong: and this interpolated piece is the best thing in the opera.

A well-known French critic, writing of *Hamlet* not long ago, observed: "There was nothing in *Hamlet* that could surprise or disconcert the listeners of 1868. It was natural that they should understand *Hamlet* on the spot, and that, satisfied with understanding it so well, and deceived by its serious exterior, they should think that they had found a great work. Thus is to be explained the immediate success of Ambroise Thomas' operas, and the uncertain destiny of Gounod's. But Gounod at his best has survived and Thomas in *Hamlet* is dead."

It is evident that *Hamlet*, both libretto and music, belongs to a state of things now, fortunately, definitely outgrown. When it was written it was considered, in France at any rate, that only certain kinds of situations could be carried on adequately in opera, and that if the dramatist had not supplied a sufficient number of them, the librettist must come to the aid of the musician and make room for them, in place of other less suitable matter. The opera begins with a meaningless piece of Court pageantry in order that the characters may be properly introduced. Hamlet flourishes a golden goblet and leads the chorus in a song in praise of "sweet liquor" when he ought to be giving the players his wholesome advice as to speaking their parts—though the librettists were no doubt right in thinking that so long as this is an opera that speech is very ill-suited to music. And finally Ophelia, in the opera, is to sail down the stream on a perfectly dry bier after fainting in the presence of the chorus, who leave her to commit suicide undisturbed, after remarking that "her reason has fled without return." Operas are written today, if not always in a better, at least in a different way.

13

The Victor Café

LEOPOLD SALTZMAN

The Victor Café on Dickinson Street in South Philadelphia is probably the most famous operatic restaurant in the world. It is only a little place in the middle of a block, across the street from a fish store and next door to a meat market, but it has brought more culture to Philadelphia than many a musical organization with much greater pretentions. In 1917 John di Stefano, its founder, started out in business with a photograph shop; with the Wall Street crash, however, he closed his doors and in 1933 opened a restaurant. While his wife, Rose, cooked in the kitchen, John presided over the customers out front, playing his opera records during slack periods. Discovering that many customers enjoyed it, he decided to play the records during the lunch and dinner hours. As a result, the world started to beat a path to his door. Not only did people come to hear the voices of Martinelli and De Luca, but Martinelli and De Luca even came to hear themselves.

When di Stefano died, in 1954, he left one of the world's largest collections of opera records, including a fabulous number of unpublished Victor releases. The RCA Victor staff used to dine at John's place, since he had named the restaurant after their company, and occasionally they would slip him an unpublished record or two; in time these gifts grew to include several hundred rare items. The two di Stefano boys, Armand and Henry, now operate the restaurant, and things haven't changed much, except that they do not object as vehemently as their father to the more popular singers.

John di Stefano loved to reminisce about "Old Man" Iannarelli, who operated an ice-cream parlor in south Philadelphia beginning in 1890. While selling his wares, he played old cylinders and opera discs, which

Courtesy of *Opera News*. First published in *Opera News*, February 19, 1966.

he kept in a large iron safe. Not everyone was welcome in this ice-cream parlor, and those admitted were bound by a strict rule—no talking during the music. Violators risked being bodily ejected, or exiled with no reprieve. One night Iannarelli played thirty-five different versions of "Di quella pira"; "After that," said John, "it took me five years before I could sit through *Il Trovatore* again." Once after a visit from "the boss," as Caruso was affectionally called, Iannarelli carved an "X" on the chair where he sat. "Why did you do that?" asked a bewildered John. Because after "the boss" sat in that chair, no one else could. And no one else ever did. Another time, a friend was pleading with Iannarelli to sell a rare record of Fernando De Lucia, the master of *bel canto*; after what seemed an eternity, Iannarelli finally agreed, "I'll sell it to you provided I can scratch out the other side." Why? "Because Magini-Coletti sings 'La Danza,' and I don't want you to have *that* in your collection!"

Perhaps the most colorful figure of all, Umberto di Curcio, di Stefano's closest friend and opera's knight in shining armor, still holds court at the Victor Café. A loyal fan since 1907, he numbered among his closest friends such Golden Age immortals as Caruso, Ruffo, Chaliapin, Zenatello and Amato. In 1912, during a performance of *Rigoletto* in which Titta Ruffo made his Philadelphia debut, bedlam broke loose. The mighty baritone displayed tones that were utterly unbelievable, and after the "Sì, vendetta" Umberto, who was seated in the gallery, commenced to slide down pillar after pillar, leaping onto the stage before a somewhat startled Ruffo, who managed to ask, "What are you doing here?"

"I wanted to see if you were human," came the reply. "Anyone who can sing like that must be a god."

All arguments, questions, controversy and doubts pertaining to opera in South Philadelphia or in the world are settled at the Victor Café. Every night, everybody has his say, and that means the record collector, the voice teacher, the singer, the impresario and the opera-lover in general. Many a promising young singer—Mario Lanza, Frank Guarrera and Anna Moffo, to mention a few—has become inspired at the Victor Café by listening to old records.

Some years ago Bernardo de Muro, a famous tenor of the past, paid a visit to his friend John di Stefano. John played some of de Muro's recordings made many years before. "Ah!" sighed de Muro, a little stogie in his mouth, "those were the days!"

"Yes," replied John, "but youth must be served."

"Perhaps," said de Muro, suddenly getting to his feet and unleashing a high C resembling a bolt of thunder. Smiling, he said, "But I can still show them a thing or two."

14

Titta Ruffo in Argentina

EDUARDO ARNOSI

There can be little doubt that Titta Ruffo was the most famous baritone of all time and one of the greatest that lived. His prodigious power and range in the upper register—although less solid in lower tones—the great volume and authentic baritonal timbre, his leonine presence and dramatic flare became almost legendary. As in the case of Caruso, he in his voice range was the King of the Lyric Stage and was acclaimed enthusiastically by the most varied audiences and particularly by those in Argentina, before whom he so often appeared.

Titta Ruffo's artistic home was the Teatro Colón, in the same sense that Caruso's was the Metropolitan in New York. He appeared before Argentine audiences more often than any other in the world. He sang in ten opera seasons in Buenos Aires: one at the Teatro de la Opera in 1902, and the other nine at the Colón between 1908 and 1931. At the latter he sang a total of 198 performances, including galas and special occasions when he appeared in a single act of an opera or sang solo numbers. He also sang in La Plata, Rosario, Córdoba, and Tucumán. By comparison, he sang only fifty-four performances with the Met, in the house and on tour, in eight consecutive seasons between 1922 and 1929.

When he made his debut as the Herald in *Lohengrin*, Francisco Viñas, who sang the title role, said to him: "I never heard a baritone voice like yours. If you study and know how to conserve it, you have much glory ahead of you." Viñas was proven right, and for three decades Ruffo reaped his share of glory as did few other baritones.

His first South American engagement took him to Chile in 1900. This journey had a special significance for him, not only because it was his

Translated by Ted Fagan.

20. Titta Ruffo as a Young Man
     From the collection of Andrew Farkas

first appearance in the Americas, but because of an occurrence of a more personal nature. On the voyage he met a singer of the company who had a lasting influence on his life, both as a man and as an artist. Wishing to conceal her identity, Ruffo refers to her in his memoirs by the expressive pseudonym "Benedetta," the Blessed One. Her identity has since been revealed by the son of the baritone. She was Adelina Fanton, whom Ruffo called the "sacred star of my life." Fanton died in 1907, but despite the relative brevity of their friendship, Ruffo writes, "she was the angel who guided the most difficult steps of my career and, with great assurance, set my feet on the path toward my final goal."[1]

His debut in Santiago was in a very successful *Africana* on August 5, 1900. He then apppeared in *Rigoletto* and *Ballo in Maschera*, and sang his first Iago in *Otello*. During that same Chilean season he sang in *Aida*, *Trovatore*, *Forza del Destino*, his first Gérard in *Andrea Chénier*, *La Salinara* (by D. Brescia), *Carmen*, *Gioconda*, *Lucia di Lammermoor*, *Ruy Blas* and *Faust*.

The year 1902 found him once again in Latin America, this time at the Teatro de la Opera in Buenos Aires, where he made his debut as Amonasro in *Aida* on May 21. The program listed him as Ruffo Titta. *La Prensa* reviewed his debut in *Aida* in the following terms: "We must remember to mention the convincing interpretation of the role of Amonasro by the Baritone Titta Ruffo who has a beautiful and sonorous voice, however, were he to sing less *dans le masque* as the French say, he would add brilliance and naturalness to his delivery." After a weak performance of *Africana* (the adjective was used in *La Prensa* and the review does not even mention him), he sang Di Luna in *Trovatore*. The same critic wrote that "although his voice, still *dans le masque*, becomes somewhat suffused, Titta Ruffo had some good moments." Leoncavallo's *Zazà* had its Buenos Aires premiere on August 9, 1902, and it gave him a chance, in the role of Cascart, to make his first truly successful impression on the Argentine public. The critic, who found little value in the opera itself, considered the singers "worthy of praise" and stated that they "gave an outstanding performance" (*La Prensa*). Although Ruffo's performance did not receive special mention, the critic did write that his last-act aria, "Zazà, piccola zingara," had to be encored. To sum it up, the Buenos Aires debut of the future great baritone passed into history with "neither sorrow nor glory," but the latter would be forthcoming at the Colón later, in 1908.

There were several important milestones in Ruffo's career between his 1902 and 1908 engagements. He made his Covent Garden debut in 1903 and his La Scala debut in the title role of *Rigoletto* in 1904. Then followed his enormously successful 1905 and 1906 Russian seasons. Taking the role of Gleby in a Paris performance of *Siberia* on May 4, 1905, he sang with Caruso for the first time. They were later reunited in a single *Rigoletto* in Vienna on October 2, 1906. The Milanese paper *Il*

Teatro Illustrato carried an article on the event by Giovanni Borelli. It deserves to be quoted here because, leaving aside the hyperbolae and panegyrics, it reflects the qualities of the great baritone and explains his well-earned renown:

A more complete and rare organ cannot be heard on the lyric stage of today.[2] Complete in its entire range, even in its volume, metallic in its attack, rare in its velvety naturalness and in the ease and measure of its breath control and golden timbre. He is the possessor of what our predecessors called the *tubatura* and which he has developed in order to produce a remarkable variety of stunning and pure sounds, using it at its widest scope with no strain and with marvelous phonic results. Thus the endless *fiato* of the ancient masters allows him seamless and captivating *legato*, powerful *crescendi* and refined *sfumature* making the very volume of the voice—a precious thing in itself—three times more so. Gradually over the last two or three years, the fine metal of his voice has acquired an evenness which is stupendous. Its distribution and coloration permit the singer to indulge in effects of incomparable *chiaro-oscuri* and *mezza-voce*. One would have to go back to the classical period of the great Italian voices to find as phenomenal a voice as that of Titta Ruffo. In my earlier reviews I have said that we had to recall the Reggio-born Bertolini, called Babaliti, the possessor of the most open and pure baritone voice of his period, or Aldighiero Aldighieri. If Titta Ruffo does not surpass them, he is certainly their peer. Some dark deviations and certain somewhat closed sounds in the lower register, which I recall hearing in Ruffo's voice a few years ago, have now acquired a fullness, roundness, and a tone that is above reproach. The column of sound possesses a bronze-like purity which gives off striking resonances. To the listener the voice offers a voluptuous joy, one that is untouched by concern of fear of limitations, since it is a vocal organ that has never been surpassed in its sincere, natural and easy production. Added to which, if you place this priceless throat at the service of an open and perceptive mind, an instinctive and refined good taste, a fine physical presence, a most noble yet exquisitely expressive face, vocal intelligence, and you heap upon all this a Tuscan diction of the purest water which sculpts the syllables in an impeccable accent so that every word carries its full meaning and grammatical intonation, then you will have the exact portrait of—and not merely fulsome praise heaped upon—an outstanding artistic personality that the name of Titta Ruffo has earned in the Halls of the Great. Some aspects of his production, grammatical expressiveness and perfection of enunciation can also be found in others who have become outstanding because of their range and tone, such as Tamagno. Now Ruffo's fame has spread throughout the civilized world. A short while ago at the Hofoper of Vienna, Titta Ruffo excelled in *Rigoletto* and excited both the audience and the press to acclaim him in words that did honor to Italian art. And it was on an evening when his companion of art and glory was none other than the thrilling monarch of cosmopolitan audiences and the heir of the legendary masters of bel canto, Enrico Caruso himself. The pair was entitled to represent the summation of the admirable gifts of which—even in these sadder and less propitious days—the Italian lyric stage can proudly boast of its world-wide supremacy. In Vienna Ruffo rose to the level of those shining few who have truly earned the daunting responsibility of carrying on an age-old tradition and further brighten and illuminate it. All hail to him. He has earned it!

He sang his first Hamlet on January 24, 1907, in Lisbon, at the Teatro San Carlos, with Esperanza Clasenti as Ophelia, under the baton of Luigi Mancinelli. It was attended by La Benedetta shortly before her death. He had a tremendous personal success, and he made his Teatro Colón debut in the same role on May 30, 1908, again with Clasenti, together with Fabbri and Nicoletti-Kormann, Mancinelli conducting. It was the second performance of the inaugural season of the new opera house of Buenos Aires and, as expected, it was highly successful. What was curious about the reviews, although the fact must have pleased him, was that in general the critics harped more on his histrionic ability than on his most uncommon vocal attributes, seemingly overlooking his artistry in that field. In fact, *La Prensa* read as follows:

Last night Titta Ruffo handed Rossini a powerful rebuttal, for, far from possessing the voice which the celebrated composer argues is the only indispensable requisite for the lyric stage, he impressed the audience with sole use of artistry, reaching the point virtually discarding the singing phrase. The choice of this opera for Ruffo in itself bespoke the confidence he possesses in his ability as a lyric artist rather than in his vocal faculties. We do not wish to imply by this that his voice was lacking, by no means that, but this artist excels mainly by the expressive intensity of his declamation. He speaks admirably and with a true talent for analysis and observation that is rarely found in singers; he interprets the text. He proved himself a consummate actor and overlooked no detail. At first the audience was somewhat diffident and although he carried off his declaration to Ophelia with fine style in the first act ("Nega se puoi la luce") it only earned him token applause and the same applied to the invocation on the terrace. It was the "Drinking Song" in the second act that stunned the packed house and especially the cadence of the reprise of "O vin discaccia la tristezza," all taken on a single breath, with the descending scale and the ascent by semi-tones to the initial phrase of the aria, which Titta Ruffo executed flawlessly. It brought forth ear-splitting, unanimous, vociferous and sweeping applause that proclaimed the success of the debuting artist.

Thus the audience, eagerly awaiting great vocal feats from the baritone on his triumphal return, was far from allowing itself to be seduced—like the critic—by the "sole use of artistry" and yielded only when the singer was allowed to let himself go, and then acclaimed him for his extraordinary and gloriously used voice which always won over his audiences. It possessed formidable resonance and resistance, "a miracle of a voice" as his colleague Giuseppe de Luca and conductor Tullio Serafin described it, which he obviously and generally utilized with potent and fierce expression, although not always with depth. In his *Voci parallele*,

Giacomo Lauri-Volpi observed: "A leonine voice, at times roaring, at others languid and it was unlike any of those that came before as it tended more to the cavernous, nasal resonances, to the spectacular *portamenti* and to the percussiveness that disguised the notes themselves."[3]

The critic of *La Razón*, doubtless closer to the truth, also stressed that fact without belittling his acting ability in the review he wrote of the baritone's debut:

When Titta Ruffo appeared on stage in the first act, he was greeted with prolonged applause, probably from the admirers he had left behind after his last season here, but the enthusiastic and genuinely logical and well-earned applause really was heard after the "Drinking Song" in the second act. Titta Ruffo sang it admirably, with undefinable vocal colorations that proved him to be an acting singer who summons up enthusiastic reactions from his listeners. After the ovation that drowned his "Drinking Song" he was prevailed upon to encore it. The worth and the recognition of the great baritone grew, if that were possible, at the conclusion of the second act, in the scene with the comedians and, in the third act, rose to enviable heights. We have said that Titta Ruffo is both an actor and a singer and, in fact, he is not only an actor who deserves praise under any of the different aspects on which he may be judged, but as far as Hamlet is concerned, he has made a careful study of his character and makes Shakespeare's Dane an admirable creation.

In his own memoirs, when writing of his debut at the Colón, Ruffo himself dwells mainly on the voice. "Hamlet was decisive," he says. "My voice, at its best, spread over the huge auditorium with overwhelming freedom. My interpretation of the complex character was admired and praised, and for the remaining performances the hall was constantly filled to capacity. They literally coined money."[4]

Because of Ruffo's lasting fascination with the protagonist, the opportunities the role gave him to exhibit the special qualities of his voice, and the enthusiastic audience response he enjoyed at every performance, Hamlet became his favorite battle horse. The role gave him the opportunity, in accord with his ambitions, to become a great tragedian as well as a superbly endowed vocalist, and the opera owed its worldwide acceptance in its Italian version as *Amleto* to Ruffo. It was his version of the "Chanson Bacchique," the drinking song of the second act, that allowed him to exhibit his astounding length of breath—the *fiato*—in the cadence; it invariably led to such applause that only an encore would satisfy his hearers. It seems that he once sang it three times.

Ruffo recorded the "Brindisi," as he sang it in Italian, on three occasions. First in 1905 on Pathé cylinder 4202, but this cut version lacks the meditative central portion "La vita è breve..." and differs from the later versions, partly because of the slow tempi of the opening phrases, but mainly because of the almost sarcastic tone in which, after the cad-

ential phrases, he returns to the words "il riso schernitor" and "O liquor
incantator...." The 1908 version, recorded with chorus in Milan (HMV
052188; Victor 92037), which brings out his phenomenal phrasing, is
the best. Finally, the 1920 recording on Victor (88619; d/f 6266) shows
less *fiato* in the cadence and thus it is less spectacular.

Apart from the "Brindisi," he also recorded the main passages of the
protagonist in Milan in 1907: the duet with Ophelia "Nega se puoi la
luce" with Maria Galvany (HMV 05418; Victor 92500), "Spettro infer-
nale" (HMV 2-52622; Victor 87153), and "Spettro santo" (HMV 2-52621;
Victor 87154); "Essere o non essere" (HMV 052189; Victor 92042); and
"Come il romito fior" (HMV 052248; Victor 92064; both on d/f 6403).
(All of these passages of Thomas' opera along with his *Rigoletto* excerpts
have been reissued on an Angel LP, COLH 155). The only one, however,
that in this writer's opinion is worthy of interest and on a level with
Shakespeare's work is the "Spettro santo."

Regarding the Shakespeare play, it is interesting to note that Ruffo
wanted to leave behind proof of his dramatic ability of which he was so
proud, and thus he recorded two spoken excerpts in Italian: the "Appearance of the Ghost" (HMV 51097; Victor 87381) and the well-known
"To be or not to be" (HMV 51098; Victor 87382; both selections coupled
on HMV DA 170 and Victor 985). The records were made in Italy
in 1914. Apart from the interest in having an example of Ruffo's speaking voice, they show him to possess the full capabilities of a dramatic
actor. His interpretation of Shakespeare in the Italian rhetorical style of
a Salvini, a Novelli, or a Zacconi is more successful in the Apparition
scene, which exhibits moments of convincing strength, than in the monologue. It should be pointed out that his voice sounds like that of an
older man than one would envisage Hamlet to be, or Ruffo actually was,
since he was only thirty-seven at the time.

In his own assessment, the other selections, especially the monologues,
were the meat of the opera, the "Brindisi" being the least successful.
"But," as he writes in his memoirs, not without a certain bitterness, "my
Hamlet was inevitably connected with it. This proves that for the masses
the force and vibration of the voice is what counts in the artist."[5] His
conclusion was ingenuous. The torrential outpouring of the voice with
which nature had blessed him and the breadth of his *fiato* which the
"Brindisi" allowed him to put to great good use naturally sparked the
plaudits and delirious reaction of the audience. They marveled at his
vocal prowess and identified his Hamlet with that selection; while as an
actor, although vigorous and truly dedicated to expressing the character
in the drama, he was not as exceptional, nor as outstanding.

Ruffo's second opera at the Colón, on June 14, 1908, was *Rigoletto*
with Clasenti, Ferraris, Nicoletti-Kormann, and Bassi, conducted by Arturo Vigna. It gave him a better opportunity to display his vocal qualities

since it was not a matter of a single blinding outburst of bravura, like the *Hamlet* "Drinking Song," but had many moments calling for great vocal resources and technical ability to successfully cope with the difficulties of the role. It also gave him a chance to show his abilities as an actor. Although possessing great dramatic strength, Rigoletto as a character is far less complex than Hamlet and considerably more extroverted, and admittedly much better defined by Verdi than the Dane is by Thomas.

The critic of *La Prensa*, focusing on the actor and, seemingly, curiously deaf to the exceptional qualities of the voice, wrote of the *Rigoletto*:

Titta Ruffo has utterly escaped the tyrannical bounds of the pentagram. He uses his [singing] voice solely as a means of ensuring melodic continuity without seeking in it the expressive intensity which he achieves entirely without vocal sonority. For this reason, very often the actor prevails over the singer and pure and simple declamation replaces singing.... His approach reminds one of some of the canavases in the Louvre because of the appropriateness of his costumes. Let us not dwell on it whether this disguises or not what he is lacking in richness or abundance of vocal wealth, for if that be the case, it proves he has talent, skill and art, and that is paramount.

The critic goes on to bemoan the fact that "the artist lets himself get carried away to the point of unduly extending some notes—albeit loudly applauded—but in open conflict with the artistry of which he usually gives proof." As an example, the critic singles out the opening phrase of the "Vendetta" duet and adds, "Since we have alluded to the not overly plentiful vocal wealth of Mr. Titta Ruffo, it is only fair to admit that his is a voice of wide range and this was attested to at the end of the third act where he delivered an exquisite high A flat."

The critic for *La Nación* was far more judicious and gave a more accurate, realistic appraisal. He pointed out the existing acting limitations and stressed the extraordinary merit and nature of the voice itself. Reporting on this same *Rigoletto*, he wrote:

The worthiness of the interpreter lies in the expressiveness that he injects into his diction and dramatics. Perhaps his personality fails to reach full bloom and it was noted that he even used identical means to represent such entirely disparate roles, however, he does infuse what he says with an intention that never errs in its aim and he acts with an amazing conjunction of all his faculties, making it difficult to analyze the infallible impression he creates. Add to this the miracle of an exceptional instrument and then you will be able to understand why every member of the audience focused his unblinking attention on the singer.

The reviewer's observations are reinforced by Henry Pleasants, who in his book *The Great Singers* (1966) writes that Titta Ruffo "was not a

21. Titta Ruffo in the Title Role of *Rigoletto* (Chicago, 1912)
Photo: Matzene
Courtesy of Kurt Binar

great actor, but the enormous voice, proceeded from a big, robust body and a massive head, and his movements on the stage had something of the assertive, compelling, overpowering force of his singing.... Ruffo's was simply the grandest voice in baritone history."[6] It must be borne in mind, of course, that Pleasants had never heard Ruffo on stage, and his judgment is just as much based on contemporary accounts, written and oral, handed down to posterity, as the efforts of present-day researchers trying to assemble the totality of Ruffo's artistic image.

With the exception of the Sparafucile-Rigoletto duet and the Quartet, Ruffo recorded all the solos and duets of the opera in 1907 and 1908. It is to be regretted that the only remake of any of these excerpts is the 1920 recording of "Pari siamo." This recording shows an artistic maturity absent in the earlier version. It also makes it easy to understand why his Rigoletto was regarded as one of his most successful characterizations by the time he presented it in the United States. The early set of records are less accomplished than one would expect and they lack interpretative depth. As such, they serve as recorded evidence in support of the reviewer's observations. Ruffo's best moments are in the "Piangi, fanciulla" duet in the flowing quality of his singing, in the "Sì, vendetta" where the vocal and dramatic forces propel the music to a stupendous climax of an A flat, and in the final duet, "Lassù in ciel." Still, the records cannot be more than a pale reflection of what his stage Rigoletto must have been. If they suffer in comparison with the polished, mature interpretation of Stracciari in his complete recording, or even with that of De Luca, whose voice was best suited to the lyrical moments of the role, it cannot be denied that these artists left a record of their interpretation after many more years of experience. Were Ruffo to have remade all the selections in the middle 1910s, say 1912 or 1915, posterity could form a more accurate idea of his interpretation of the role.

During the inaugural 1908 season of the Teatro Colón he also sang in *Tosca, La Gioconda, Otello, Barber of Seville, Pagliacci, Don Giovanni*, the part of Don Ignacio in the world premiere of *Aurora* by Panizza on September 5, and also that of Gianciotto in the local premiere of *Paolo e Francesca* by Mancinelli on July 4. In this last he was partnered by Maria Farneti and Amedeo Bassi in the three performances of the work which were given under the direction of the composer. In short, he presented the most celebrated roles of his repertoire.

The review in *La Prensa* of his June 16 Scarpia in *Tosca* reads as follows: "Titta Ruffo has given too much importance to the 'old satyr' side of his interpretation of the role, overlooking the other facets of Scarpia's personality.... Moreover, he allows himself to be swept away by the outburst of anger which does not fit the character of Scarpia, the all-powerful police chief." Writing of the second act, the critic finds "Sammarco's to be a more logical interpretation." Then, discussing Ruffo's version, he goes on: "We also note that he permits his characterization to go so far as to show an exaggeratedly weak senility, yet, at a given moment, this feebleness does not stop him from grabbing the young and burly Spoletta by the scruff of the neck and hurling him to the ground, an act that is surely impossible for the tired old man Ruffo is trying to portray.... The declamatory portion was pronounced in his own unique style and apart from his approach to the character, we cannot but applaud him."

In the June 24 *La Gioconda*, Ruffo "again heard the enthusiastic and unstinted acclamations that always greet his performances," as *La Nación* wrote, and he even had to repeat the second-act "Barcarola." According to *La Prensa*, "his interpretation of Barnaba was a personal one which differs from the one to which we have been accustomed." The critic continues: "In the role of the vile spy he was unable to bring out the fine and subtle shadings with which he virtually vivisects his characters," but he reserved his finest depiction of "the psychology of the abject human beast for the last act, filled to overflowing with brutal hungers and, as usual, he captured his audience with the verismo style of exteriorizing the feelings that rule him." The audience's demand for an encore of the "Barcarola" is understandable if his singing equaled the superb rendition preserved on the 1912 recording (HMV 052378; Victor 88394; d/f 6265). This recording truly shows the prodigiousness of his voice, the powerful middle and the amazing high notes, and the explosive vigor he was wont to attach to certain phrases. The "O monumento" he recorded from *Gioconda* in the same year (HMV 052376; Victor 88396; d/f 6398) is a good but not exceptional performance. Although he sings the written *portamento*, the high note on "Parla!" is somewhat disappointing. He impales the the first syllable of the word on the high G and does not spit it out as imperiously as—to cite one example—Leonard Warren.

Of his Iago in *Otello*, performed on July 18 with tenor Antonio Paoli and Maria Farneti under Mancinelli, *La Prensa*'s review read, in part: "Ruffo performed the role and by saying that, we are already saying that it was outstandingly done. Perhaps we might cavil at the excessive indifference with which he tossed off the first act 'Brindisi,' but the distinguished baritone very soon came to the fore and began to paint the character, giving it the necessary duplicity and skepticism it calls for. The enthusiastic audience insisted on an encore of the 'Credo' but we would select 'Cassio's Dream' as the moment when he brought out his finest vocal efforts." Ruffo's recording of the "Credo" (Victor 88466; d/f 6267 and 8045) is one of the best versions on disk. It shows the dark quality of his voice and the sinister overtones that made his Iago a superb characterization. The second act duet, "Sì, pel ciel," must also be mentioned as the only surviving record made by the most celebrated *divi* of the period: Titta Ruffo and Enrico Caruso. Without a doubt it ranks as one of the outstanding recordings of the century (Victor 89075; HMV 2-054049; d/f Victor 8045; HMV DK 114).

After that he delivered his very successful Figaro for the public of Buenos Aires. It took place on July 28 and he was supported by Polverosi, Clasenti, Chaliapin, and Pini-Corsi under the baton of Mancinelli. Praising the performance, the critic of *La Prensa* wrote:

Titta Ruffo embodied the jovial barber with a brilliant control of the vocal part and as far as the interpretation was concerned, he dimmed out the traditional memories of all his predecessors. This was surprising since the part is so different from his usually preferred roles.... His first act cavatina was delivered with brio and although thunderous applause urged an encore, he had the good taste to refrain which added immeasurably to the aesthetics of the action, without interrupting its natural flow. Then, in the duet with the tenor, he moderated his voice to accommodate that of the very weak one of his colleague, thus impressing on the selection a commendable fusion and unity. He also sang his next act duet with Rosina very well.... His very lively performance was at one and the same time natural and not exaggerated and the entire evening went without a flaw, in fact, his was the performance that clung to the correct artistic line which the rest of the cast seemed unable to manage as would have been desired.

In a review of the second performance of the work, the critic, who had found in Ruffo's other characters a "slight Hamletian after-taste," pointed to the "amazing metamorphosis" undergone by the artist when performing the Rossini role. "He offered the frankest and most jovial characterization one could imagine of the hero of Beaumarchais' creation, behaving with abandon and true Andalusian inventiveness and mischief." In short, this was a "real triumph for Ruffo, thanks to his unfettered brilliance and his admirable stage movements. He overlooked not the slightest gesture, no successful subtle stress, yet all without falling into clowning and vulgarities."

Ruffo sang his first *Pagliacci* at the Colón on August 5, 1908. *La Prensa* wrote that "praise is worthless.... His amazingly original Tonio was a veritable psychological study of the wretched, deformed being in whom Nedda awakens brutal desires and who avenges her rejection in the vilest and most cowardly fashion. The beauty of the enunciation which he showed in the 'Prologue' was so remarkable that the audience pressed for a repetition of the second part."

On August 18 Mozart's *Don Giovanni* was staged with Ruffo, Chaliapin, Pinto, Clasenti, Polverosi, and Farneti under the direction of Mancinelli. Despite the excellent, albeit "somewhat heterogeneous," cast, "the performance was colorless and cold, did not hold together and was turgid and grey," according to *La Prensa*'s critic. "The only outstanding moment was the serenade, 'Deh vieni alla finestra,' by Titta Ruffo, who sang with good taste and fine enunciation, to say nothing of the glorious F sharp which he held admirably in the final phrase and which earned him the only burst of applause of the evening, and the only request for an encore which was granted." Thus the only artist singled out in this first *Don Giovanni* of the Colón's was Ruffo, whose vocal attributes did not indicate him as the ideal performer of the role. It is ironic that his delivery should be singled out for the unwritten high note at the end of the "Serenade." It should be noted that in singing it Ruffo was only yielding to the aesthetically distasteful practice of the period, as all baritones sang the interpolated high note for which he was roundly panned in Chicago a few years later.

Ruffo took part in the premiere of an Argentine opera, which at the time was sung in Italian, by Ettore Panizza, called *Aurora*. It took place on August 5, 1908. *La Prensa* found that "Titta Ruffo imbued Governor del Puente with the authority that is the hallmark of the celebrated baritone. His stance and presence evoked the true image of the great heroes of the heroic age. His fleeting appearance in the act did not permit us to more than admire him as the impeccable personification of the representative of the Monarchy."

The triumphal performances during that inaugural season of the Teatro Colón in 1908 made him one of the idols of Argentine audiences. According to *La Prensa*, he was "the cornerstone of the house, for there is no other way to describe him." In his memoirs, Ruffo went on to write, "I had had a feeling that that season would be the beginning of a great fortune of colossal popularity for me and my prescience was fulfilled."[7] Shortly prior to their departure on September 2, the company gave a benefit *Rigoletto* in his honor and, according to *La Prensa*, "the great auditorium was too small to hold the immense numbers who wanted to bestow the warmest applause on their celebrated baritone. The evening was punctuated by ovations. At the end, there were numerous presentations and among them, mention should be made of an artistic bronze casket filled with American gold coins, a gift as original as it was valuable."

Ruffo returned to sing at the Colón for the next three seasons—1909, 1910, 1911—and later he would return for those of 1915, 1916, 1926, 1928, and 1931. He was, during the first three of these later seasons, acclaimed in the works of his basic repertoire: *Rigoletto*, *Barber of Seville*, *Hamlet* (the last being dropped only from his third season), *Pagliacci*, and *Gioconda*. He was also heard in as diverse works as *Lucia di Lammermoor*, *Demon*, *Thaïs*, *Cristoforo Colombo*, *Fanciulla del West*, *Don Carlo*, and *Eugene Onegin*.

When on May 23, 1909, Titta Ruffo returned to the Colón to sing in *La Gioconda, La Prensa* reported that at the end of the duet with the tenor Constantino, "he let go with a series of unison high notes with Enzo that electrified the whole house and made all else look pale. Needless to say, this sparked a noisy ovation from the entire audience." He then sang a *Rigoletto* with Bonci and Pareto. "Ruffo, singing the name part, was, as usual, the lion whose powerful claw is made uniquely felt and turned out to be the outstanding presence of the evening" (*La Prensa*). In addition to his standard repertory he sang the title role in the Buenos Aires premiere of Rubinstein's *Demon* on August 31. According to *La Prensa*, "The celebrated baritone as the Demon brought into play his usual art, and unraveling the composer's intentions, highlighted them superbly. The second act arioso, which he delivered magnificently, had to be encored, and it was thanks to his own performance that the lengthy dialogues were heard with attention. The same can be said of the immensely long drawn-out seduction scene in the last act." His partners on this occasion were Hariclea Darclée in the role of Tamara, Florencio Constantino as Sinodal, and Mansueto Gaudio as Gudal, conducted by Giuseppe Barone.

During his 1909 engagement he gave a joint recital at the Teatro Odeón on July 26 with the famous soprano Elena Teodorini. Their accompanist was the Argentine pianist Ernesto Drangosch. "As usual," *La Prensa* wrote, "he was the darling of the audience. We do not need to describe the great baritone's sublime interpretation of the 'Serenade' from *Don Giovanni*, which earned him such endless applause at the Colón last year—but again, yesterday, it had to be encored as did the 'Là ci darem la mano' with Mme. Teodorini. However, where he truly surprised us and proved that a great artist can always find ways to shine even in the simplest selections, was in the short salon pieces which, one after the other, he was called upon to satisfy—but not to satiate—the desires of the public. He made of 'Torna a Surriento' a poem of expressive sentiment. Then 'Maria, Marì' was adorned with the bursts of crescendi that are the hallmarks of this great artist. A 'Tuscan Song' and another from. . .we know not where, brought the series to an end, but did not put a stop to the ovations which went on and on, bringing Titta Ruffo back time and time again to the stage to bow and wave in acknowledgment. In short: another triumph. . .and that makes a thousand!"

This review in *La Prensa* reveals the popularity and the immense success that Ruffo had achieved in Buenos Aires, as does the following, from another of the many newspapers of the time. The unidentified clipping is from 1910:

Titta Ruffo, the colossal baritone, appeared on stage and was greeted by a deafening ovation as soon as he was seen. This was no claque, this was a spontaneous and sincere outburst of love for the outstanding singer who earns bravos from the public. The "divo" smiles. It is his triumph over a multitude that he enslaves and subjugates by his charming presence. We understand it all when we see the stance of a sincere man, one who lives above misery and envy and is convinced of his own worth. The public quiets down and from that privileged throat emerges a torrent of vocal harmony that at times caresses the ear like a gently moving murmur, lulling the mind, and then, suddenly, startling it into wakefulness, shaking it into the outburst of a "Bravo!" that is echoed and re-echoed by two thousand throats that can only thus give expression to the influence of this monument of a singer over that mass that is a slave to his vocal cords. And he sings once, twice, three, four, and five times but the greedy public wants their pound of flesh and calls for more—but that is it! He has given in five times and everyone applauds: ladies, gentlemen and children all scream their deafening "Bravos!" and Titta Ruffo continues to smile.... Who remembers anything or anyone while he is there? Now the public seeks no further spectacle, all it wants is the intensely pleasing impression of the great Titta, and with that, they leave; but it is like enjoying a wonderful dream, and one refuses to awaken. The public mills about the lobby of the theater awaiting the appearance of the great baritone, and when he finally does come through to get to his carriage they embrace him, they crush him, they cry out to him "Viva Titta Ruffo!"

Although Ruffo was not a recitalist in the usual sense, he recorded salon songs and *canzonettas* like other famous Italian *divi*, although they constitute only a small portion of his total recorded output. He was the only baritone of this century to achieve an international status which rivaled that usually reserved for tenors. As Lauri-Volpi points out in his book *Voci parallele*: "It was *the* historic baritone voice, as were those of Duprez, Tamagno and Caruso among the tenors and Chaliapin's among the basses."[8]

Ruffo sang the title role in a gala *Rigoletto* on May 25, 1910, celebrating the Centenary of the Revolution of May, the hundredth anniversary of the birth of the Argentine Republic. He also sang in *La Gioconda, Barber of Seville, Cristoforo Colombo, Hamlet*, and *Pagliacci*. Of the first performance he gave of *Cristoforo Colombo* on June 21, *La Prensa* wrote: "Last night, Christopher Columbus was Titta Ruffo. As was to be expected, thanks to his powerful vocal endowments the artist was able to derive more from the role than had been possible for his predecessor.[9] During the first and second acts, the memory of Giraldoni was not entirely obscured, and it took the epilogue to decide the issue and proclaim Titta Ruffo the victor in the comparison."

At the conclusion of the 1910 season a special performance was mounted in Ruffo's honor. He sang Tonio in a complete performance of *Pagliacci* with Rousselière and Agostinelli, and then the third act of *Rigoletto* with Graziella Pareto. Being his farewell, it developed into an apotheosis and the greatest demonstration to date of the unlimited admiration on the part of the Buenos Aires public for the great baritone. Describing that evening, *La Prensa* wrote:

Words cannot recount what took place last night at the Colón at the gala held in honor of Titta Ruffo who received a demonstration that can only deserve the term "delirious." It was an evening of triumph and enthusiasm. There were the makings of an ovation after the "Prologue" to *Pagliacci*, which opened the proceedings and needless to say the celebrated baritone had to repeat it for the electrified audience.[10] It is true that the singer turns this musical selection into something sublime through the vocal effects that reach the highest degree of intensity.... The peak of the demonstration was reached after the "Sì, vendetta" from *Rigoletto*, also encored, and which ended the evening. We could not keep count of the curtain calls but the stage was literally carpeted with flowers thrown from the boxes, the tiers and balconies. Then the stage itself was gradually filled with servants carrying innumerable gifts to be presented and among them we will only mention a huge engraved golden chalice, a pin with a priceless pearl the size of a large pea and an oil painting.[11] So the evening will be a memorable one for Titta Ruffo—as it will be indelibly marked in the annals of the theater.

The reviewer of *La Prensa* was by no means exaggerating or carried away by enthusiasm. His description of that jubilant evening is corroborated by the reports of other newspapers. One of them wrote:

The evening reached unimaginable heights that surpassed the most ardent dreams. Monstrous is the only word that can describe the tempest of enthusiasm engendered by the great singer. The packed hall, whose occupants stood crushed together in the aisles, was on pins and needles. The "Prologue" from *Pagliacci* which the great baritone delivered with a fullness of voice and variety of expression that far surpassed expectations, unleashed an ovation never equalled before in any of our theaters. Palms beat heatedly and from the boxes, the stalls, the tiers, circles and balconies the noise gathered momentum and became a uniform and lasting tribute. To describe those impetuous outpourings that have never before been heard in any of our theaters before would be a hard task indeed.... After *Pagliacci*, came the third act of *Rigoletto*, sung with Signora Pareto, and after the "Sì, vendetta"—to which he imparts special expressiveness, the whole house jumped to its feet to acclaim its favorite artist with the wildest and loudest applause known in the annals of the lyric stage.

Another paper describes the event in the same enthusiastic terms:

Last night was an exceptional one in that it was announced as a farewell to the most beloved of the artists before the public: the baritone Titta Ruffo. It was a nonsubscription performance but the hall has seldom presented a more imposing appearance nor have its walls ever resounded to such endless ovations to prove that the love of the public for its favorite artist borders on fanaticism. In the history of our theaters—from the days of Tamagno to the present—no name appears that has had the popularity and general acclaim of that of Titta Ruffo.

"And finally," wrote still another, "it was a farewell that was worthy of being sent in review, to Milan."

Following the 1910 season at the Colón, he traveled to Montevideo. He made his Uruguayan debut at the Teatro Urquiza (which later be-

came the Teatro of the S.O.D.R.E.). He sang the four roles that were
regarded his most accomplished interpretations: Figaro (first with Pareto, later with Galli-Curci), Rigoletto, Hamlet, and Tonio in *Pagliacci*. In
the last he was partnered by his lifelong friend, Manuel Izquierdo.

Ruffo's great success in Madrid in 1910 prompted the Spanish music
critic Vicente Contreras to write a critical essay about him.[12] He made
the same deep impression on the Argentine reporters. Following his
performance in 1910, Mariano Antonio Barrenechea, music critic of *La
Nación*, published an article in the magazine *Música* in 1911 under the
title "Titta Ruffo: Notes of Artistic Psychology." (It was later republished
as an appendix to the third edition of his *Historia Estética della Música*.[13])
Despite a few contradictions it makes for interesting reading, particularly
for those who never heard or saw Titta Ruffo on stage and must therefore judge him solely on the basis of recorded excerpts from his repertory
and through eyewitness accounts. The article describes his delivery of
several roles in complete performances during his heyday, in 1910. A
few excerpts from Barrenechea's essay deserve to be quoted in order to
convey the impression Ruffo created on his hearers and to make the
essay more accessible to the international readership of operatic history.

Titta Ruffo is of great interest and I have to devote these pages to him for he
is the most finished and admirable example of the modern singer. Today's great
practitioners of the lyric art more or less talentedly follow and respect the virtually lost traditions of the old school. They sing. That is to say, they follow the
text and they interpret it according to the measures, the intonations and the
rhythm of the phrases. If Titta Ruffo is asked how he prepares and studies his
role, he will answer: "To create the role of Tonio in *Pagliacci*, I try to reproduce
the image of a poor idiot I encountered in a village lying between Italy and
Switzerland. On stage I mimic his gestures, his cries and even his broken front
tooth. For Cascart I emulate the sort of fellow we meet in our daily visits to
cafés. To Hamlet I bring all that is suggested to me by the troubles afflicting
the poor Prince and the same for Rigoletto whose tribulations could be visited
on any of us. To bring these two characters to life, all I need to do is remember
the pains of my own youth." These are surprising remarks coming from a singer.
He says nothing of his vocal range, his high notes, his modulations: He only
speaks of the veracity of his dramatic creations. Yet it would be difficult to find
a more marvelously endowed singer. His voice goes from low A to high B natural,
two and a half tones beyond the overall range of the normal baritone: two tones
higher and one-half lower.[14] That voice possesses a texture, a roundness and a
purity that caress the senses more completely than any other that we can imagine.
These qualities acquire an additional beauty when they reach the higher register
from the middle C up, and by their fullness, assurance and beautiful timbre,
they acquire an almost tenor-like quality. As he travels down the scale, it does
not retain the same purity nor beauty. The length of his breath is truly phenomenal: a veritable marvel of nature. As an example we can cite the somewhat

unlovely cadence in the *Hamlet* "Drinking Song" which he delivers without a break and which includes four truly radiant Gs.

* * *

The expressive changes he is able to bring, the vocal *tours de force* that he manages with incredible ease are indescribable. It is also difficult to decide whether Titta Ruffo has succeeded because of the glory of that voice, the attractiveness of his person or the pathos of his style and the depth of his expression. Yet all these qualities, admirable when alone, are blended into a harmonious whole that justifies the success enjoyed by the artist: one that is unequalled in the last twenty years of singing. Titta Ruffo is a weak musician and asserted himself through the expression of his dramatic feeling obtained by a simple but deeply felt declamation, and by the portentous notes of his high register. Essentially he is a dramatic baritone, far richer in his intuitive expression than in his musical knowledge. He studies his roles from a literary standpoint: He tries to gather all possible information on the type of character he is to portray and once he feels sure that he has penetrated the dramatics of the character, he sings, and in an entirely natural way, gives free rein to the feelings that his contact with the role has awakened in him. Thus *Hamlet*, a feebly composed opera, when interpreted by this artist seems to become a work of genius. It is in this composition of Ambroise Thomas, perhaps thanks to his own special characteristics, that Titta Ruffo stands lifesize before us.... If Titta Ruffo can become Hamlet, movingly incarnate, if when he sings Rigoletto he can overpower us with his impressive realism, if his Figaro is more joyous than any other's—if he fleshes out all these three disparate types of personalities and presents them to us, not as lyric or operatic stage creatures, but as truly human beings, it must be due not only to his being a great singer or an intelligent actor. It is because he understands and lives his characters, because there is something of him in Hamlet, because he feels in his heart the sorrows of Rigoletto and because his spirit rejoices in the mischief of Figaro.... In the character of Hamlet, Titta Ruffo found the ideal that galvanized and developed the most characteristic instincts of his artistic nature.... The talent of the celebrated artist is nowhere as admirably shown as in his Hamlet. In none of his other *personae* have I found him to show such style, that is to say, to show how his reason controls the expression of his sensibility; nowhere else is there such a mellifluous blending of the many vocal resources at his command, the admirable intuition with which he expresses the most pathetic phrases and the dramatic knowledge of how best to guess and translate the true interplay of events. In Tonio of *Pagliacci*, attracted by what I would call the picturesque side of the role, he somewhat tends to overlook the true psychological make-up of the character and creates a charged and violent caricature. Tonio is a pathetic wretch hopelessly enamoured, but lacking in energy, will and character. He is not an imbecile in the clinical sense of the word. In *Cristoforo Colombo* of Franchetti, the artist's favorite score, Ruffo never once engendered in me an impression of greatness. Barnaba, as a stage figure, does not measure up to Ruffo's abilities.

* * *

In Figaro he re-emerges in all his facets and personality. All the talents and style of the artist shine through, but now in a more diverting and amusing way which is, however, no less interesting for that. This book would be endless were I to try to analyze all the admirable qualities possessed by the singer and shown in the cavatina and in the allegro of the difficult duet between Almaviva and Figaro: "All'idea di quel metallo," or in the tender expressions of the duet with Rosina: "Di Lindoro il vago oggetto siete voi bella Rosina," and particularly in the *recitativi* which he pours out in absolutely classical style. It becomes virtually impossible to decide whether his enunciation is clearer than agile, for his musical stress is as impeccable as his intention. To proceed, I shall say that the admirable artist has managed to play with equal firmness and gusto, with an equally flexible talent, two extreme chords of the soul: He brings out the laughter of Beaumarchais and the tears of Shakespeare. . . . In *Rigoletto*, Titta Ruffo shines particularly for the expansiveness with which he expresses the imperious phrases, which is why I prefer him in the admirable scene with the courtiers to any other in the opera. . . . Titta Ruffo knows how to sing and he sings well when he wants to; for the proof of this suffice it to hear and analyze the gusto and technical niceties he puts into the recitatives and arias of *The Barber of Seville*. But he gladly sacrifices the beauties of his art on the altar of dramatic verities when required to do so. He is the prototype of the artist of our day, of this period in music when, to attach a new meaning to the fine dictum of the old and great creator of *Alceste*, "the muses have silenced the song of the Sirens.". . . Titta Ruffo is specially attracted to the art of drama. He is an unconditional admirer of Grasso, Zacconi, and, above all, of Novelli from whom he has borrowed many of the details of his impersonation of Hamlet. Whenever possible he enjoys theater going. In private, he delights in tirelessly declaiming Italian poetry and reiterates complacently that when the glories of his voice have faded, and if his age allows, he will yield to the temptations of a dramatic career. It well may be that this young artist, in the full flower of good health and possessing magnificent powers may yet have a surprise in reserve for his admirers and that the artist who is today the fine glory of the lyric stage may later gather new laurels from the groves of Italian drama. . . . Yet Titta Ruffo has risen so high in the admiration of his contemporaries, his glory has become so great and unchallenged, that it will be hard for him to climb to such a pinnacle if he turns his artistic abilities to a different field. His fame, like these very abilities themselves, are full justification for my having gathered together the notes and observations that I have put down after friendly contacts with him as an artist and as a man with a heart and soul. Titta Ruffo has earned the admiration of all those who concern themselves lovingly with matters of the lyric theater and the evolution of artistic customs and tastes. He deserves a careful study if only because of his privileged position in the eyes of audiences of the world, to which he stands as an idol. . . .

* * *

His charming and voluble conversation touches on the most difficult and diverse subjects, and always in an interesting manner. Just as on stage, in private life also he can slip with the same ease from a light and playful tone to the grave and dramatic. He is the same in public and private: His face reflects with great fidelity the effects, feelings or emotions he experiences or evokes....This man, who has struggled so hard and experienced pain so profoundly, still retains the heart of a child, a great naivete, which does not exclude a certain pride and *hauteur*.

For the 1911 season Ruffo brought a much wider variety of roles, which showed his versatility as well as his limitations. Besides two of the old stand-bys, Rigoletto and Figaro, he sang in *Thaïs, Lucia di Lammermoor, Don Carlo, Fanciulla del West, Tristan und Isolde*, and *Eugene Onegin*; in other words, he appeared in Italian, French, German, and Russian operas.

According to *La Prensa*, "he made a valuable contribution to the evening with his usual vocal prowess" in the May 24 performance of *Thaïs*. The May 25 *Lucia* was a special event, as it signaled the return to the stage of Maria Barrientos following a temporary retirement because of her marriage. Of Ruffo's performance *La Prensa* wrote: "Although he plays a relatively minor role, that of Enrico, Titta Ruffo still made his presence felt, bringing it into the foreground in the first scene with his aria 'Cruda, funesta smania' and then in the duet with Lucia. In the first, he showed off his superb high notes and in the second, he successfully toned down the power of his voice to blend musically with that of Mme. Barrientos, thus avoiding a tasteless overshadowing."

Of his Rodrigo in *Don Carlo* on July 1, *La Prensa* carried the following notice: "Like an eagle on the wing, the baritone Titta Ruffo soared above all the others—as an actor and as a singer—with his irreproachable and elegant costuming and carriage, careful enunciation and the nobility of phrasing which he carried to insuperable magnificence with the full power of the voice that is so admired by all."

La Fanciulla del West was having its Buenos Aires premiere on July 25 with Agostinelli, and *La Prensa* wrote: "Among the main protagonists, Titta Ruffo stood out for the way he portrayed the role of Rance and the effectiveness of his dramatic action, supported by his beautiful and powerful vocal gifts."

As for *Tristan und Isolde* on August 10, *La Prensa* wrote: "Kurwenal was sung by Titta Ruffo. That says it all"—which is a nice way of saying nothing although the praise is implicit.

La Nación was more explicit: "The baritone Titta Ruffo repeatedly gave proof that this was his first essay of the part of Kurwenal.[15] It was demonstrated in the way he studiously watched the conductor for his 'entrances' and in the tenseness with which he performed the role. He did, however, sing the first scene of Act 3 accurately and pleasingly."

As far as Tchaikovsky's *Eugene Onegin* was concerned, it had its Buenos Aires premiere on August 20, 1911, with Ruffo, Lina Pasini Vitale, and the tenor Angelo Pintucci. The only thing *La Prensa* said was that the opera only barely made the stage and that only because a baritone of

22. Tittà Ruffo as Rodrigo in *Don Carlo* (1912)
    Photo: Carlo Edwards
    Courtesy of Ruffo Titta, Jr.

the caliber of Titta Ruffo was available to do the title role. *La Nación* merely pointed out that "his great faculties found little to exploit in the title role."

After the season at the Colón in Buenos Aires he sang for the first time in Rosario at the Teatro Colón of that city on September 3, 1911, in *Rigoletto* with Maria Barrientos, and on September 5 he sang Hamlet. Afterward he made his Brazilian debut on September 12 at the inaugural performance of the Teatro Municipal in São Paulo in *Hamlet*. Then, still in 1911, he appeared at the Teatro Lyrico for the first time, in *Rigoletto* on October 3.

Ruffo made his enormously successful North American debut in 1912. The lucrative offers that followed kept him busy on that continent and in Europe until 1915. He made his Cuban debut in *Aida* at the Teatro Nacional in Havana on April 22, 1915. At the conclusion of his month-long Cuban engagement he briefly returned to the United States, and after a stormy voyage from New York he arrived in Buenos Aires. His first performance of the season at the Colón was in *L'Africana*, on July 6, 1915.

This was a particularly important season which signaled not only the return of Titta Ruffo, but the Colón debut of Enrico Caruso who had not been heard in the Argentine capital since 1903. Yet it would seem that the triumphal reappearance of Ruffo was such an eagerly awaited event that it outshone even Caruso's return.

At a time when newspapers rarely printed illustrations, *La Prensa* departed from the usual practice and published a photograph of Ruffo (which it had not done even for Caruso) at the top of a lengthy review of the opera in which he was appearing, and spoke of him in the following terms:

Last night Ruffo brought together at the Colón, all the many audiences that Caruso had attracted in all his performances.... Although our idea of the character of Nelusko differs entirely in certain passages from the version presented by Ruffo, last night taught us what can be wrought by the will and the art of one man. Titta Ruffo appears before us now possessing admirable qualities as an interpreter, qualities that have been acquired by a surprising constancy linked to profound intuition. As he appeared on stage, he was greeted by a great salvo of applause which was repeated at the end of his first act aria. After the "Invocation to Brahma" in the second act and the "Ballad" of the third the same thing happened, although the enthusiasm may have been less evident perhaps because certain *portamenti* and *rallentamenti* in the rhythm tended to make his singing somewhat monochromatic, but he was showered with considerable applause. We feel, however, that in the scene in the fourth act, Ruffo really hit his stride. The phrase "Averla tanto amata" was admirably delivered. In that passage, Titta gave us the superstitious personage in all his rough reality: He made clear the respectful love felt for the unhappy Queen and moved us with the terrible despair born of the betrayal he has committed in obedience to the command of his beloved Sovereign. However, we do feel that he might have been well advised to have selected a different opera in which to return to this audience.... If in *Africana* Titta had his moments, in another, more human vehicle he might have kept the enthusiasm boiling throughout the evening.

Ruffo recorded two selections from the third act of *Africana*: "All'erta, marinar" in 1915 (Victor 87223; d/f 817), and "Adamastor" on two occasions, acoustically in 1920 (Victor 88622; d/f 6262) and electrically in 1929 (Victor d/f 7153). In the first selection he left the most stunning document of his voice as it is shown here, more than in any other recording, what the prodigious bronze-like voice sounded like. The stentorian virility, immense volume, and unbelievable flights into the higher reaches are all preserved on this record and helps one understand the sweeping enthusiasm of his public and the ovations. One can also comprehend the tribute of the printed leaflets (formerly on exhibit in the Museum of the Colón) tossed from the balconies and boxes by his admirers with the text "Viva Titta Ruffo, the One and Only!" and "Viva the King of the Baritones!" Another would plead, "Come back next year!"

During the balance of the 1915 season in Buenos Aires he sang Figaro, Rigoletto, Hamlet, and Escamillo. Apart from these roles, at a memorable evening organized by the Asociación de la Critica on August 4, he sang the part of Tonio to Caruso's Canio in the first act of *Pagliacci*, which was part of the festive program. Hina Spani in the role of Nedda shared the limelight with this illustrious team.

Regarding Ruffo's work during the Buenos Aires season the critic of *La Prensa* makes some curious observations following the *Barber of Seville* performance on July 7:

With the transformation from Nelusko to Figaro, the baritone has regained all the highest prestige he has always enjoyed among us. From the very first "cavatina" of the first act, Titta received a veritable ovation from the public for the incomparable torrent of voice that filled the vast auditorium of the Colón. But aside from the voice there is also the genius of the artist in his interpretation. His Figaro is the result of profound observation. The artist reveals to us the rustic, playful intriguer, if one can use the word, that lies in the character of Figaro, and he does it forcefully and truthfully. In fact, there are times when he might seem to go too far in his injection of interpretative and technical details. If in the first act his spoken recitatives always retain the cadences of the sung phrases, in the second the rhythms were very often altered. Then, at times, he seemed to abandon his voice (!?) and impress a character on the declamation that bears no resemblance to any other artist's version of the part. We do not believe that he needs to resort to such means.

Could the critic have meant perhaps that instead of singing certain passages he delivered them in a spoken voice? It seems to be a logical explanation. Of his July 26 Rigoletto *La Prensa* writes:

Despite certain moments when he seemed to 'abandon' or 'drag' his voice, Titta Ruffo was the focus of the audience's attention and he gained it by the enormous vigor and shining beauty of his vocal prowess. The second act monologue, ending in a powerful G and the famous third act imprecation earned him indescribable acclamations.

La Prensa devotes a lengthy article to his Hamlet of that year and gives a detailed analysis of his performance:

Last night (July 30), the celebrated baritone, with a voice of magnificent timbre and its amazing and powerful range once again captivated the audience. After the "Drinking Song" in which he delivered a B flat of rare brilliance, he was recalled nine times and finally prevailed upon to repeat the *cadenza* which is his hallmark of the aria and the high point of his delivery, for apart from his agility, we admire the range and sounds that constitute the segment. We can swear that Titta Ruffo has no rival in that passage. In the duet with Ophelia (Galli-Curci) and more specifically reaching the words "No, lasciarti non vo," the idea of doubt was expressed with great intensity, as was also a sense of premonition when Laertes informs him that the King has ordered that he leave the Court. But in the Ghost scene, perhaps because the melody in that portion is symmetrical, he did not quite get across the idea of true awe. . . . In the other two acts he rose to great thespian heights, except in the last part of the third act where we found he was somewhat overacting. In the monologue, we would have preferred the dilemma to have been expressed with a greater musical variation. In "Esser o non essere," there are two indications, one in crescendo and one in diminuendo, which define the choice perfectly and which Titta overlooked. We can understand that he tried to present the meditative aspect of the phrase, but we would point out to him that in Hamlet, doubt and skepticism are constants in the mind of the protagonist. Be that as it may, the public applauded the baritone to the rafters.

   In the middle of the 1915 Colón season, on August 16, members of the company performed *Cavalleria rusticana* and *Pagliacci* at the Teatro Urquiza in Montevideo. The latter work reunited once more, and for the last time, Ruffo and Caruso in a complete performance. One can gauge the significance of this operatic event from the unusually large number of South American newspapers that carried a review.

   The *Tiempo* singled out his Prologue which "unleashed a tempest of applause. . . . he delivered the 'Incominciate!' in one breath of overwhelming power, with two successive diminuendi and crescendi which earned a renewed wave of applause. Showered with flowers, Ruffo left the stage and the tragedy could begin." All reviews mention the fact that Ruffo was obliged to encore the second half of the Prologue.

The review of *La Razón* is no less complimentary, praising "his astounding vocal prowess."

Rio de Janeiro's *O Paiz* had the following to say:

Titta Ruffo is an irresistible force—his is one of the most captivating of the world's great voices. From the moment of his appearance he swept away the public, not only as an extraordinary singer but also as an actor.

His Tonio is a true creation. A naturally comic character, he endowed him with a nervous tic he was able to sustain throughout the whole performance, and he held the attention of the audience all evening. . . . Quite appropriately we regard him as one of the most perfect artists in the way he colors and shapes even the slightest words of the libretto.

In addition to giving unreserved praise to his singing, the *Diario del Plata* was no less complimentary of his acting. The reviewer wrote: ". . . And Tonio laughs and sobs at the same time, and his sobs are so real in the play within the play, that the public does not know whether to laugh at the weeping of the histrionic wretch or to weep at his pathetic laughter, so inextricably enmeshed are the voice of the artist and his interpretation of the character."

The extensive review published in the *Tribuna Popular* deserves to be quoted at length. The critic's admiration for the baritone is quite obvious and would seem excessive were his judgments not corroborated by his colleagues. It is noteworthy that Ruffo commanded more attention than Caruso himself.

No, the public did not pay fabulous prices simply to hear Caruso's "Vesti la giubba." Beside the setting sun there shone that other sun that is at its zenith and in all its shining glory: Titta Ruffo.

Quite sincerely, and moreover without any desire to underestimate the merits of others, I can say that I would have been more than satisfied with the Prologue alone as sung by Titta Ruffo.

Earlier, on another memorable occasion, the great baritone sang the role of Tonio on the stage of the Teatro Urquiza. At that time he amazed the public with the perfect and thorough study he has made of the character which he portrays with such deep psychological insights. But between that admirable Tonio we unreservedly applauded then and last night's Tonio who exposed his tragic impotence, his venomous physical and moral inferiority and his tortured passion for Nedda on the humble pantomime stage, there is a wide difference—there is such an improvement that at times one wondered whether this was not a different artist from the one we applauded earlier.

Some have vaunted the great interpretative abilities of Caruso. Ah! But those of Titta Ruffo are more amazing still! One cannot hesitate to say so in a sober and fair review. Titta Ruffo is almost a greater interpreter than a singer, yet even as a singer one cannot do less than to say that he is the greatest living baritone.

23. Titta Ruffo as Tonio and Enrico Caruso as Canio in *Pagliacci* (Buenos Aires, 1915)
    Courtesy of Ruffo Titta, Jr.

His Prologue last night was the most outstanding moment of the evening: a formidable voice at the service of his remarkable artistry.

He is a singer who does not spare the treasures of his throat. At all moments, not only when following the directions of the score, but when another singer might have made do with a colorless recitative, Titta applies the full harmonious potential of his voice. What usually have been merely unremarkable phrases, suddenly, thanks to his unique artistry, become imbued with power and with his very personal creative genius. They emerge with a brilliance and color that we did not think possible.

It was not only his superb delivery of the Prologue, which itself usually turns out to be such a hurdle to many and he renders without apparent effort—one might even say "scherzando"—but also in the duet with Nedda, in his exchanges with Canio after Colombina's betrayal has been exposed, and in the whole of the first part of the farce, Ruffo showed himself an extraordinary singer and an extraordinary actor.

Never, never have we heard such artistic singing of a role that by the very nature of the part seems ungrateful and arid and hardly conducive to the display of great ability. But Titta vanquished all and his Tonio will remain as an example for all time.

Still in 1915 Ruffo sang a single performance in Rosario, at the Teatro de la Opera, a *Barber of Seville* opposite Galli-Curci. He concluded his South American engagements in Brazil, making his debut in *Hamlet* on September 4, 1915, at the Teatro Municipal of Rio de Janeiro. During the same engagement he appered in *Rigoletto, Pagliacci, Africana, Barbiere,* and *Tosca.* This was the only year he sang at the Municipal at Rio. Ruffo spent the first half of 1916 singing in Spain and then returned to the Colón for the 1916 season with three new roles in addition to his standard repertory: the title roles of *Boris Godunov* and *Falstaff,* and Carlo Gérard in *Andrea Chénier.* His first role was *Boris* (on May 20) whose dramatic possibilities he must have known from Chaliapin's characterizations. Different sources report that it was not one of his major successes, but the critic of *La Prensa* praised it highly.

Last night *Boris Godunov* had a protagonist worthy of the work. Titta Ruffo performed a task of interpretative genius. The depiction of the tragic character may well be considered one of the most polished creations of the notable artist who has studied the role with great love. In *Boris Godunov,* Titta Ruffo has unfurled all his faculties: not only those of his huge and powerful voice, but also that of his dramatic talent and he was able to breathe life into the somber character of Boris and develop it in its own sinister and mysterious glow. From the "Coronation" to the "Death Scenes," he riveted the increasing attention of the public and reached great heights in the second act monologue when he believes himself haunted by the ghost of his victim.

It is a matter of some speculation that if Ruffo's Boris was indeed as outstanding as the critic of *La Prensa* claims, why wasn't he asked to

24. Titta Ruffo in the Title Role of *Boris Godunov* (Buenos Aires, 1916)
Courtesy of Horacio Sanguinetti

perform the role elsewhere? This is an especially valid question since Chaliapin, the foremost exponent of the role, was held captive in his native Russia first by the war and later by the Revolution and its consequences, until 1921. There can be no doubt that Ruffo would have liked to sing the role again—he talked about it as late as 1944! Yet his two Colón performances remained the only occasions that he donned the costume of Tsar Boris.

Andrea Chénier followed on June 3, with Edoardo di Giovanni (Edward Johnson) in the title role. The part of Carlo Gérard seemed to suit both Ruffo's voice and temperament as was confirmed by the reviewer of *La Prensa*, though not without some reservations.

In the interpretation of Gérard, Titta Ruffo again achieved one of his customary successes. Perhaps the Gérard he gave us was not the Gérard we ourselves envisage: certain inflections and misplaced stresses—or perhaps some accents not entirely reflective of the text, especially in the first act and the monologue of the third—somewhat marred the work of Titta Ruffo. Needless to say, vocally the baritone achieved extraordinarily sonorous effects.

The reviewer's judgment is difficult to reconcile with the recorded evidence left by Ruffo. In 1920 he recorded both of Gérard's monologues: "Son sessant'anni" (Victor 87325; d/f 817) is very good; his powerful notes stand out on the words "Io dei servi"; only the final sustained high note in the phrase "Nell'ora della morte" is disappointing if measured against his own high standards. "Nemico della patria," however, is one of Ruffo's outstanding recordings vocally as well as from the standpoint of characterization. One of the most impressive moments is the F sharp in the phrase "e in un sol bacio." It is not a mere coincidence that Henry Pleasants in *The Great Singers* chose to single out Gérard's great monologue:

Maurel used to say that Ruffo's D-flat, D, E-flat and the following notes to the top A-flat were the most glorious baritone sounds he had ever heard. Anyone who has listened to his cadence on C-sharp, A, D at the end of his recording of the "Nemico della patria" from *Andrea Chénier* will know what Maurel was talking about, and anyone who has heard his "Brindisi" from *Hamlet* will know what they all were talking about.[16]

Even the 1929 electric version (Victor 7153), which is less brilliant and shows some wear and tear in the voice, is an impressive recording with, perhaps, even better characterization.

Regarding Falstaff, which he sang for the first time in Buenos Aires on July 27, 1916, it was obvious that the part was not truly suitable to his artistic temperament, essentially dramatic. As he had often demonstrated in *The Barber of Seville*, he was able to express humor, joviality, even exuberance. But Verdi's Sir John is a more complex personality than Figaro, whose essence Ruffo was able neither to capture entirely nor to express convincingly. The subtle shadings and flexibility the part calls for did not come naturally to him. His "L'onore! Ladri!" recording of 1921 (Victor 88637; d/f 6264) is excellent and shows a vocal plenitude that few interpreters of this Verdi character were able to offer. But he is much less convincing in the 1922 "Quand'ero paggio" (Victor 87360; d/f 876) where his voice lacks the agility and light touch that is the essence of the piece.

The review in *La Prensa* of his 1916 Colón Falstaff is surprisingly succinct. "Surprisingly" because the critic traditionally gave a detailed analysis of Ruffo's performances, expressing praise or criticism. On this occasion the reviewer seems to tell more by omission. Following a lengthy description of Verdi's comedy he writes, "The baritone, Titta Ruffo, who was performing his first Falstaff, did it in a commendable fashion."

The critic of *La Razón*, however, is more explicit and more generous in his praise. "Titta Ruffo was truly fortunate in his new creation, with words and gestures of a most expressive nature, he used his powerful voice with discretion while imbuing it with delicate subtleties of which we did not know him capable, and thus made a most interesting figure of his creation."

In 1916, Ruffo made a single appearance at the Teatro Rivera Indarte in Córdoba, singing *Andrea Chénier* with Adelina Agostinelli and Edward Johnson. Then in Tucumán at the Teatro Odeon he sang Rigoletto on July 6, and on July 9, in a performance that celebrated the Centenary of the Republic's Independence, he sang *Andrea Chénier* again with Edward Johnson and Gilda della Rizza. Before returning to Europe he gave a benefit performance of *Pagliacci* at the Coliseo of Buenos Aires on August 14 for the Comité Italiano de Guerra (the Italian War Committee).

When Ruffo left Argentina in 1916 nobody suspected that a decade would pass before he would be heard again in Buenos Aires. His military obligations kept him in Italy—and in uniform—for the balance of World War I, and following the war he first returned to North America. His immense success produced so many offers that he was hard-pressed to fulfill all his engagements. In 1924 he toured the Caribbean and made it as far south as Caracas and Bogotá. His engagement in Bogotá was abruptly ended when he received the news of the assassination of his brother-in-law, Matteotti. Ruffo took the next ship back to Italy. He finally returned to Buenos Aires in 1926. He performed in *Hamlet, Andrea Chénier* with Lauri-Volpi, *Pagliacci* with Pertile, *Barber of Seville, Tosca* with Muzio and Lauri-Volpi, and *La Bohéme* with Pertile. On his return to the Colón after an absence of ten years, his first Hamlet (on May 29, 1926) was greeted with the same enthusiasm as before. The critic of *La Prensa* wrote:

To tell the truth, last evening's performance could have been entitled "Titta Ruffo," for the music of Thomas was purely incidental. The return of the celebrated baritone after a decade, was warmly welcomed by the audience who recalled him time and again after every act. Between 1916 and 1926, Ruffo's powers have lost very little of their strength or beauty, and his warmth, volume and expressiveness have not changed, although in the higher ranges they may be a trifle less free-flowing. His interpretation of Hamlet is the same as it always was: dramatic, moving at times, full of vigor and life.

Ruffo earned the usual critical praise for his singing during the rest of the season, and then appeared in Rio de Janeiro at the Teatro Lyrico. Because of his open hostility toward the Fascist regime he refused to sing in Italy after 1925 despite entreaties and threats from the government. He had a handful of European engagements in 1927, along with a few performances at the Metropolitan and Philadelphia. It is therefore surprising that he did not participate in the 1927 season of the Colón. When he returned there in 1928, it was not to sing in the official season but in the so-called Spring Season which, in that year, brought to Buenos Aires a number of important dignitaries. Ruffo himself was arriving from a series of performances in Chile, where he had last been heard in 1900!

During the spring season of 1928 Ruffo appeared at the Colón in the first and second acts of *Hamlet* in a gala performance given on October 14 in honor of the distinguished foreign notables who were invited to be present at the transfer of the presidency. The program also included *Cavalleria*, the Triumphal Scene from *Aida*, and the Kermesse Scene from *Faust*—a veritable feast.

His first complete opera was *Otello* on October 23, which had not been heard at the Colón since the inaugural season of 1908, also with Ruffo. In this performance the demanding title role was taken by its famous interpreter, the Chilean Renato Zanelli. The critic of *La Nación* wrote:

The availability of an Iago of the caliber of Titta Ruffo inspired the Board of Directors to stage *Otello* and the success it enjoyed was proof of their felicitous decision. The famous baritone, who has so often been applauded in trivial works of the repertoire, was finally able to place his amazing abilities at the service of an opera of worth and Titta Ruffo can very seldom have obtained a more deserved triumph than last night. His dramatic art was given full and free range and his voice rang out as it had on his finest nights. The sinister Iago is without doubt one of Titta Ruffo's great creations. Last night our audience was facing again the outstanding tragedian and gave him the acclamation he had earned. A trifle nervous in the first act, his vocalism improved until the "Credo" in the second act which is somewhat too much for him, but he overcame the difficulties and drew all the artistic possibilities from the piece.

Ruffo concluded his engagement with a complete performance of *Hamlet* on October 27, 1928. According to *La Razón*, he invested the part with "the authority of a great actor and burnished it with a still magnificent vocal polish."

His last visit to Argentina and, as it turned out, to South America came in 1931. He held a special affection for Buenos Aires, the city of some of his greatest triumphs, and he didn't hesitate to say so in an interview published in *La Nación*.

Every time I come to this city, I do so with immense enthusiasm, with infinite happiness, as though I were arriving for the first time at a place of which I had heard a lot. But then, I have given Buenos Aires the most vigorous and emotional moments of my artistic career, besides which, I inaugurated its main lyric theater. I have been returning for twenty-three years[17] and have landed ten times, as I have today, after a long sea journey, and have always been imbued with a great sense of excitement when approaching the Colón. This theater has a very personal and unique warmth, its audience possesses an aura that I do not recognize in any public anywhere else, in any other theater. I sang at the Colón's opening night[18] and so I love it more than any other theater in the world. I am not being flattering but speaking of a deep passion, a true one, which seems to possess me. I am linked to the Colón by a moral force. I have seen it develop, and on many different nights I have given it great moments most satisfying to my soul. Its popularity moves me personally, and the attraction of the hall exercises an extraordinary invigorating force over me. Yes, I love the Teatro Colón as I love no other theater in the world.

Ruffo's first appearance of the season (May 25, 1931) was the old standby, Hamlet, the role to which he clung to the very end. (In fact, it turned out to be the very last role he was ever to perform, in Nice on March 10, 1934.) Reviewing the performance, *La Prensa* wrote: "The public greeted Titta Ruffo warmly on his return. Many years ago, he earned a most well-deserved triumph in the title role of which he makes an intensely and piercingly dramatic creation, more by the passion of his temperament than by the theatricality of the part. He sang with a voice that still retains its beautiful colorations, particularly in the middle register."

He then sang in *Tosca* on June 23 with Giuseppina Cobelli and Georges Thill. "His Scarpia garnered almost all the applause," *La Prensa* reported. "It was a melodramatic and effective Scarpia that brought out the nature of the character; vocally, the celebrated baritone had moments of power and was remarkable for the clarity of his diction."

The reporter who interviewed Ruffo (and found him "still youthful and vigorous") was told by the baritone that apart from concerts and recitals he may be asked to give he would also do a *Barber of Seville* and Leoncavallo's *Edipo Re*. Contrary to his expectations, these plans did not materialize. He gave a single recital on June 14, 1931, and on July 2, 1931, Ruffo bade farewell for the last time to his beloved Teatro Colón in the role of Scarpia.

His South American engagements spanned thirty-one years—twenty-nine in Buenos Aires, where his devoted public heard him during all phases of his career: in his apprentice years, upon reaching artistic maturity, at the absolute peak of his powers, in his days of decline, and in his very last operatic season anywhere. His performance set a standard for audiences there and, conversely, the expectations of his Argentine and South American publics affected his style and manner of delivery which resulted in his frequent use and occasional overuse of power at the expense of subtlety and shadings. It would seem that during his active years no other theater or audience could equal his affection for that of the Colón and, at the same time, the public remained faithful to him to the very end of his career. Artistically speaking, for Titta Ruffo the Colón was home.

Notes

1. Titta Ruffo, *La mia parabola; memorie* (Rome: Staderini, 1977), p. 173.
2. He is obviously referring to the baritone register.
3. Giacomo Lauri-Volpi, *Voci parallele* (Rome: Garzanti, 1960), pp. 184-185.
4. Titta Ruffo, *La mia parabola*, p. 244.
5. Ibid., p. 225.
6. Henry Pleasants, *The Great Singers* (New York: Simon and Schuster, 1966), p. 289.
7. Titta Ruffo, *La mia parabola*, p. 244.
8. Giacomo Lauri-Volpi, *Voci parallele*, p. 185.
9. Eugenio Giraldoni, who is fondly remembered for his interpretation of the part and "whose presence and appearance perfectly fitted the tradition or the legend surrounding the great navigator from Genoa."
10. "In the *Pagliacci* 'Prologue' the legendary Titta, at the 'Andiam, incominciate,' tossed into his leonine nostrils such a formidable high G that it shook the theater and drove the audience wild." Giacomo Lauri-Volpi, *Voci parallele*, p. 185.
11. It was a canvas of Titta Ruffo as Hamlet, the work of the painter Gobbi. Among the other gifts received by the artist were a "superb antique sword," an autographed photograph of the president of the Republic, Dr. Figueroa Alcorta, and a medal from the mayor of the city of Buenos Aires.
12. Vincente Contreras, *Titta Ruffo y su arte: biografia y estudio en dos idiomas del eminente baritono* (Madrid, 1910).
13. Mariano Antonio Barrenechea, *Historia estetica della musica* (Buenos Aires: Claridad, 1941, 3rd ed.), Appendix: "Titta Ruffo, notas de psicologia artistica."
14. This is not accurate. Although at this time there is still no agreed criterion regarding the delimitation of the baritone range, generally speaking, a normal

baritone—that is, a good baritone—should encompass the range from low A flat to high A flat. Therefore, Ruffo's voice was only one and a half tones higher—and not two tones—and a half-tone less low than that of a "normal baritone."

15. In fact, it was the first time he performed the role in nearly a decade; but not "his first essay" since he had sung Kurwenal in Cairo, in 1902.

16. Henry Pleasants, *The Great Singers*, p. 289.

17. He was obviously referring to his arrival on the stage of the Colón, since he had set foot in Buenos Aires itself twenty-nine years earlier, in 1902.

18. That had been the plan, but due to the indisposition of the tenor Paoli, *Otello*, in which Ruffo was to have appeared, was postponed and the theater actually opened with *Aida*, Ruffo making his debut at the second performance, which was *Hamlet*.

Ruffo in Retrospect

GEORGE JELLINEK

At the peak of his success Titta Ruffo was asked about the factors that had influenced his career. "I have had many teachers," he declared, "but I think that listening to my own tone in the talking machine has been of the greatest help to me." Coming from one of the outstanding operatic figures of all time, this was a tribute indeed to the phonograph! And by grace of that "talking machine" the mighty voice of the late singer continues to teach and delight a new generation of music lovers.

Records, of course, provide no more than a reasonable approximation of the Ruffo voice. That was a phenomenon beyond all convention and comparison. What made it so? In the words of the late baritone himself, "...My voice was Nature's gift, to be sure—and I am grateful to Providence for it—but also the result of constant study and severe self-discipline."

Teachers had relatively little to do with that "constant study." The famous Persichini, teacher of Battistini and De Luca, was completely baffled by Ruffo's vocal material and held a low opinion of his pupil's operatic future. This matched Ruffo's dim view of his teacher's methods. Since teacher and pupil did not hesitate to voice their opinions, Ruffo's studies at the Rome Conservatory came to a sudden end. Lelio Casini, a noted vocal teacher in Milan with whom Ruffo continued his studies, recognized the baritone's unusual talent and coached him with patience and understanding: this despite the fact that the young singer, beset by constant financial troubles, could offer hardly anything in the way of compensation.

Ruffo's poverty actually hastened the time of his debut (1898) at a

Courtesy of George Jellinek. First published in *Saturday Review*, August 29, 1953. © 1953 Saturday Review Magazine Co. Reprinted by permission.

point when he was not yet, by academic standards, a fully accomplished singer. Nevertheless, his first stage appearance, in the small role of the Herald in *Lohengrin*, was such a success that it led to one engagement after another, and the singer was on his way.

Somehow, in these early years, Ruffo completed his development into an artist of the first order. His autobiography reveals an indebtedness to such prominent baritones of the day as Pacini, Menotti, and Giraldoni. Ruffo admired these artists on the stage and learned much from them in matters of operatic tradition, stage deportment, and vocal nuances. There may have been other influences of varying importance. But there can be no question about it—his ultimate evolution as a singer came primarily from his own efforts, as a result of a fiery determination to succeed and "severe self-discipline," which supplemented his genius of intuition and his unique vocal endowments.

The voice had but few limitations. It was somewhat hollow in the lower regions with an occasional tendency to huskiness. But the massive power and richness of the middle and upper registers, with a seemingly inexhaustible breath support behind them, defies description. At its peak it boasted a fully sustained B flat, yet retained the support and resonance of the baritonal timbre even at that dizzy altitude. Belittlers of his art often classify him as a "shouter." It is true that Ruffo's thunderous tones were ideal to express the vengeful cry of Rigoletto, the injured rage of Renato, and the fulminations of Iago. But who can ignore the richly documented fact that his skillful use of the mezzavoce, his ravishing pianissimi were just as remarkable as his range and power?

Ruffo is never mentioned alongside the paragons of bel canto singing. Forty years ago, a singing style breaking away from the traditions of a Bonci or Battistini inevitably had to give cause to adverse comments. But here Ruffo was in excellent company. Like Caruso and Chaliapin, he went beyond creating beautiful sound per se. To him singing was dramatic expression, with every phrase colored and shaded to convey a meaning. An easily accessible example of this is his recently issued "Gioconda" duet with Gigli (RCA Victor LCT 1004). What malice and irony is packed into the phrasing of the final "Buona fortuna," so vividly expressed in that inimitable musical sneer!

Through the maze of contradictory comments on Ruffo's acting, the baritone emerges as a striking—if at times an unsubtle—singing actor. His portrayal of Tonio did not end with the tremendous high G that concludes the "Prologue." It went on to create a figure that was "mournful, tragic, imbecilic, trembling on the verge of epilepsy, a condition portrayed with almost the accuracy of a clinic," according to Edward C. Moore in his *Forty Years of Opera in Chicago*. This was typical of the study and dedication with which he approached his roles.

There were traces of exhibitionism in his singing—interpolated high notes, showy cadenzas, occasional deviations from tempo to achieve an unusual effect. Critical reaction to these was justly unfavorable. Subsequent doubts about his musicianship, on the other hand, were highly exaggerated. Opera singers, as a rule, are not selfless interpreters of music, and Ruffo was no exception. But the transgressions were minor compared with the vocal accomplishments. Production of a beautiful tone is not a gift of nature and it cannot be taken for granted. It takes an artist and a musician to produce the kind of tone we hear in Ruffo's records, vibrant yet free of the controversial vibrato, with never an impure intonation or an improperly focused note.

The singer's autobiography tells us that his first recording session took place in 1897, a very early stage for both phonograph and singer. These early recordings—wax cylinders, undoubtedly—have disappeared without a trace. Eight years later, already an artist of established reputation with successful European and South American tours behind him, he recorded sixteen sides for Pathé. This rare group is mainly of curio interest. Judging by the examples this writer has heard, the Pathé recordings already showed Ruffo's vocal personality, but little of his control and polish. Yet, it was a bright promise from a singer of twenty-eight.

Promise turned to fulfillment with the first group of pressings made for G & T (1907-08). They show a vocal technique already fully developed and a tone quality that was nearing perfection. Most significant among these recordings was the appearance of several scenes featuring the artist in his two favorite roles: Rigoletto and Hamlet. His Rigoletto was a powerful characterization without quite matching the widely admired portrayal of Renaud, according to the critics of the day. As Hamlet, however, Ruffo had no rival. When he was studying the role, Victor Maurel, the great Hamlet of a bygone age, offered to coach him in it. Ruffo, with his characteristic pride and independence, politely but firmly declined the honor, preferring to develop his own conception. It turned out to be a characterization of which the artist could be justly proud. On records its strength and authority are clearly evident. The spectacular "Apparition Scene," short as it is, leaves the listener fairly stunned. No less remarkable are the vocal pyrotechnics of the "Drinking Song," while the moving and lyrical "Come il romito fior" is a fine example of legato singing.

The year 1912 marks Ruffo's first appearance in the United States as a member of the Chicago Opera Company. His Chicago successes are well remembered. A star attraction from his first appearance to his last, he filled the theater with a throng of personal devotees like no other baritone. (The fees he commanded were likewise unprecedented.) It was in the same year that his first Victor records were issued, carrying his voice to places far beyond the reach of the Chicago troupe. They were enthusiastically received and sold at such a rate that Victor rapidly followed the first issue with pressings of his earlier European masters. The acclaim was justified, for these selections show the singer at the peak of his vocal glory (1912-15). Such items as "Alla vita che t'arride" (*Masked Ball*), "Sei vendicata assai" (*Dinorah*), the *Zazà* arias, and that amazing display of vocal acrobatics, the unaccompanied "All'erta, marinar" (*Africana*), are on a particularly high level of excellence. It was in this period, too, that he recorded such conventional baritone fare as the "Prologue," "Largo al factotum," "Credo," and others, setting a vocal standard that is quite out of reach of present-day operatic competitors.

On January 8, 1914, Enrico Caruso and Titta Ruffo held their only joint recording session at Victor's Camden studios. The two vocal giants had previously sung together in Paris and Vienna (and were to be united a year later in Buenos Aires) and greatly admired each other's art. At this stage of their respective careers, however, they evidenced no particular desire to appear together on the stage. Both artists had the prestige and authority to dominate any performance in which they participated. Both were accustomed to give all they had on all occasions. And both felt that the added pressure to try to outperform one another would have been excessive. Apparently the atmosphere of the recording studio gave rise to no such tensions, for it resulted in a definitive recorded performance of the Act II finale from *Otello*. This recording has remained in the Victor catalogue ever since its first issue and has been available on several LP transfers. It remains the hope of phonophiles everywhere that the so far unpublished *Gioconda* duet, another memento of that memorable Camden meeting, will also some day be brought to light.

The outbreak of World War I interrupted Ruffo's career, and the singer entered Italian military service. This disruption of his established pattern of activity and exposure to wartime conditions left a temporary mark on his vocal equipment. It was not until 1920 that he returned to regular operatic work and resumed recording.

Ruffo's long-awaited Metropolitan debut took place on January 19, 1922. Interestingly enough, Victor issued two selections each from *Ernani* and *Andrea Chénier* in this period (1920-23), two works in which the singer was prominent during his Metropolitan career. A number of Spanish songs were also issued during these years, and beamed toward the singer's devoted South American audience. Some of these recordings may show a hardly noticeable decline from the summit attained earlier, but such items as "Era la notte" from *Otello* and the later version of Hamlet's "Drinking Song" still rate with the very best. The Act II monologue from *Rigoletto* was also rerecorded in 1920. This version has been recently reissued on RCA Victor LCT 1039.

Between 1926 and 1929 Ruffo made a few electrical recordings. The microphone, that maker of mountains out of vocal molehills, did not benefit the voice that had electric qualities of its own and was now fading after thirty years of unsparing use. Nevertheless, while far from the best Ruffo, his electrical recordings still require no apologies. His "Nemico della patria" (*Andrea Chénier*) of 1929 vintage is vocally inferior to the earlier 1920 version, but benefits by a more lifelike orchestral framework and remains an absorbing and dramatically convincing performance. (This selection is available on RCA Victor LCT 1006.)

Turning now to the singer's repertory, we find it adequately represented on records. Certain interesting portrayals—notably Boris Godunov, Amonasro, and Telramund—remained unrecorded, but we have fine examples of such unhackneyed music as the aria from Rubinstein's *Demon* (sung in Russian) and excerpts from one of the two operas composed especially for Ruffo: Franchetti's *Cristoforo Colombo*. The other, Leoncavallo's *Edipo re*, a one acter tailor-made for Ruffo's dynamic stage manners and lung power, provided the artist with nearly a full hour of incessant storming and raving, but only occasional singing. Its score was evidently considered too violent for recording purposes.

The overwhelming majority of Ruffo records are sung in Italian. This includes his only excursion into the realm of the Lied, "I due Granatieri." The selection was a happy one, for the rendition is superb and the Schumann song remains highly effective in the fine Italian translation. Ruffo was a master of diction. His singular gifts in this direction were commemorated by an interesting oddity of a record containing two spoken monologues from Shakespeare's *Hamlet*, titled "Essere o non essere" and "Apparizione."

Not counting his obsolete Pathés, Ruffo completed about 120 sides in a quarter of a century of recording. His records are sought by singers as well as collectors today. Both groups would be happier if a large number would be made available to them.

The dynamic qualities in Ruffo's singing and acting were not accidental. They matched his temperamental, self-propelling personality. The singer was born in extreme poverty—never even attending school—and was self-taught in every way. He rose to the top with the drive and determination of a self-made man. His impulsive nature clashed with many a contemporary. Ruffo was not always right, but was always true to his convictions. An ardent anti-Fascist, he preferred disfavor and obscurity during Mussolini's regime to courting official honors. He fought with impresarios, from his early stock company days to his Metropolitan period, over matters of repertory and, frequently, money. Purists took exception to his vigorous singing style and innovations. Many of his colleagues resented his vast popular appeal. Indeed, Titta Ruffo made few people completely happy: few, that is, except the thousands who applauded him from Petrograd to Rio de Janeiro, and the new generation of thousands who listen to the recorded echo of his tremendous voice.

16

Titta Ruffo

EUGENIO MONTALE

It is five years today that Titta Ruffo died in Florence on July 5, 1953. Although a quinquennial is too short a time for a commemorative celebration (one usually waits half a century at least), a few friends and admirers of the great baritone of Pisa wrote me asking to remember him. Undoubtedly Titta Ruffo, the world-famous singer and model of Italian tenacity, who suffered persecution and even confinement for having maintained his independence of thought in a time of dark servility, does not deserve the oblivion into which he seems to have fallen. But that is the way it is: Titta was a singer, and among all performers they are the ones who are most easily forgotten. Only some woman, some illustrious primadonna—from Malibran to Patti, from Cavalieri to Callas—did or will add her name to the chronicles, not always for artistic reasons. (Peach Melba pertains to gastronomy, not to bel canto.) Other artists started a fashion, introduced a dress, and entered the culture of their time through the back door.

But what trace could a Titta Ruffo and a Viglione Borghese leave on the history of our clothing, artists who did not have a legend behind them, not even the romantic-sentimental kind of a Caruso?

Unfortunately, I had little contact with Titta Ruffo and did not hear him sing much. The man I knew in Florence was fascinating by the simplicity of his manner. The artist I heard only twice: in *Pagliacci* and in Thomas' *Hamlet,* around 1920, but I may be mistaken.

For many years I have had a Pathé disk of his, recorded around 1905, which has the "Il balen" from *Trovatore* and "Vien Leonora" from *La Favorita.* These records (or cylinders) are far from perfect but are per-

Reprinted by permission of Arnoldo Mondadori Editore, Milan. First published in *Corriere d'Informazioni,* July 5-6, 1958, no. 1104. Translated by Andrew Farkas.

haps the only ones that faithfully reproduce the color of his voice. I
believe that some of the recordings made between 1905 and 1914 were
transferred to microgroove with dubious results. If distant memories
don't fail me, the most modern disks do not reproduce at all the bronze-
like, incomparable color of his voice.

The old His Master's Voice catalogs list Ruffo as a representative of
the "modern school," which he was if compared for instance to Battistini
and De Luca, artists less suited to the great dramatic Verdi repertory
and the verismo operas that followed. But here the singer's modernity
stops because his singing was of a strictly classical nature. His voice
seemed, and was, exceptional for its fullness and unbroken sonic arch
and for its incredible range. About this aspect one can read medical
reports made about him which contain the measurements of his vocal
cords, the cavities of his broad forehead and all the resonators of his
"mask" (there is a medical report of his in the archives of the Colón in
Buenos Aires that was transcribed by Giuseppe de Luca a few years ago).
And yet how could a singer like him succeed today faced with the shallow
demands of the most modern repertory, or the like of Nazzareno de
Angelis, blessed with a voice that could be likened to the roar of an
avalanche?

With Titta Ruffo and other rare specimens of his kind singing isn't
dead, but heroic singing is. He himself made a distinction between vocal
art (Caruso) and declamatory art (Chaliapin). In his time Titta, who was
proud of having studied recitation with Virginia Marini, sensed and
attempted to reconcile the two opposing qualities. This explains the
various ways of his singing: the powerful sonority of his "Adamastor"
(*L'Africaine*) or "Sei vendicata assai" (*Dinorah*) or "Zazà, piccola zingara";
and at the other extreme the almost dragging lament he gave to the
character of Hamlet in an opera that cannot be performed today, a role
he inherited from Victor Maurel, one of his earliest friends and admirers.

If we survey Titta's recordings we must recognize the conspicuous
eclecticism of this nearly autodidactic artist in an epoch particularly noted
for hamming and cheap effects. We find not only *Rigoletto* and *Trovatore*,
Don Carlos and *Aida*, *Chénier* and *Tosca*, but also operas like Rubinstein's
Demon, sung in Russian with an admittedly Pisan accent; and we find
popular songs like Padilla's "El relicario" turned into a masterpiece by
him. And what can one say of some apparently minor interpretations
like the one in *Siberia*? His Gleby was considered a discovery.

The old records made by Titta Ruffo are not short on some curiosities:
Take, for instance, the 1914 "Tremin gl'insani" from *Nabucco* in which
Titta sings both the baritone and bass parts. Taken as a whole, the
roughly one hundred fifty recordings left by the artist reveal a taste, a
temperament, and a musical character of a long period on our lyric
stage. In the study of a new score, Titta was scrupulous to the point of

folly; it was not without reason that his art as an actor was compared with that of Salvini—a veristic art of the first magnitude. It has been told that while he studied *Otello*, one of his faithful servants resigned saying that he greatly enjoyed being employed by Titta Ruffo but found it impossible to live at the side of Iago! I don't know if there is an album today, an anthology of the best interpretations of the artist. The one of Caruso, made of old matrices, must have discouraged initiatives of a purely commercial nature. I am not aware that in institutions where singing is taught (at Santa Cecilia, for instance, where I don't believe there is a new Cotogni at the teacher's desk) some old and important recording of the great Titta is being recommended to students, not to imitate but to instruct. In any case the recorded voice of Titta, even when it is barely more than the monochromatic photograph of a beautiful painting, with its merits and defects could always teach something.

Coming from a family of simple artisans, a blacksmith himself in his youth, Titta Ruffo became a man of exemplary simplicity, a stranger to glamour. One wouldn't think so listening to the marvelous vocal pyrotechnics of the *Hamlet* "Drinking song," his most famous interpretation. But those who were close to the artist know that as much for his character as for his stature as a man he deserved, and deserves in the future, an enduring memorial in operatic history.

17

Lion of Pisa

MAX DE SCHAUENSEE

Titta Ruffo was not a singer, he was a phenomenon. Everywhere delirious crowds hailed the storms of his stentorian tones. Never a repertory-house baritone, Ruffo—like Patti, Chaliapin and Tetrazzini—reigned as an international star, whose guest appearances became the focal part of seasons in which he took a limited part. Appearing in North and South America, Europe, North Africa, Russia, wherever his fame preceded him, he created an excitement usually reserved for coloratura sopranos and tenors.

Ruffo attained his vocal peak during the years 1907-16. "Not a voice but a miracle!" Giuseppe de Luca used to exclaim, his blue eyes fairly jumping at you; other baritones seem to have admired this voice, among them the legendary Victor Maurel, who maintained that Ruffo's D-flat, D, E-flat and then up to top A-flat were the most glorious baritone notes he had ever heard. As for tonal quality, Emilio de Gogorza called Ruffo's "a black voice"—a term usually reserved for the richest basses.

When Ruffo finally reached the Metropolitan Opera as a member of the company, on the night of January 19, 1922, in Rossini's *Barbiere di Siviglia*, he arrived as the most famous baritone of his era. But people had begun to doubt that he would ever appear at the Opera House; illness had caused him to cancel his performances from the time of his scheduled debut in *Ernani* (specially revived for him) on December 8. In the final event the New York *Sun* noted, "The fabulously large voice which used to swamp the Manhattan, filled the further spaces of the Metropolitan to the great rapture of Mr. Ruffo's friends." And the *Journal* reported, "Indubitably, his is now the biggest voice discoverable anywhere in the operatic universe...the loudest thing heard in the

Reprinted with permission of *Opera News*. First published in *Opera News*, April 8, 1967.

Metropolitan since Caruso departed, but its quality was rather that of brass than gold; still it is a voice, a stupendous voice." "Ruffo is the baritonal Tamagno," said Henry T. Finck in the *Evening Post*.

Even so, when Ruffo came to the Metropolitan he was forty-five, and the voice had lost some of its ease and phenomenal resonance, especially in the lower register. There were rumors that the singer had been approached by Gatti-Casazza during the preceding season for possible appearances with Caruso in *Otello*; nothing came of it. From the vantage point of our day, it is fascinating to speculate why the Opera House waited so long to engage this vocal titan, why it neglected to enlist him during his supremacy.

It was claimed, for example, that Ruffo's fee of $2,500 (at that time the highest of any baritone in the world) delayed his engagement by the Metropolitan, but the company, bolstered by the generosity of Otto Kahn, was hardly averse to expensive stars. It may have been that Gatti was happy with the long-established elegance of Scotti, with the undoubted brilliance of Amato. When Ruffo first appeared in the United States— Rigoletto in Philadelphia on November 4, 1912—he created a sensation, giving rise to comparisons with Caruso, not always to the advantage of the New York idol. In the same role at the Paris Opéra that year, with Caruso and the popular Russian soprano Neshdanova, Ruffo had carried off the honors. Perhaps Gatti and Kahn did not wish to ruffle the surface or to cause the prestige of Caruso, whom they worshiped, any embarrassment. In support of this rises the fact that Ruffo was promptly engaged by Gatti following Caruso's death.

Ruffo appeared for eight seasons as a member of the Metropolitan, singing forty-five complete performances and one Sunday evening concert. His roles included Figaro, Don Carlo in *Ernani*, Tonio, Amonasro, Gérard, Barnaba and Neri Chiaramantesi (in Giordano's *Cena delle Beffe*). Still, he sang in New York only sporadically, perhaps as few as three or four times a season. Unlike De Luca, Danise, Basiola and the regulars, his performances always carried the aura of a guest appearance, of something special. He bade farewell to the Company on February 22, 1929, as Amonasro; oddly, he never appeared as Rigoletto or as Cascart in Leoncavallo's *Zazà*, two of his most famous roles, though both operas were in repertory during his tenure. The baritone's retirement was voluntary: he announced that he now contemplated the broader field of motion pictures.

Despite his fabulous voice, Titta Ruffo emerges as a controversial artist. Those who enjoyed the mellifluous "flower-of-the-lips" *bel canto* of De Luca were apt to find fault with Ruffo's heaven-storming effects. Giacomo Lauri-Volpi in his *Voci Parallele* (Aldo Garzanti, 1955) writes, "The velvety singing of Battistini, De Luca and Stracciari, conducted with knowledge and filled with inner nuances, received a rude shock with the sonorous manifestation of a biting and audacious Tuscan voice, which skyrocketed the price of baritones in the theatrical stock exchange. A leonine voice, sometimes roaring, sometimes languid and dragged out, it did not resemble any other that had preceded it, because it featured cavernous nasal resonances, spectacular *portamenti* and notes that were dark and percussive." Ruffo's art offered elements both sinister and emotional. I remember that once at Montecatini, he and I were talking about singers. When we came to Pinza, he looked at me and said, "Senza dolore" (He sings without any sorrow). As an actor, Ruffo was elemental and compelling but given to melodramatic excess. I don't know how we would react to him today. Many people have written that Ruffo's thunderous style shortened his career. When one considers that he was vocally active from 1898—he made his debut in Rome as the *Lohengrin* Herald—until the 1930's, such contentions have a hollow ring.

A native of Pisa, the baritone fought for Italy in 1916 and proclaimed himself a rabid anti-Fascist during World War II. He was married and had two children. One heard little about his family during the sad final years of his life. The highest-paid baritone the world had known came to end his days in solitude—a disheartened old man, out of step with the "new order"—in a fourth-floor walk-up, with a small upright piano, a chiseled silver box and a fine picture among his few remaining reminders of days that had been. Titta Ruffo died in Florence of heart disease on the night of July 5, 1953. Those four flights of stairs must have taxed the fading strength of this lion among singers.*

*See Dr. Ruffo Titta, Jr.'s comment under (c) on page 37, chapter 3.

18

Titta Ruffo

ALBERT WOLF

This is one record lover speaking to others. No attempt has been made to write a biography or a critical essay about Titta Ruffo or his art. Most of the statements are the author's own opinions, in some instances so much his very own that collectors as well as students and experts in the history of operatic singing may sharply disagree.

There is nothing more prominent, and more compelling about Ruffo than his voice. All other elements in his personal and artistic makeup fade into unimportance beside it. He may have had more than his share of personality; he may or may not have been an artist in the truest sense; he may be judged to have had good, bad or indifferent vocal technique; he may have been an outstanding actor, but it is to the voice that future generations will listen. The voice, of true Italian color, strongly reminiscent of Caruso's in his middle period, was indeed a unique one. The listener is tempted at times to label it "short tenor" because of its effortless brilliance in the high register, and its lack of security in the low. Yet, no matter how one describes it, the instrument was a phenomenal one, sonorous, and overwhelming in its prime.

There is an ever recurrent story that Ruffo was counselled to discontinue his studies by the directors of the Santa Cecilia Conservatory in Rome because his vocal equipment was deemed inadequate for an operatic career. I have it on good authority that the true reason for Ruffo's dismissal was not for lack of voice, but rather his unwillingness or inability to learn the Conservatory's set method of correct singing. He refused to apply himself to the study of traditional "bel canto" because nature had already given him a great gift of song, unfashioned by the style of

Courtesy of James F. Dennis, editor, *The Record Collector*. First published in *The Record Collector* in May 1947.

the great maestri. After his dismissal from the Conservatory, like all aspiring singers, he went from maestro to maestro, learning something from each, but with no one did he stay long. As a matter of fact, the wiser teachers found that mutual satisfaction was reached only when they modified their principles, and were content to limit their instruction to enlarging Ruffo's operatic repertoire. Of all these diverse maestri, Lelio Casini was perhaps the most successful, and to him Ruffo is indebted for his impeccable treatment of "Figaro" in the Rossini opera.

Ruffo was by no means the only musical aspirant in the Titta family (Titta, not Ruffo, was the family name); his sister Fosca made quite a fair career as a soprano, and made recordings with her brother, and another brother, Ettore, was the successful composer of the opera *Malena*, and numerous songs; his name, too, is often encountered in Ruffo's recorded repertoire.

In the Winter of 1906-7, Ruffo's first lateral cut records were made in Milan for the Gramophone Company. From the outset he was accorded the Red (celebrity) label, and when the Pink (Star celebrity) series was introduced, he was immediately transferred to that class. Despite a modest success at Convent Garden in 1903, and a full engagement book for Italy and elsewhere, it is doubtful whether Ruffo had yet become a true "celebrity," but his recordings were so successful and popular that the honour seemed merited. His fellow artists on concerted recordings would seem of a like category.

On these early recordings made in Milan until 1910, we find the vocal quality light compared with his later discs, but nevertheless of a masculine timbre. There is no obvious determination to sing according to the principles of the great "bel canto" school. Niceties, such as cadenzas in what I would call "semi piano" are in evidence here, though completely absent in later discs. In Tosti's "Marechiare" (C52383), and in the recordings of his brother's compositions, one will even detect a trace of gaiety, a quality quite alien to his later interpretations.

AlthoughRuffo's voice in itself was something to be proud of, the artist seems to have rated his ability to enunciate clearly and rapidly as worthy of equal admiration. The "Largo al factotum" is a cavatina known to be immensely difficult to sing and render comprehensively word for word. It has defied the efforts of such notables as Battistini, Campanari, De Luca, and Stracciari as well as many others. To my knowledge, Ancona and Renaud have not recorded this selection. In many recordings, singers resort to the substitute of La, la la and artful whistles for the true vocal line. Ruffo's first recording (052132/ V-92039) is a fine rendition bettered by the later Milan recording (052380/V-88391); however, in the writer's opinion both are surpassed by the third version recorded in America (V-88391/2-052184); every word is clear, every note is sung, and the tempi are exact. Here is one selection which the singer felt could not be improved, and rightly so. Some collectors may prefer other renditions of this aria, but the Ruffo version holds first place in general popularity. Other Milan recordings include interpretations of Rigoletto, di Luna, Hamlet, and Tonio strongly foreshadowing the singer's eventual development into a performer of the highly dramatic type.

Having matured and gathered laurels in Europe and South America, Ruffo descended in all his glory on New York in 1912. After a single performance, he held the public in the palm of his hand, and it was not long before the Metropolitan offered him a tempting contract. One may safely say that never before had there been a baritone who so completely overwhelmed his audiences. Exhibitions of superior singing perhaps, a greater depth of acting, and certainly truer teamwork with conductor and ensemble granted all these things, but still Ruffo's performances were unique in their effect.

Ruffo's first American recordings were made in 1912; they reveal a high degree of vocal proficiency. In fairness, it must be noted in most of them: a golden full voice pouring out gorgeous notes especially in the middle and high registers; there are frequent regrettable transpositions, and other liberties taken with the original score sometimes for the sake of convenience, but more often to enhance desired effects. In addition to "Largo al factotum," the "Credo" and "Era la notte" from *Otello* are especially convincing. Here, Ruffo's interpretative powers are much in evidence; only rarely do they appear in later recordings. The Victor record 985 (HMV DA352) has curious subject matter. On one side is a selection from Thomas' setting of *Hamlet*, and on the reverse a declamation of Hamlet's soliloquy in the Italian translation of the original Shakespeare text. Ruffo must have thought highly of his diction, rightly so, to attempt this difficult speaking role, and to present a characterization which is moving even to those who cannot understand Italian. Generally, this artist's records give the impression that he recorded with great gusto, and even enjoyed the presence of an audience at his recording sessions—a habit firmly barred by most artists. A clearly audible "Bravo" at the end of his "Di Provenza" from *Traviata* (2-52529/V 87141) bears out the above.

His voice became progressively heavier, and the tendency to resort to fortes above other means more accentuated. Despite this, all of his recordings with the possible exception of 6429 *Faust*: "Dio possente," *Cristoforo Colombo*: "Dunque ho sognato," 963 arias from *Damnation of Faust*, and *The Demon* (this latter in Russian!), 995 "Santa Lucia/Marechiare," 1019 "Lolita/Perjura," and 1076 "Mia sposa sarà/Chitarrata Abruzzese" may be said to range from good to outstanding. Eight electrical recordings were released (Victor numbers 1038, 1401, 1406 & 7153); all that can be said is that it would have been better not to have released them.

Several unreleased recordings which were in the archives of the Victor company have disappeared with the exception of "Urna fatale" from *Forza* which was once issued by the Historic Record Society (2015). The others were:—

Tannhäuser: "O tu bell 'astro" (12″ matrix no. C 25216), recorded 15 April 1921;

Gioconda: "Enzo Grimaldo," with Enrico Caruso (12″ matrix no. C 14273), recorded on 18 January, 1914.

The many tales involving Ruffo and Caruso may account for the non-release of the *Gioconda* duet. It is said that Caruso, finding himself "robbed" of a great share of his accustomed laurels on the occasions when he appeared with Ruffo elsewhere, had a clause in his contract with the Metropolitan restricting Ruffo's appearances to pre- and post-season engagements when he was not singing. It is a fact that these two artists never sang together at the Metropolitan. The one duet to be issued (*Otello*: "Sì, pel ciel marmoreo giuro") is indeed a thrilling record, even if the impression is given that the two giants vied to outsing each other.

A number of Pathé hill and dale records of Ruffo may also be found; they are of immature vintage, and are of particular interest only when the recorded selections are not duplicated by his later recordings. The more interesting titles include "The Death of Valentine," *Bohème* duets with Bassi, and an extract from *Siberia*.

Unlike many recorded singers, very few of Ruffo's acoustic recordings merit as low a rating as "poor," therefore the opportunity to acquire a record by him may be regarded as a highly potential source of enjoyment.

The writer has found it essential to play Ruffo recordings with ample volume in order to gain maximum pleasure, and to hear the highly individual timbre of a great baritone—perhaps the greatest ever to perform on records.

APPENDIXES

APPENDIX A

Chronology of Titta Ruffo's Public Performances

RUFFO TITTA, JR., with C. MARINELLI ROSCIONI

I am glad to be able to contribute the most accurate chronology compiled to date of my father's artistic career. It is a revision of the one that first appeared in the 1977 centenary edition of Titta Ruffo's autobiography, published on the 100th anniversary of his birth.

This re-publication was made possible by additions and corrections supplied by several individuals. I want to thank Eduardo Arnosi, Antonio Massísimo, Vincenzo Mesiano, Mário Moreau and Horacio Sanguinetti who helped me, to various extents, to correct errors and fill in lacunae. Special thanks are due to Thomas G. Kaufman for his contribution of valuable information about a large number of Titta Ruffo's operatic and concert engagements least accessible to the researcher, particularly those in Russia, Uruguay and Cuba.

Arrangement

The theaters and other sites of Titta Ruffo's public appearances are identified according to contemporary usage and in the language of the country.

The operas in which he interpreted a role for the first time are indicated by **bold face** type.

When it could be ascertained, the number of performances of the same work is indicated by parentheses ( ) following the title of the opera; the number in square brackets [ ] following the city or the theater denotes the total number of performances in the course of that engagement.

If, in a series of performances, there was a cast change, the names of the artists singing the same role on different occasions are separated by a slash /.

Abbreviations

::	missing data	s	soprano
?	data uncertain	ms	mezzosoprano or contralto
***	world premiere	t	tenor
**	national premiere	b	baritone
*	local premiere	bs	bass

Date of First Performance		City/Theater	Opera and Other Performances	Conductor: Principal Soloists
1898				
9	IV	ROME Costanzi	**Lohengrin** (14)	V. Mingardi: L. De Benedetto s, A. Degli Abbati ms, F. Viñas t, A. Gnaccarini/O. Benedetti b, F. Spangher bs.
19	V	»	**Lucia di Lammermoor** (1)	T. De Angelis: A. Padovani s, F. Granados t, F. Spangher bs.
16	VII	LIVORNO Arena Alfieri	**Il trovatore** (7)	A. Torri: A. Grippa s, M. Pignani ms, F. Nieddu t.
28	VII	»	Lucia di Lammermoor (6)	A. Torri: G. Longone s, F. Nieddu t, C. Di Ciolo bs.
6	VIII	»	**Rigoletto** (2)	A. Torri: G. Longone s, C. Dani t. ::
::	VIII	*Bagni Pancaldi*	*Concert*	
14	VIII	PISA Politeama	Il trovatore (2)	A. Torri: A. Grippa s, M. Pignani ms, G. Cesaroni/ C. Dani t, C. Di Ciolo bs.
18	IX	»	Lucia di Lammermoor (3)	A. Torri: D. Tanfani/G. Longone s, C. Dani t, A. Bini/C. Di Ciolo bs.
25	IX	»	*Concert*[a]	A. Bini bs.
22	XII	CATANZARO Comunale	**La forza del destino**	A. Doncich: E. Adaberto s, E. Cavara t, G. Rebonato b, R. Di Falco bs.
1899				
11	I	»	**Ruy Blas**	A. Doncich: T. Chelotti s, Marenzi s, E. Cavara t.
25	I	»	**La bohème**	A. Doncich: E. Adaberto s, Marenzi s, M. Izquierdo t.
20	II	SYRACUSE Massimo	La bohème	A. Doncich: E. Adaberto s, Marenzi s, E. Cavara t.

[a]*Lucia di Lammermoor*, Act III, Scene 1.

Date of First Performance		City/Theater	Opera and Other Performances	Conductor: Principal Soloists
1899				
15	III	SYRACUSE Massimo	Rigoletto	A. Doncich: E. Adaberto s, F. Farelli ms, A. Sarcoli t, A. Venturini bs.
7	IV	ACIREALE Bellini	**Manon Lescaut**	:: :: :: :: :: :: ::
::	V	»	La bohème	A. Doncich: E. Adaberto s, T. Chelotti s, A. Sarcoli t.
::	V	»	Ruy Blas	A. Doncich: E. Adaberto s, T. Chelotti s, E. Cavara t.
::	V	»	**Un ballo in maschera**	A. Doncich: E. Adaberto s, F. Farelli ms, A. Dianni t.
::	V	»	Rigoletto	A. Doncich: E. Adaberto s, F. Farelli ms, A. Sarcoli t, A. Venturini bs.
16	V	CATANIA Nazionale	La bohème (3)	A. Doncich: E. Adaberto s, T. Chelotti/Scalera s, A. Sarcoli t.
26	V	»	Rigoletto	A. Doncich: E. Adaberto s, F. Farelli ms, A. Sarcoli t, A. Venturini bs.
26	VI	»	Un ballo in maschera	A. Doncich: E. Adaberto s, F. Farelli ms, A. Dianni t.
20	VII	*Chiesa dei Benedettini*	*La risurrezione di Lazzaro* (oratorio)* (2)	F. Tarallo: A. Antinori s, M. Pozzi ms, A. Sarcoli t.
::	VII	Nazionale	**La Gioconda** (8)	G. Serrao/F. Tarallo: A. Giuliani/A. Antinori s, M. Pozzi ms, A. Sarcoli t, F. Fabro bs.
20	VIII	SYRACUSE Massimo	La Gioconda (2)	G. Serrao/F. Tarallo: A. Giuliani s, M. Pozzi ms, A. Sarcoli t, F. Fabro bs.
25	VIII	CATANIA Nazionale	**La favorita** (2)	F. Tarallo: M. Pozzi ms, A. Sarcoli t.
13	IX	SALERNO Municipale	La bohème	C. Sebastiani: G. Tosi s, J. Massa s, A. Sarcoli t.

Date of First Performance		City/Theater	Opera and Other Performances	Conductor: Principal Soloists
1899				
::	IX	SALERNO Municipale	**Faust**	:: :: :: :: :: :: ::
23	IX	*Duomo*	«*Messa*» di Luigi Barella*** (2)	:: J. Massa s, A. Sarcoli t.
23	IX	Municipale	Rigoletto	C. Sebastiani: J. Massa s, G. Del Prato ms, A. Sarcoli t, G. Berenzone bs.
::	IX	»	La Gioconda	C. Sebastiani: J. Massa s, G. Del Prato ms, A. Sarcoli t.
7	XI	PADUA Garibaldi	**Carmen** (3)	S. Boscarini: E. Bruno ms, A. Matassini t.
24	XII	BOLOGNA Duse	**Cavalleria rusticana**	A. Siragusa: A. Busi s, O. Frosini t.
			Pagliacci	A. Siragusa: Drudi s, O. Frosini t.
1900				
6	I	BOLOGNA Duse	Carmen (1)	A. Siragusa: Z. Montalcino ms, O. Frosini t.
21	I	GENOA Carlo Felice	**La traviata** (2)	O. Anselmi: A. Pandolfi, s, E. Ventura t.
14	II	»	Rigoletto	O. Anselmi: A. Occhiolini s, G. Marchi ms, A. Stampanoni t, R. Ercolani bs.
10	III	PARMA Regio	Il trovatore (5)	A. Franzoni: I. Paoli s, E. Ghibaudo ms, V. Bieletto t, F. Fabro bs.
9	V	FERRARA Tosi-Borghi	**Ernani** (8)	D. Varola: M. Pizzagalli s, A. Gamba t, A. Brondi bs.
3	VI	LUCERNE Kursaal	Rigoletto	A. Fumagalli: G. Raschke-Lucignani s, C. Dani t, A. Dadò bs.

Date of First Performance		City/Theater	Opera and Other Performances	Conductor: Principal Soloists
1900				
		SANTIAGO (Chile)		
5	VIII	Municipal	**L'Africaine**	Arturo Padovani: N. Mazzi s. G. Piccoletti s, M. Izquierdo t, A. Venturini bs, P. Wulmann bs.
::	VIII	»	Rigoletto	A. Padovani: G. Piccoletti s, E. Castellano t.
		VALPARAISO		
13	VIII	Victoria	L'Africaine	A. Padovani: N. Mazzi s, G. Piccoletti s, M. Izquierdo t, P. Wulmann bs.
27	VIII	»	Il trovatore	A. Padovani: N. Mazzi s, M. Pozzi ms, M. Izquierdo t, F. Cerri bs.
29	VIII	»	La Gioconda	A. Padovani: N. Mazzi s, M. Pozzi ms, E. Castellano t, P. Wulmann bs.
		SANTIAGO		
::	IX	Municipal	**Aida**	A. Padovani: N. Mazzi s, M. Pozzi ms, M. Izquierdo t, A. Venturini bs.
::	IX	»	Il trovatore	A. Padovani: N. Mazzi s, M. Pozzi ms, M. Izquierdo t, A. Venturini bs.
		VALPARAISO		
1	X	Victoria	Ruy Blas	A. Padovani: N. Mazzi s, M. Pozzi ms, M. Izquierdo t.
		SANTIAGO		
::	X	Municipal	La forza del destino	A. Padovani: N. Mazzi s, M. Pozzi ms, M. Izquierdo t, A. Cerratelli b, P. Wulmann bs.
::	X	»	**Andrea Chénier**	A. Padovani: E. Miotti s, M. Izquierdo t.
11	X	»	**La salinara*****	A. Padovani: E. Miotti s, M. Pozzi ms, M. Izquierdo t.

Date of First Performance		City/Theater	Opera and Other Performances	Conductor: Principal Soloists
1900				
23	X	VALPARAISO Victoria	Andrea Chénier	A. Padovani: E. Miotti s., M. Izquierdo t.
28	X	»	**Otello**	A. Padovani: N. Mazzi s, M. Izquierdo t.
::	XI	SANTIAGO Municipal	Carmen	A. Padovani: M. Pozzi ms, M. Izquierdo t.
::	XI	»	La Gioconda	A. Padovani: N. Mazzi s, M. Pozzi ms, E. Castellano t, P. Wulmann bs.
::	XI	»	Lucia di Lammermoor	A. Padovani: G. Piccoletti s, M. Izquierdo t.
::	XI	»	Ruy Blas	A. Padovani: N. Mazzi s, M. Pozzi ms, M. Izquierdo t.
::	XI	»	Un ballo in maschera	A. Padovani: N. Mazzi s, G. Piccoletti s, M. Pozzi ms, M. Izquierdo t.
::	XII	»	Otello (1)	A. Padovani: N. Mazzi s, M. Izquierdo t.
::	XII	»	Faust	A. Padovani: I. Myrtea s, E. Castellano t, P. Wulmann bs.
1901				
21	I	SIENA dei Rinnovati	Ernani	U. Zanetti: E. Canovas s, F. De Grandi t.
2	III	PISA R. Teatro Nuovo	Otello (20 ?)	R. Bracale: T. Maragliano/M. Sirti s, E. Galli t.
19	III	»	Ernani (3)	R. Bracale: A. Stinco Palermini s, M. Izquierdo t, U. Ceccarelli bs.
2	IV	»	*Benefit concert*	M. Rosselli Nissim (piano): M. Sirti s, U. Ceccarelli bs.
::	III/IV	LIVORNO Goldoni	*Concert in memory of G. Verdi*	

Date of First Performance		City/Theater	Opera and Other Performances	Conductor: Principal Soloists
1901				
		PALERMO		
12	IV	Massimo	**Tosca**	R. Ferrari: E. Bianchini Cappelli s, G. Anselmi t.
13	IV	»	Rigoletto	R. Ferrari: B. Morello s, G. Giaconia ms, E. Ventura t, G. Tisci Rubini bs.
		TRIESTE		
1	IX	La Fenice	**Nabucco**	E. Perosio: I. De Frate s, A. Fanton ms, A. Zennaro t, C. Thos bs.
14	IX	»	La Gioconda	G. Gialdini: I. De Frate s, C. Pagnoni ms, A. Fanton ms, A. Maurini t, C. Thos bs.
		CAIRO		
3	XII	Khedival	La bohème	A. Pomè: A. Pandolfini s, A. Barone s, E. Garbin t.
16	XII	»	**Samson et Dalila**	A. Pomè: V. Guerrini s, C. Barrera t.
18	XII	»	**Fedora**	A. Pomè: A. Pandolfini s, A. Fusco s, F. Giraud t.
::	XII	»	Otello (1)	A. Pomè: A. Carrera s, C. Barrera t.
::	XII	»	**Iris**	A. Pomè: A. Pandolfini s, F. Giraud t, G. Tisci Rubini bs.
1902				
		ALEXANDRIA (Egypt)		
28	I	Zizinia	Aida (6)	A. Pomè: A. Carrera s, V. Guerrini ms, C. Carrera t, G. Tisci Rubini bs.
5	II	»	Fedora (3)	A. Pomè: A. Pandolfini s, A. Barone s, F. Giraud t.
12	II	»	Samson et Dalila (7)	A. Pomè: V. Guerrini s, C. Barrera t.
14	II	»	La bohème	A. Pomè: A. Pandolfini s, A. Barone s, F. Giraud t.
		BUENOS AIRES		
21	V	La Opera	Aida (4)	L. Mugnone: M. De Lerma s, A. Cucini ms, J. Biel t, M. Boudouresque bs.

Date of First Performance	City/Theater	Opera and Other Performances	Conductor: Principal Soloists
1902			
	BUENOS AIRES		
9 VI	La Opera	L'Africaine (2)	L. Mugnone: M. De Lerma s, I. Timroth s, J. Biel t, R. Ercolani bs.
17 VII	»	Il trovatore (2)	L. Mugnone: H. Darclée s, A. Cucini ms, J. Biel t, R. Ercolani bs.
9 VIII	»	**Zazà**** (2)	L. Mugnone: H. Darclée s, E. Garbin t, M. Boudouresque bs.
13 VIII	»	Cavalleria rusticana (1)	L. Mugnone: H. Darclée s, E. Garbin t.
	MONTEVIDEO		
19 VIII	Solis	Aida	L. Mugnone: M. De Lerma s, A. Cucini ms, J. Biel t, M. Boudouresque bs.
29 VIII	"	Il trovatore	:: H. Darclée s., A. Cucini ms, J. Biel t.
31 VIII	"	Zazà	:: H. Darclée s, E. Garbin t.
	SALSOMAG-GIORE		
2 X	Ferrario	*Benefit concert*	A. Dianni t.
	ALEXANDRIA		
:: XII	Zizinia	La bohème	G. Zuccani: A. Stehle s, C. Rommel s, E. Garbin t.
1903			
5 I	»	**Proserpina****	G. Zuccani: C. Wyns s, E. Trentini s, G. Borgatti t, C. Walter bs.
:: I/II	»	Manon Lescaut	G. Zuccani: A. Santarelli s, G. Borgatti t, C. Walter bs.
:: I/II	»	Fedora	G. Zuccani: A. Pandolfini s. :: ::
:: I/II	»	Carmen	G. Zuccani: C. Wyns s, G. Borgatti t.
	CAIRO		
16 II	Khedival	Fedora	G. Zuccani: A. Pandolfini s. :: ::

Date of First Performance		City/Theater	Opera and Other Performances	Conductor: Principal Soloists
1903				
::	II/III	CAIRO Khedival	Manon Lescaut	G. Zuccani: A. Santarelli s, G. Borgatti t, C. Walter bs.
::	II/III	»	Carmen	G. Zuccani: C. Wyns s, G. Borgatti t.
::	II/III	»	Proserpina*	G. Zuccani: C. Wyns s, E. Trentini s, G. Borgatti t, C. Walter bs.
6	III	»	La bohème	G. Zuccani: C. Wyns s, C. Rommel s, E. Garbin t.
16	III	»	**Tristan und Isolde** (2)	G. Zuccani: G. Borgatti t. :: :: ::
::	III	»	**Lohengrin**	G. Zuccani: G. Borgatti t. :: :: ::
18	IV	VENICE La Fenice	Il trovatore (10)	R. Ferrari: R. Calligaris-Marti s, M. Julia ms, A. Paoli t, T. Montico bs.
7	V	»	**Il santo***** (6)	R. Ferrari: E. Canovas s, S. Ronconi ms, A. Cecchi t.
5	VI	LONDON Covent Garden	Lucia di Lammer-moor (1)	L. Mancinelli: E. Wedekind s, A. Bonci t, M. Journet bs.
25	VI	*33, Grosvenor Square*	*Concert given by Sir Philip Livine*	
1	VII	Covent Garden	**Il barbiere di Siviglia**	L. Mancinelli: M. Barrientos s, A. Bonci t, M. Journet bs, C. Gilibert bs.
4	XI	VENICE Rossini	Nabucco (6)	F. Tanara: P. Roluti s, A. Fanton ms, L. Penso-Boldrini t, E. Masini bs.
1904				
7	I	MILAN Scala	Rigoletto (16)	C. Campanini: G. Wermez/F. Toresella s, G. Giaconia/I. Monti-Baldini ms, G. Anselmi/G. Ibos/G. Krismer t, A. Didur bs.

Date of First Performance		City/Theater	Opera and Other Performances	Conductor: Principal Soloists
1904				
		MILAN		
30	I	Scala	**Germania** (9)	C. Campanini: C. Pasini s, E. Trentini s, F. Viñas/G. Zenatello t, A. Pini-Corsi bs, A. Didur bs.
10	IV	»	**Griselda** (2)	C. Campanini: C. Pasini s, I. Monti-Baldini ms, G. Bazelli t, G. De Luca b.
::	IV	*La Famiglia Artistica Milanese*	*Concert*	
		FLORENCE		
20	IV	La Pergola	Rigoletto (3)	S. Boscarini: M. Galvany s, A. Colombo ms, I. Cristalli t, O. Banti/E. Vannuccini bs.
		MILAN		
6	X	Lirico	**Siberia** (6)	L. Mugnone: E. Carelli s, A. Franceschini t, A. Sabellico bs.
22	X	»	Zazà	L. Mugnone: E. Carelli s, E. Leliva t.
25	X	»	**Adriana Lecouvreur** (4)	L. Mugnone: S. Krusceniski s, N. Frascani s, P. Zeni t, E. Sottolana bs.
		BERGAMO		
4	XII	Donizetti	*L'Immacolata* (oratorio) (3)	G. Mattioli: P. Sassi s, A. Alemanni t, A. Bendinelli t, E. Brancaleoni bs.
1905				
		ODESSA		
8	I	Municipal	Rigoletto	A. Bernardi: A. Gonzaga s, G. Giaconia ms, A. Dianni/G. Anselmi t, G. Gravina bs.
11	I	»	Tosca (5)	I.V. Pribic: A. Santarelli s, R. De Rosa/A. Dianni/ G. Anselmi t.
12	I	»	Il trovatore	I.V. Pribic: Ristori/M. Santoliva s, M. Verger ms, M. Gilion t.
20	I	»	Aida	I.V. Pribic: M. Santoliva/ Ristori s, M. Verger ms, M. Gilion t, A. Sabellico bs.

Date of First Performance		City/Theater	Opera and Other Performances	Conductor: Principal Soloists
1905				
31	I	ODESSA Municipal	**Demon**	A. Bernardi: J. Korolew-icz-Wayda s, M. Gilion t, A. Sabellico/O. Villani bs.
11	II	»	Pagliacci	A. Bernardi: J. Korolew-icz-Wayda s, A. Dianni t.
17	II	»	Il barbiere di Siviglia	A. Bernardi: A. Gonzaga s, G. Anselmi t, A. Sabel-lico bs, E. Coletti bs.
21	II	»	Otello	A. Bernardi: J. Korolew-icz-Wayda s, M. Gilion t.
4	III	»	Germania**	A. Bernardi: A. Santarelli s, A. Gonzaga s, M. Gilion t, G. Gravina bs.
20	III	PETERSBURG New Conservatory	Rigoletto (11)	E.D. Esposito: Van der Brandt s, E. de Cisneros ms, L. Sobinov t, A. Sa-bellico bs.
21	III	»	Il trovatore	E.D. Esposito: T. Chelotti s, E. de Cisneros ms, A. Paoli t.
24	III	»	Faust	E.D. Esposito: Van der Brandt s, L. Sobinov t, A. Sabellico bs.
26	III	»	Demon	E.D. Esposito: Sardgevi s, Sibiriakov t.
27	III	»	Aida	E.D. Esposito: T. Chelotti s, E. de Cisneros ms, A. Paoli t, A. Sabellico bs.
11	IV	»	Otello	:: A. Paoli t. :: :: :: :: ::
16	IV	»	Il barbiere di Siviglia	E.D. Esposito: A. Gon-zaga s. ::
19	IV	»	La traviata	:: L. Sobinov t. :: :: :: ::
::	IV	»	Pagliacci	.. :: :: :: :: :: :: :: :: ::
4	V	PARIS Sarah Bernhardt	Siberia**	C. Campanini: A. Pinto s, A. Bassi t.
13	V	»	Fedora**	C. Campanini: L. Cavali-eri s, A. Barone s, E. Ca-ruso t.
22	V	::	*Concert organized by the newspaper "Le Figaro"*	

Date of First Performance		City/Theater	Opera and Other Performances	Conductor: Principal Soloists
1905				
		PARIS		
30	V	Sarah Bernhardt	Il barbiere di Siviglia	R. Ferrari: R. Pacini s, A. Masini t, O. Luppi bs. A. Baldelli bs.
2	VI	*Palais Comtesse Château*	*Concert*	
5	VI	::	*Concert*	L. Cavalieri s.
8	VI	*Palais du Trocadéro*	*Concert* (La traviata, act II)	M. Mangin: G. Bellincioni s, A. Bendinelli t.
		MILAN		
18	X	Lirico	**Le jongleur de Nôtre-Dame****	R. Ferrari: E. Leliva t, U. Cocchi bs.
		MOSCOW		
::	XII	Imperial	Il barbiere di Siviglia	:: :: :: :: :: :: :: :: :: ::
::	XII	»	Demon	:: :: :: :: :: :: :: :: :: ::
		PETERSBURG		
15	XII	New Conservatory	Rigoletto	:: :: :: :: :: :: :: :: :: ::
19	XII	»	Demon	:: :: :: :: :: :: :: :: :: ::
20	XII	»	Tosca	:: :: :: :: :: :: :: :: :: ::
31	XII	»	La Gioconda	:: :: :: :: :: :: :: :: :: ::
1906				
		PETERSBURG		
5	III	New Conservatory	Tosca	:: E. Carelli s, A. Giorgini t.
8	III	»	**Linda di Chamonix**	G. Golisciani: M. Galvany s, G. Fabbri ms, A. Giorgini t, A. Sabellico bs.
13	III	»	Il barbiere di Siviglia	:: :: :: :: :: :: :: :: :: ::
		MOSCOW		
16	III	Imperial	Rigoletto	G. Golisciani: M. Galvany s, A. Gramegna ms, R. Andreini/G.Armanini t, A. Sabellico bs.
		PETERSBURG		
25	III	New Conservatory	La Gioconda	:: E. Carelli s, G. Fabbri ms, G. Armanini t.
26	III	*Hall of the Cadets*	*Benefit concert*	F. Titta s.
26	III	New Conservatory	Linda di Chamonix	:: R. Andreini t. :: :: ::
28	III	Imperial	Zazà	:: E. Carelli s, G. Armanini t.
3	IV	Imperial	Il barbiere di Siviglia	:: :: :: :: :: :: :: :: :: ::

Date of First Performance		City/Theater	Opera and Other Performances	Conductor: Principal Soloists
1906				
16	IV	KHAR'KOV Municipal	Il barbiere di Siviglia	A. Bernardi: M. Galvany s, G. Gasparri t.
19	IV	»	Demon	A. Bernardi: J. Korolew-icz-Wayda s, G. Gasparri t.
21	IV	»	Faust	A. Bernardi: J. Korolew-icz-Wayda s.:: :: :: :: ::
22	IV	»	La traviata	A. Bernardi: M. Galvany s. :: :: :: :: ::
23	IV	»	Il trovatore	A. Bernardi: J. Korolew-icz-Wayda s. :: :: :: :: ::
::	IV	»	Rigoletto	:: :: :: :: :: :: :: :: :: ::
::	IV	KIEV Solovzov	Demon	A. Margulian: J. Koro-lewicz-Wayda s, Machin t. :: :: :: ::
::	IV	»	Il trovatore	A. Margulian: :: :: :: :: ::
28	IV	»	Il barbiere di Siviglia	A. Margulian: M. Galvany s. :: :: ::
::	IV/V	»	Rigoletto	A. Margulian: M. Galvany s, Dobronskaia ms, G. Gasparri/V. Coppola t, Segievich bs.
::	IV/V	»	La traviata	:: :: :: :: :: :: :: :: :: ::
::	IV/V	»	Ernani	:: :: :: :: :: :: :: :: :: ::
3	V	ODESSA Sibiriak ?	*Benefit concert* (La traviata, act II)	M. Galvany s.
13	V	Municipal	Il barbiere di Siviglia	I.V. Pribic: M. Galvany s, Askochenski t.
::	V/VI	Sibiriak ?	Rigoletto	I.V. Pribic: M. Galvany s, Kovielkova ms, Asko-chenski t, Nezhdikov bs.
::	V/VI	»	Demon	I.V. Pribic: J. Korolewicz-Wayda s. :: :: :: :: :: ::
5	IX	MILAN Lirico	Zazà (12)	G. Baroni: E. Carelli s, P. Schiavazzi t.
2	X	VIENNA Hofoper	Rigoletto (1)	F. Spetrino: S. Kurz s, H. Kittel ms, E. Caruso t.

Date of First Performance		City/Theater	Opera and Other Performances	Conductor: Principal Soloists
1906				
::	XI	PETERSBURG Aquarium	La Gioconda	:: L. Berlendi s, Dolina ms, Klementiev t.
19	XI	*Nikolai I. Orphanage*	*Benefit concert*	
::	::	New Opera ?	Rigoletto	:: Antonova s, Dobronskaia ms, Klementiev t, Segievich bs.
22	XI	Aquarium	Il barbiere di Siviglia	:: M. Galvany s, Riera bs.
23	XI	New Conservatory	Rigoletto	:: M. Galvany/Turkianinova s, Nikitina ms, Saianov t, Zhukov bs.
29	XI	Aquarium	Demon	:: :: :: :: :: :: :: :: :: ::
30	XI	"	Il trovatore	:: L. Berlendi/F. Titta s, Iakarova ms, Klementiev t.
7	XII	New Conservatory	Pagliacci & Ernani, Act III	:: Dolina s, Klementiev t.
16	XII	Aquarium	L'Africaine	:: :: :: :: :: :: :: :: :: ::
::	XII	New Conservatory	Demon	Sierk: Gushina s, Polshiakov t.
25	XII	MOSCOW Imperial [7]	Rigoletto	E. Plotnikov: (*possible cointerpreters* H. Darclée, O. Boronat, S. Arnoldson ss.—M. Bastia-Pagnoni, L. Hotkovska mss.—A. Paoli, G. Anselmi, F. Marconi, U. Colombini tt.—G. Tansini, G. Bossè bss).
::	XII	»	Il barbiere di Siviglia	
27	XII	»	Demon	
::	XII	»	Zazà	
::	XII	»	*Concert*	F. Titta s.
1907				
14	I	PETERSBURG New Conservatory	*Benefit concert*	
15	I	"	Tosca	:: L. Berlendi s, Klementiev t.
21	I	*School of Technology*	*Benefit concert for famine victims*	
::	I	New Conservatory	Pagliacci	:: :: :: :: :: :: :: :: :: ::

Date of First Performance		City/Theater	Opera and Other Performances	Conductor: Principal Soloists
1907				
24	I	LISBON »	**Hamlet** (6)	L. Mancinelli: E. Clasenti s, A. Torretta ms, G. Cirino bs.
2	II	São Carlos	Rigoletto (1)	V. Lombardi: E. Clasenti s, A. Torretta ms, P. Schiavazzi t, A. Brondi bs.
12	II	MONTE CARLO Grand-Théâtre	Un ballo in maschera, acts III & IV (1)	A. Pomè: L. De Benedetto s, S. Kurz s, N. Zerola t.
16	II	»	**Don Pasquale** (3)	A. Pomè: R. Storchio s, L. Sobinov t, A. Pini-Corsi bs.
1	III	»	*Concert*	
8	III	»	*Concert*	
14	III	»	Il barbiere di Siviglia (2)	A. Pomè: R. Storchio s, F. De Lucia t, F. Chaliapin bs, A. Pini-Corsi bs.
::	IV	BERLIN Königliches Opernhaus[a]	Il barbiere di Siviglia (1)	A. Pomè: R. Storchio s, F. De Lucia t, F. Chaliapin bs, A. Pini-Corsi bs.
16	X	MILAN Lirico	Hamlet (8)	E. Perosio: L. Grenville s, M. Grassé ms, G. Quinzi-Tapergi bs.
2	XI	BUCHAREST National [10]	Rigoletto	F. Spetrino: B. Morello s, T. Di Angelo ms, G. Armanini t, J. Torres de Luna bs.
5	XI	»	Ernani	F. Spetrino: T. Poli-Randaccio s, A. Angioletti t, J. Torres de Luna bs.
7	XI	»	Il barbiere di Siviglia	F. Spetrino: B. Morello s, G. Armanini t, J. Torres de Luna bs.
9	XI	»	Un ballo in maschera	F. Spetrino: T. Poli-Randaccio s, T. Di Angelo ms, A. Angioletti t.

[a] Company of the Grand-Théâtre of Monte Carlo.

Date of First Performance		City/Theater	Opera and Other Performances	Conductor: Principal Soloists
1907				
12	XI	BUCHAREST National	Il trovatore	F. Spetrino: T. Poli-Randaccio s, T. Di Angelo ms, A. Angioletti t.
::	XI	»	*Concert*	
3	XII	WARSAW Wielki	Rigoletto (2)	A. Vigna: W. Stajewska s, H. Oleska ms, Lowczynski t, A. Ostrowski bs.
10	XII	»	Hamlet (2)	A. Vigna: W. Stajewska s, H. Oleska ms, A. Ostrowski bs.
13	XII	*Filharmonji*	*Concert*	
14	XII	Wielki	Il demone (3)	E.N. Reznicek: J. Korolewicz-Wayda s, H. Oleska ms, A. Ostrowski bs.
17	XII	»	Pagliacci (1)	A. Vigna: J. Korolewicz-Wayda s, W. Alberti t.
1908				
7	I	MADRID Real	Rigoletto	R. Villa: G. Pareto s, M. De Marsan ms, G. Anselmi t, F. Navarrini bs.
13	I	*Palacio Real*	*Concert*	G. Pareto s.
14	I	Real	Tosca	R. Villa: E. Bianchini Cappelli s, G. Anselmi t.
22	I	»	Hamlet	G. Golisciani: Solis s, L. Hotkovska ms, F. Navarrini bs.
4	II	MONTE CARLO Grand-Théâtre	La Gioconda (2)	A. Pomé: F. Litvinne s, M. Talaisi ms, Bailac ms, G. Anselmi t, J. Nivette bs.
::	II	VALENCIA Principal	Hamlet	J. Tolosa: A. Alaban s, C. Mas ms, Landerer bs.
::	II	»	Rigoletto	:: G. Rubio s, D. Eguileor t. :: ::
::	II	»	Il barbiere di Siviglia	Baratta: Salas s, L. Iribarne t, Cajal bs, Leoni bs.

Date of First Performance	City/Theater	Opera and Other Performances	Conductor: Principal Soloists
1908			
26 II	MONTE CARLO Grand-Théâtre	Il barbiere di Siviglia (1)	A. Pomé: S. Kurz s, D. Smirnov t, F. Chaliapin bs, A. Pini-Corsi bs.
29 II	LISBON São Carlos	**Paolo e Francesca****(4)ᵃ	L. Mancinelli: G. Piccoletti s, G. Krismer t.
9 III	»	Hamlet (4)	L. Mancinelli: E. Clasenti s, E. Mantelli ms, O. Luppi bs.
2 IV	NAPLES San Carlo	La Gioconda (2)	G. Papi: T. Burchi s, T. Di Angelo ms, B. Wheeler ms, G. Taccani t, A. Perelló de Segurola bs.
6 IV	»	L'Africaine (3)	E. Mascheroni: S. Krusceniski, s, E. Scafidi s, F. Viñas t, A. Perelló de Segurola bs, G. Tisci Rubini bs.
10 IV	»	Rigoletto (1)	G. Papi: E. Scafidi s, T. Di Angelo ms, G. Armanini t, G. Berenzone bs.
17 IV	BARCELONA Liceo	Hamlet	E. Vitale: G. Pareto s, M. Pozzi ms, S. Cirotto bs.
22 IV	»	Tosca	E. Vitale: L. Pasini-Vitale s, F. Fazzini t.
30 V	BUENOS AIRES Colón	Hamlet (6)	L. Mancinelli: E. Clasenti s, G. Fabri ms, L. Nicoletti-Kormann bs.
14 VI	»	Rigoletto (5)	A. Vigna: E. Clasenti s, T. Ferraris ms, A. Bassi/ M. Polverosi t, L. Nicoletti-Kormann bs.
16 VI	»	Tosca (2)	A. Vigna: A. Pinto/L. Crestani s, A. Bassi t.
24 VI	»	La Gioconda (5)	A. Vigna: A. Pinto s, T. Ferraris ms, G. Fabbri ms, M. Polverosi t, V. Arimondi bs.

ᵃPerformed three times with Act I of *Il barbiere di Siviglia* (E. Perea t.); once with Act III of *Rigoletto*.

Date of First Performance		City/Theater	Opera and Other Performances	Conductor: Principal Soloists
1908				
4	VII	BUENOS AIRES Colón	Paolo e Francesca** (3)	L. Mancinelli: M. Farneti ms, A. Bassi t, C. Bonfanti t.
9	VII	LA PLATA Argentino	Rigoletto (1)[a]	G. Falconi: E. Clasenti s, T. Ferraris ms, M. Polverosi t, L. Nicoletti-Kormann bs.
18	VII	BUENOS AIRES Colón	Otello (4)	L. Mancinelli: M. Farneti s, A. Paoli t.
28	VII	»	Il barbiere di Siviglia (6)	L. Mancinelli: E. Clasenti s, M. Polverosi t, F. Chaliapin bs, A. Pini-Corsi bs.
5	VIII	»	Pagliacci (4)	A. Vigna: E. Reussi s, A. Bassi t, F. Sarmiento b.
18	VIII	»	**Don Giovanni** (3)	L. Mancinelli: A. Pinto s, M. Farneti s, E. Clasenti s, M. Polverosi t, F. Chaliapin bs, A. Pini-Corsi bs.
6	IX	»	**Aurora***** (3)	H. Panizza: M. Farneti s, E. Clasenti s, A. Bassi t.
10	IX	*Salon La Argentina*	*Concert*	
14	XI	MONTEVIDEO Solis	Pagliacci and Hamlet, Act IV	E. Vitale: A. Galli-Curci s, M. Izquierdo t, G. La Puma bs.
16	XII	MADRID Real	Hamlet	R. Villa: A. Alaban/G. Pareto s, G. Lukacewska/A. Parsi-Pettinella ms, M. Gaudio bs.
30	XII	»	Il barbiere di Siviglia	:: :: :: :: :: :: :: :: ::
1909				
1	I	»	Il barbiere di Siviglia	R. Villa: G. Pareto s, E. Perea t, M. Gaudio bs, M. Verdaguer bs.
7	I	*Palacio Real*	*Concert*	

[a]Gala performance with the company of the Colón in celebration of the national holiday.

Date of First Performance		City/Theater	Opera and Other Performances	Conductor: Principal Soloists
1909				
12	I	MADRID Real	Linda di Chamonix	P. Urrutia: R. Storchio s, G. Lukacewska ms, E. Perea t, F. Meana bs.
24	I	»	Rigoletto	R. Villa: G. Pareto s, G. Lukacewska ms, I. Cristalli t, A. Vidal bs.
::	I	»	*Benefit concert for the victims of the Siculo-Calabrese earthquake of 1908*	
29	I		*Concert for the Society of the Press* (Il barbiere di Siviglia Acts II & III)	R. Villa: G. Pareto s, E. Perea t, M. Gaudio bs, M. Verdaguer bs.
9	II	MONTE CARLO Grand-Théâtre	**Cristoforo Colombo** (2)	A. Pomé: Y. Dubels, s, G. De Tura t, J. Vallier bs.
18	II	»	Rigoletto (2)	A. Pomé: F. Hempel s, De Kowska ms, D. Smirnov t, J. Vallier bs.
27	II	»	Il barbiere di Siviglia (2)	A. Pomé: E. de Hidalgo s, D. Smirnov t, F. Chaliapin bs, A. Pini-Corsi bs.
::	II	NICE *Vaisseau Amiral «Patrie»*	*Concert*	
2	III	MONTE CARLO Grand-Théâtre	La Gioconda (1)	A. Pomé: F. Litvinne s, De Kowska ms, J. Spennert ms, G. Anselmi t, J. Vallier bs.
::	III	VALENCIA Principal	Rigoletto	Baratta: G. Rubio s, D. Eguileor t.
13	III	ROME Costanzi	Hamlet (4)	G. Polacco: G. Pareto s, E. Ceresoli Salvatori ms, B. Berardi bs.
31	III	»	La Gioconda (4)	G. Polacco: G. Russ s, E. Ceresoli Salvatori ms, M. Claessens ms, J. Palet t, A. Masini-Pieralli bs.

Date of First Performance		City/Theater	Opera and Other Performances	Conductor: Principal Soloists
1909				
11	IV	NAPLES San Carlo	Hamlet (2)	G. Zuccani: G. Pareto s, N. Frascani ms, A. Ricceri bs.
13	IV	»	Il barbiere di Siviglia (3)	G. Zuccani: G. Pareto s, E. Perea t, A. Ricceri bs. P. Poggi bs.
23	V	BUENOS AIRES Colón	La Gioconda (5)	G. Baroni: E. Burzio s, E. Petri ms, M. Claessens ms, F. Constantino t, C. Walter bs.
25	V	»	Rigoletto (5)	L. Mancinelli: G. Pareto s, E. Lucci ms, A. Bonci t, M. Gaudio bs.
20	VI	»	Il barbiere di Siviglia (7)	L. Mancinelli: G. Pareto s, A. Bonci t, M. Gaudio bs, A. Pini-Corsi bs.
29	VI	»	Hamlet (8)	L. Mancinelli: G. Pareto s, E. Petri ms, C. Walter bs.
6	VII	»	Aurora (3)	G. Baroni: H. Darclée s, G. Grazioli s, F. Constantino t.
26	VII	*Odeón*	*Concert*	E. Drangosch: E. Theodorini s, F. Dereyne s.
17	VIII	Colón	Pagliacci (2)	G. Baroni: F. Dereyne s, A. Rosanov t, G. Novelli b.
18	VIII	*Odeón*	*Concert for «Colegio-Taller»*	E. Drangosch: A. Leander Flodin s, A. Bonci t, R. Oltman bs.
31	VIII	Colón	Demon** (2)	G. Baroni: H. Darclée s, F. Constantino t, M. Gaudio bs.
::	::	MONTEVIDEO Urquiza	Rigoletto	L. Mancinelli: G. Pareto s, E. Lucci ms, A. Bonci t, M. Gaudio bs.
24	X	RACCONIGI *Castello Reale*	*Concert in honor of Tsar Nicholas II*[a]	P. Mascagni (piano): M. Farneti s, A. Parsi-Pettinella ms, R. Grassi t.

[a]Brindisi from *Hamlet* and Quartet from *Rigoletto*.

Date of First Performance		City/Theater	Opera and Other Performances	Conductor: Principal Soloists
1909				
21	XI	**LONDON** *Lady Kleinwort's Palace*	*Concert*	
30	XII	**PARIS** *Palais Stern*	*Concert*	
1910				
4	I	**MADRID** Real	Hamlet	R. Villa: G. Finzi-Magrini s, E. Petri/F. Perini ms, A. Ricceri bs.
11	I	*Palacio Real*	*Concert*	
20	I	Real	Rigoletto	G. Marinuzzi: G. Finzi-Magrini s, F. Perini ms, G. Taccani t, A. Ricceri bs.
23	I	»	La Gioconda	G. Marinuzzi: T. Poli-Randaccio s, E. Petri ms, F. Perini ms, G. Taccani t, A. Ricceri bs.
24	I	"	*Concert for the Society of the Press*	
9	II	**MONTE CARLO** Grand-Théâtre	Il barbiere di Siviglia	:: E. de Hidalgo s, D. Smirnov t, F. Chaliapin bs, V. Chalmin bs.
17	II	»	Otello	A. Pomé: L. Edvina/J. Spennert s, C. Rousselière t.
::	III	»	Rigoletto	:: G. Pareto s, Mati ms, D. Smirnov t, Marvini bs.
13	III	»	La traviata	:: A. Zeppilli s, D. Smirnov t.
15	III	»	Fedora**	A. Pomé: M. Chénal s, J. Spennert s, D. Smirnov t.
4	IV	**ROME** Costanzi	Il barbiere di Siviglia (1)	P. Mascagni: R. Pinkert s, U. Macnez t, C. Walter bs. P. Malatesta bs.
7	IV	**NAPLES** San Carlo	Il barbiere di Siviglia (2)	C. Campanini: S. Michelini s, M. Polverosi t, V. Arimondi bs. P. Poggi bs.

Date of First Performance		City/Theater	Opera and Other Performances	Conductor: Principal Soloists
1910				
13	IV	NAPLES San Carlo	Zazà* (1)	E. Perosio: A. Agostinelli s, R. Andreini t.
12	IV	*Circolo artistico*	*Concert*	
25	V	BUENOS AIRES Colón	Rigoletto (5)	E. Vitale: G. Pareto s, F. Perini ms, G. Anselmi t, S. Cirotto bs.
4	VI	»	La Gioconda (2)	E. Vitale: E. Mazzoleni s, F. Perini ms, A. Cucini ms, G. Taccani t, G. Cirino bs.
12	VI	»	Il barbiere di Siviglia (6)	E. Vitale: G. Pareto s, G. Anselmi t, A. Didur/G. Cirino bs, C. Paterna bs.
21	VI	»	Cristoforo Colombo (4)	E. Vitale: E. Mazzoleni s, A. Pintucci t, G. Cirino bs.
::	VI	*Palacio de Castellis*	*Concert in honor of the Infanta Isabella of Spain*	
::	VI	*Palacio Mihanovich*	*Concert in honor of the President of Chile*	
14	VII	Colón	Hamlet (8)	E. Vitale: G. Pareto/E. Clasenti s, F. Perini ms, G. Cirino bs.
30	VII	Avenida	*Concert in honor of Riccardo de la Vega*	M. Gay ms; M. Guerrero & F. Díaz de Mendoza (actors)
14	VIII	Coliseo	Pagliacci[a]	A. De Angelis: Cracoppo s, E. Bergamaschi t.
18	VIII	Odeón	*Concert for "Colegio-Taller"*	
1	IX	Colón	Pagliacci (1) and Rigoletto, Act III	E. Vitale: A. Agostinelli s, C. Rousselière t, R. Rasponi b. :: G. Pareto s.
7	IX	MONTEVIDEO Urquiza	Il barbiere di Siviglia	E. Vitale: G. Pareto/A. Galli-Curci s, F. Carpi t, G. Cirino bs, G. La Puma bs.

[a]Benefit performance for the Comité Italiano di Guerra.

Date of First Performance		City/Theater	Opera and Other Performances	Conductor: Principal Soloists
1910				
8	IX	MONTEVIDEO Urquiza	Rigoletto	E. Vitale: G. Pareto s, F. Carpi t, C. Paterna bs.
13	IX	»	Pagliacci	:: :: :: :: :: :: :: ::
17	IX	»	Hamlet	:: :: :: :: :: :: :: ::
1911				
2	II	NAPLES San Carlo	L'Africaine (2)	I. Nini Bellucci: E. Mazzoleni s, E. Scafidi s, M. Gilion t, L. Contini bs, O. Luppi bs.
6	II	»	Tosca (1)	I. Nini Bellucci: A. Karola s, A. Giorgini t.
8	II	»	Il barbiere di Siviglia (2)	V. Gui: S. Michelini s, E. Perea t, L. Contini bs, V. Trevisan bs.
9	III	MONTE CARLO Grand-Théâtre	Il barbiere di Siviglia (3)	A. Pomé: E. de Hidalgo s, A. Giorgini t, F. Chaliapin bs, V. Chalmin bs.
21	III	»	Linda di Chamonix (2)	A. Pomé: E. de Hidalgo s, N. Lollini ms, A. Giorgini t.
28	III	»	La Gioconda (3)	A. Pomé: F. Litvinne s, M. Borga ms, C. Croiza ms, F. Carpi t, Marvini bs.
3	IV	NAPLES San Carlo	La Gioconda (2)	V. Gui: E. Mazzoleni s, E. Petri ms, M. Verger ms, R. Grassi/G. Genzardi t, O. Luppi bs.
7	IV	Politeama Giacosa	*Concert*	
8	IV	San Carlo	Aida (1)	V. Gui: E. Mazzoleni s, E. Petri ms, N. Fusati t, O. Luppi bs.
16	IV	ROME Costanzi	Il barbiere di Siviglia (4)	L. Mancinelli/T. De Angelis: G. Pareto s, U. Macnez t, N. De Angelis bs, G. Kaschmann bs.

Date of First Performance	City/Theater	Opera and Other Performances	Conductor: Principal Soloists
1911			
24 V	BUENOS AIRES Colón	**Thaïs** (2)	E. Vitale: A. Agostinelli s, A. Bada t.
25 V	»	Lucia di Lammermoor (6)	E. Vitale: M. Barrientos s, F. Constantino t, N. De Angelis bs.
1 VI	»	Rigoletto (6)	E. Vitale: M. Barrientos s, F. Perini ms, F. Constantino t, P. Ludikar bs.
25 VI	»	Il barbiere di Siviglia (6)	E. Vitale: M. Barrientos s, A. Bonci t, N. De Angelis bs, C. Paterna bs.
7 VII	»	**Don Carlo** (5)	E. Vitale: A. Agostinelli s, L. Garibaldi ms, F. Constantino t, N. De Angelis bs, P. Ludikar bs.
25 VII	»	**La fanciulla del West**** (4)	E. Vitale: A. Agostinelli s, E. Ferrari-Fontana t.
10 VIII	»	Tristan und Isolde (2)	E. Vitale: L. Pasini Vitale s, L. Garibaldi ms, E. Ferrari-Fontana t, N. De Angelis bs.
20 VIII	»	**Evgenii Onegin**** (2)	E. Vitale: L. Pasini Vitale s, F. Anitúa ms, A. Pintucci t, P. Ludikar bs.
25 VIII	MONTEVIDEO Urquiza	Il barbiere di Siviglia	E. Vitale: M. Barrientos s, A. Bonci t, P. Ludikar bs, C. Paterna bs.
26 VIII	»	La fanciulla del West**	E. Vitale: A. Agostinelli s, E. Ferrari-Fontana t.
30 VIII	»	Rigoletto	E. Vitale: M. Barrientos s, F. Perini ms, A. Pintucci t, P. Ludikar bs.
2 IX	ROSARIO DI SANTA FE Colón	Il barbiere di Siviglia	E. Vitale: M. Barrientos s, A. Bonci t, P. Ludikar bs, C. Paterna bs.
4 IX	»	Rigoletto	E. Vitale: M. Barrientos s, F. Perini ms, A. Pintucci t, P. Ludikar bs.

Date of First Performance		City/Theater	Opera and Other Performances	Conductor: Principal Soloists
1911				
		ROSARIO DI SANTA FE		
::	IX	Colón	Hamlet	E. Vitale: A. Gonzaga s, F. Perini ms, P. Ludikar bs.
		SÃO PAULO		
12	IX	Municipal	Hamlet (2)	E. Vitale: G. Pareto s, F. Perini ms, P. Ludikar bs.
17	IX	»	La bohème (3)	E. Vitale: A. Agostinelli s, R. Garavaglia s, A. Bonci t, V. Bettoni bs, P. Ludikar bs.
19	IX	»	Tristan und Isolde (2)	E. Vitale: L. Pasini Vitale s, F. Perini ms, E. Ferrari-Fontana t, P. Ludikar bs.
24	IX	»	Il barbiere di Siviglia (3)	E. Vitale: G. Pareto s, A. Bonci t, P. Ludikar bs, C. Paterna bs.
26	IX	»	Rigoletto (1)	E. Vitale: G. Pareto s, F. Perini ms, A. Bonci t, P. Ludikar bs.
29	IX	»	Don Pasquale (1)	E. Vitale: A. Agostinelli s, A. Bonci t, C. Paterna bs.
		RIO DE JANEIRO		
3	X	Lyrico [7]	Rigoletto	E. Vitale: G. Pareto s, F. Perini ms, A. Bonci t, P. Ludikar bs.
5	X	»	Hamlet	E. Vitale: G. Pareto s, F. Perini ms, P. Ludikar bs.
7	X	»	Il barbiere di Siviglia	E. Vitale: G. Pareto s, A. Bonci t, P. Ludikar bs, C. Paterna bs.
10	X	»	Don Pasquale	:: A. Agostinelli s, A. Bonci t, C. Paterna bs.
		ROME		
18	XI	Costanzi	Il barbiere di Siviglia (4)	L. Mancinelli: E. de Hidalgo s, F. Carpi t, N. De Angelis bs, G. Schottler bs.
		PARIS		
18	XII	Opéra	Rigoletto	:: Y. Gall s, L. Charny ms, R. Lassalle t, M. Journet bs.

Date of First Performance		City/Theater	Opera and Other Performances	Conductor: Principal Soloists
1911				
::	XII	PARIS Opéra	Hamlet	:: J. Campredon s. :: :: ::
20	XII	*Trocadéro*	*Concert*	
22	XII	Opéra	Hamlet	P. Vidal: Y. Gall s, K. La-peyrette ms, M. Journet bs.
1912				
20	I	MADRID Real	Il barbiere di Siviglia	G. Marinuzzi: P. Sanz s, U. Macnez t, A. Masini-Pieralli bs, M. Verdaguer bs.
30	I	»	L'Africaine	R. Villa: M. de Lerma s, E. Fiorin s, F. Viñas t, A. Masini-Pieralli bs.
17	II	»	Pagliacci	G. Marinuzzi: G. Baldas-sarre Tedeschi s, M. Iz-quierdo t, C. Patino b.
::	II	»	*Concert for the wounded of the Rif campaign*	
13	II	FLORENCE Verdi	Il barbiere di Siviglia (2)	A. Alvisi: E. Gomez s, G. Vogliotti t, E. Benazzo bs, C. Rossi bs.
::	II/III	MONTE CARLO Grand-Théâtre	Il barbiere di Siviglia	:: E. de Hidalgo s, M. Polverosi t, F. Chaliapin bs, V. Chalmin bs.
::	II/III	»	Don Carlo	:: Lambert Willaume s, Mattei ms, C. Rousselière t, F. Chaliapin bs, P. Clauzure bs.
26	III	BUDAPEST Operaház	Il barbiere di Siviglia (1)	E. Ábrányi: E. Sándor s, D. Arányi t, R. Kornai bs, F. Hegedüs bs.
29	III	»	Rigoletto	A. Szikla: E. Sándor s, D. Bársony ms, D. Arányi t, R. Kornai bs.

Date of First Performance		City/Theater	Opera and Other Performances	Conductor: Principal Soloists
1912				
1	IV	»	Hamlet	E. Ábrányi: E. Sándor s, A. Fodor ms, F. Székely-hidy t, B. Venczell bs, R. Kornai bs.
		VENICE		
21	IV	La Fenice	Il barbiere di Siviglia (4)	R. Ferrari: E. De Hidalgo s, E. Perea t, F. Navarrini bs, G. Kaschmann b.
		PARIS		
12	V	Opéra	Rigoletto	L. Jéhin: A. Nezhdanova s, N. Lollini ms, E. Caruso t, J. Torres de Luna bs.
16	V	»	La fanciulla del West**	T. Serafin: C. Melis/T. Poli Randaccio s, E. Caruso t.
19	V	»	Il barbiere di Siviglia	A. Pomé: E. de Hidalgo s, D. Smirnov t, F. Chaliapin bs, V. Chalmin bs.
31	V	*31, rue Nitot*	*Benefit concert*	C. Melis s, E. Caruso t.
		DEAUVILLE		
11	VIII	Casino	Il barbiere di Siviglia	:: :: :: :: :: :: :: :: ::
		PHILADELPHIA		
4	XI	Metropolitan	Rigoletto	C. Campanini: A. Gluck s, M. Keyes ms, O. Harrold t, H. Scott bs.
::	XI	»	Il barbiere di Siviglia	G. Sturani: J. Dufau s, A. Giorgini t, H. Scott bs, V. Trevisan bs.
::	XI	»	Un ballo in maschera	E. Perosio: C. Gagliardi s, M. Gay ms, G. Zenatello t.
::	XI	"	Il trovatore	C. Campanini: C. Gagliardi s, M. Gay ms, C. Nicolay t, E. Venturini t.
		NEW YORK		
19	XI	Metropolitan[a]	Hamlet	C. Campanini: A. Zeppilli s, E. de Cisneros ms, G. Huberdeau bs.
25	XI	*Carnegie Hall*	*Concert*	E. Perosio: H. Stanley s.

[a]Philadelphia Chicago Opera Company.

Date of First Performance		City/Theater	Opera and Other Performances	Conductor: Principal Soloists
1912				
29	XI	CHICAGO Auditorium	Rigoletto (2)	C. Campanini: A. Zeppilli/J. Dufau s, O. Harrold t, G. Huberdeau/H. Scott bs.
3	XII	»	Hamlet (1)	C. Campanini: A. Zeppilli s, E. de Cisneros ms, G. Huberdeau bs.
5	XII	»	Pagliacci (2)	E. Perosio: A. Zeppilli s, I. Calleja/G. Zenatello t.
15	XII	New York *Hippodrome*	*Concert*	E. Perosio: H. Stanley s.
1913				
7	I	BARCELONA Liceo	Il barbiere di Siviglia	G. Falconi: E. de Hidalgo s, M. Polverosi t, L. Rossato bs.
10	I	»	Rigoletto	G. Falconi: M. Llopart s, M. Blanco Sadun ms, M. Polverosi t, E. Sesona bs.
14	I	»	Pagliacci	G. Falconi: M. Llopart s, L. Colazza t, A. Pacini b.
16	I	MADRID Real	Tristan und Isolde	G. Zuccani: C. Gagliardi s, V. Guerrini ms, F. Viñas t, O. Luppi bs.
21	I	»	Don Carlo	G. Zuccani: C. Gagliardi s, V. Guerrini ms, J. Palet t, A. Masini Pierralli bs.
26	I	»	Pagliacci	G. Zuccani: M. Moscicka s, J. Palet t, C. Patino b.
1	II	»	Rigoletto	G. Zuccani: A. Gonzaga s, R. Cesaretti ms, G. Rotondi/J. Palet t, A. Vidal bs.
19	II	»	Hamlet	G. Zuccani: A. Gonzaga s, V. Guerrini ms, O. Luppi bs.
27	II	»	Tristan und Isolde	:: :: :: :: :: :: :: :: ::
1	III	»	Il trovatore	G. Zuccani: C. Gagliardi s, Buisan ms, F. Burroni t, A. Vidal bs.

Date of First Performance		City/Theater	Opera and Other Performances	Conductor: Principal Soloists
1913				
::	III	MADRID Real	*Concert for the Society of the Press*	
4/14	III	VALENCIA Principal	Pagliacci	G. Zuccani: M. Moscicka s, F. Burroni t, C. Patino b.
4/14	III	»	Hamlet	G. Zuccani: A. Gonzaga s, V. Guerrini ms, O. Luppi bs.
11	IV	BUDAPEST Népopera	Il trovatore (1)	F. Reiner: M. Jávor s, I. Durigo ms, P. Seidler t.
15	IV	»	Hamlet (3)	F. Reiner: A. Ádler s, M. Basilides ms, S. Bihar bs.
18	IV	»	Il barbiere di Siviglia (2)	F. Reiner: A. Ádler s, A. Tedeschi t, S. Bihar bs, E. Mátrai bs.
22	IV	»	**Faust** (1)	F. Reiner: A. Ádler s, M. Basilides ms, P. Seidler t, J. Gábor b, S. Bihar bs.
28	IV	»	Rigoletto (1)	F. Reiner: M. Jávor s, M. Basilides ms, F. Kurt t, S. Bihar bs.
1	VI	PARIS Champs-Elysées	*Benefit concert* (Il barbiere di Siviglia, Act II)	Camilleri: L. Lipkowska s, F. Carpi t.
13	VIII	S. SEBASTIANO Gran Teatro Circo[a]	Pagliacci	:: L. Cavalieri s, Gaudenzi t.
::	VIII	?	*Concert*	
5	XI	PHILADELPHIA Metropolitan[b]	Il barbiere di Siviglia (1)	G. Sturani: J. Dufau s, A. Giorgini t, H. Scott bs, V. Trevisan bs.

[a] One of three performances given to commemorate the centenary of the liberation of the city from French occupation.

[b] Tour of the Chicago Opera Company.

Date of First Performance		City/Theater	Opera and Other Performances	Conductor: Principal Soloists
1913				
7	XI	BALTIMORE Ford's Grand Opera ?ª	Rigoletto (1)	C. Campanini: A. Zeppilli s, M. Keyes ms, A. Giorgini t, G. Huberdeau bs.
10	XI	PHILADELPHIA Metropolitanª	Rigoletto (1)	E. Perosio: A. Zeppilli s, A. Giorgini t.
13	XI	»	Pagliacci (1)	G. Sturani: J. Osborn-Hannah s, A. Bassi t, A. Crabbé b.
17	XI	»	La Gioconda (1)	G. Sturani: C. White s, J. Claussen ms, A. Bassi t, H. Scott bs.
20	XI	»	Cristoforo Colombo** (2)	C. Campanini: R. Raisa s, A. Bassi t, G. Huberdeau bs.
25	XI	CHICAGO Auditorium	La Gioconda (1)	G. Sturani: C. White s, J. Claussen ms, A. Giorgini t, H. Scott bs.
1	XII	»	Rigoletto (2)	C. Campanini: A. Zeppilli/J. Dufau s, M. Keyes ms, A. Giorgini t, G. Huberdeau/H. Scott bs.
4	XII	»	Cristoforo Colombo (2)	C. Campanini: R. Raisa s, A. Bassi t, G. Huberdeau bs.
15	XII	»	Il barbiere di Siviglia (1)	C. Campanini: J. Dufau s, A. Giorgini t, H. Scott bs, V. Trevisan bs.
18	XII	»	Don Giovanni (1)	C. Campanini: Dorda s, J. Dufau s, C. White s, A. Giorgini t, G. Huberdeau bs.
19	XII	»	Pagliacci (2)	C. Campanini: J. Osborn-Hannah s, A. Bassi t.
26	XII	»	Thaïs (2)	C. Campanini: M. Garden s, C. Dalmorès t, G. Huberdeau bs.

ªTour of the Chicago Opera Company.

Date of First Performance		City/Theater	Opera and Other Performances	Conductor: Principal Soloists
1914				
4	I	NEW YORK *Hippodrome*	*Concert*	N. Franko: F. Hinkle s, W. M. Rummel (violin), A. Rosenstein (piano), Mona Krog (piano)
9	I	WASHINGTON ?	*Private concert at the Vanderbilt's*	
11	I	BOSTON ?	*Concert*	
16	I	DETROIT *Armory*	*Concert*	
19	I	COLUMBUS ?	*Concert*	
21	I	CINCINNATI *Music Hall*	*Concert*	L. Tetrazzini s.
23	I	MINNEAPOLIS *Armory*	*Concert*	L. Tetrazzini s.
26	I	TOLEDO ?	*Concert*	
28	I	TORONTO Massen Hall	*Concert*	L. Tetrazzini s.
30	I	BUFFALO Broadway	*Concert*	L. Tetrazzini s.
1	II	NEW YORK *Hippodrome*	*Concert*	
2	II	PHILADELPHIA Metropolitan	Pagliacci	C. Campanini: A. Zeppilli s, A. Bassi t, A. Crabbé b.
5	II	BOSTON ?	*Concert*	
16	II	CHICAGO ?	*Concert*	L. Tetrazzini s.
18	II	PHILADELPHIA Metropolitan	Rigoletto	C. Campanini: N. Melba s, M. Keyes ms, A. Gior- gini t, H. Scott bs.
21	II	»	Don Giovanni	C. Campanini: R. Raisa s, C. White s, Z. Zeppilli s, A. Giorgini t, G. Huber- deau bs.

Date of First Performance		City/Theater	Opera and Other Performances	Conductor: Principal Soloists
1914				
23	II	PHILADELPHIA Metropolitan	Cristoforo Colombo	C. Campanini: R. Raisa s, A. Bassi t, G. Huberdeau bs.
28	II	»	Hamlet	C. Campanini: A. Zeppilli s, J. Claussen ms, G. Huberdeau bs.
4	III	? DALLAS Coliseum[a]	Rigoletto	C. Campanini: F. Macbeth s, M. Keyes ms, A. Giorgini t, H. Scott bs.
7	III	»	Pagliacci	C. Campanini: J. Osborn-Hannah s, O. Marak t.
10	III	LOS ANGELES *Philharmonic Auditorium*[a]	Rigoletto	C. Campanini: F. Macbeth s, M. Keyes ms, A. Giorgini t, H. Scott bs.
14	III	»	Pagliacci	G. Sturani: J. Osborn-Hannah s, A. Bassi t, A. Crabbé bs.
30	III	? SEATTLE Orpheum[a]	Pagliacci	G. Sturani: J. Osborn-Hannah s, A. Bassi t, A. Crabbé bs.
2	IV	PORTLAND Orpheum[a]	Pagliacci	G. Sturani: J. Osborn-Hannah s, A. Bassi t, A. Crabbé bs.
8	IV	DENVER Auditorium[a]	Pagliacci	C. Campanini: J. Osborn-Hannah s, A. Bassi t, F. Federici b.
17	IV	ST. LOUIS Odeon[a]	Pagliacci	:: A. Zeppilli s, O. Marak t.
20	IV	ST. PAUL Auditorium[a]	Rigoletto	C. Campanini: F. Macbeth s, M. Keyes ms, A. Giorgini t, G. Huberdeau bs.
22	IV	»	Pagliacci	:: :: :: :: :: :: :: :: :: ::

[a] Tour of the Chicago Opera Company.

Date of First Performance		City/Theater	Opera and Other Performances	Conductor: Principal Soloists
1914				
27	IV	NEW YORK St. Denis	Concert	A. Fitziu s.
1	V	PATERSON Regent	Benefit concert	
15	VIII	OSTENDE Kursaal	Concert	
23	VIII	»	Concert	
16	X	MILAN Carcano[a]	Il barbiere di Siviglia (1)	L. Mancinelli: A. Galli-Curci s, E. Perea t, A. Masini-Pieralli bs, A. Pini-Corsi bs.
29	X	BOLOGNA Corso	Il barbiere di Siviglia (2)	A. Alvisi: E. Angelini-Borelli s, A. Salvaneschi t, A. Masini-Pieralli bs, A. Pini-Corsi bs.
17	XII	FLORENCE Verdi	Hamlet (4)	E. Mascheroni: E. Angelini-Borelli s, A. Gramegna ms, G. La Puma bs.
27	XII	»	Il barbiere di Siviglia (2)	A. Alvisi: E. Angelini-Borelli s, G. Paganelli t, O. Carozzi bs, G. La Puma bs.
1915				
5	I	GENOA Politeama Genovese	Pagliacci (2)	G. Baroni: M. Rago/M. Llacer s, G. Gaudenzi t, M. Aineto b.
2	II	»	Hamlet (3)	G. Baroni: B. Morello s, L. Garibaldi ms, L. Manfrini bs.
22	IV	HAVANA Nacional	Aida	T. Serafin: J. Capella s, R. Alvarez/M. Gay ms, J. Palet t, M. Gaudio bs.
24	IV	»	Pagliacci	A. Bovi: C. Muzio s, G. Zenatello/J. Palet t.

[a] For the unemployed lyric artists and the Verdi Society of Mutual Aid.

Date of First Performance		City/Theater	Opera and Other Performances	Conductor: Principal Soloists
1915				
29	IV	HAVANA Nacional	Rigoletto	T. Serafin: B. De Pasquali s, M. Polverosi t, M. Gaudio bs.
1	V	»	Il barbiere di Siviglia	T. Serafin: B. De Pasquali s, M. Polverosi t, M. Gaudio bs, G. La Puma bs.
6	V	»	Otello	T. Serafin: C. Muzio s, G. Zenatello t.
9	V	»	Un ballo in maschera	:: J. Capella s, R. Alvarez ms, J. Palet t.
11	V	»	La bohème	T. Serafin/A. Bovi: C. Muzio s, A. Giana s, G. Zenatello t.
13	V	»	Carmen	T. Serafin: M. Gay ms, C. Muzio s, G. Zenatello t.
22	V	»	La Gioconda	:: E. Rakowska s, Alvarez ms, Luci ms, J. Palet t, M. Gaudio bs.
::	V	MATANZAS Sauto	Pagliacci	A. Bovi: C. Muzio s, J. Palet t.
::	V	»	Il barbiere di Siviglia	T. Serafin: B. De Pasquali s, M. Gaudio bs, G. La Puma bs.
::	V	»	La bohème	A. Bovi: C. Muzio s, A. Giana s, G. Zenatello t.
1	VI	NEW YORK Manhattan	*Concert*	
3	VI	»	*Concert*	
6	VII	BUENOS AIRES Colón	L'Africaine (3)	G. Marinuzzi: R. Raisa s, M. Melsa/H. Spani s, B. De Muro t, G. Cirino bs, T. Dantale bs.
7	VII	»	Il barbiere di Siviglia (5)	G. Marinuzzi: A. Galli-Curci s, A. Tedeschi t, G. Cirino bs, G. Niola bs.
26	VII	»	Rigoletto (2)	G. Marinuzzi: A. Galli-Curci s, F. Perini ms, H. Lázaro t, B. Berardi bs.

Date of First Performance	City/Theater	Opera and Other Performances	Conductor: Principal Soloists
1915			
	BUENOS AIRES		
30 VII	Colón	Hamlet (4)	G. Marinuzzi: A. Galli-Curci s, N. Frascani ms, B. Berardi bs.
2 VIII	?	*Concert*	G. Marinuzzi: :: ::
4 VIII	Colón	Pagliacci, Act I[a]	G. Marinuzzi: H. Spani s, E. Caruso t, E. Caronna b.
11 VIII	»	Carmen, Act II[b]	G. Sturani: G. Vix s, B. De Muro t.
13 VIII	»	Carmen & "Prologo" of Pagliacci (1)	G. Sturani: N. Frascani ms, B. De Muro t.
	MONTEVIDEO		
16 VIII	Urquiza	Pagliacci	G. Marinuzzi: H. Spani s, E. Caruso t.
:: VIII	»	Il barbiere di Siviglia	:: A. Tedeschi t, G. Cirino bs. :: :: ::
:: VIII	»	Rigoletto	:: H. Lázaro t. :: :: :: ::
:: VIII	»	Hamlet	:: :: :: :: :: :: :: :: :: ::
	BUENOS AIRES		
18 VIII	Colón	Anfione e Zeto (2)	P. De Rogatis: G. Salvini
	RIO DE JANEIRO		
4 IX	Municipal	Hamlet (1)	G. Marinuzzi: A. Galli-Curci s, N. Frascani ms, G. Cirino bs.
8 IX	»	Rigoletto (1)	G. Marinuzzi: A. Galli-Curci s, F. Perini ms, H. Lázaro t, B. Berardi bs.
11 IX	»	Pagliacci (1)	G. Sturani: A. Giacomucci s, J. Martins t, E. Caronna b.
13 IX	»	L'Africaine (1)	G. Marinuzzi: R. Raisa s, A. Galli-Curci s, B. De Muro t, G. Cirino bs, B. Berardi bs.

[a] In a concert given for the Society of the Press.

[b] In a concert given for the Red Cross.

Date of First Performance		City/Theater	Opera and Other Performances	Conductor: Principal Soloists
1915				
16	IX	RIO DE JANEIRO Municipal	Il barbiere di Siviglia (1)	G. Marinuzzi: A. Galli-Curci s, A. Tedeschi t, G. Cirino bs, G. Niola bs.
18	IX	»	Tosca (1)	G. Marinuzzi: G. Dalla Rizza s, H. Lázaro t.
21	IX	SÃO PAULO Municipal	Rigoletto (1)	G. Marinuzzi: A. Galli-Curci s, N. Frascani ms, H. Lázaro t, B. Berardi bs.
23	IX	»	L'Africaine (1)	G. Marinuzzi: R. Raisa s, A. Giacomucci s, B. De Muro t, G. Cirino bs, B. Berardi bs.
26	IX	»	Il barbiere di Siviglia (1)	G. Marinuzzi: A. Galli-Curci s, A. Tedeschi t, G. Cirino bs, G. Niola bs.
28	IX	»	Pagliacci (1)	G. Sturani: A. Giacomucci s, J. Martins t, E. Caronna b.
1	X	»	La fanciulla del West (1)	G. Marinuzzi: G. Dalla Rizza s, B. De Muro t.
4	X	»	Hamlet (1)	G. Marinuzzi: A. Galli-Curci s, N. Frascani ms, B. Berardi bs.
1916				
11	II	BARCELONA Liceo	Hamlet	Alfredo Padovani: G. Pareto s, N. Frascani ms, L. Manfrini bs.
13	II	»	Pagliacci	A. Padovani: P. Barti/A. Agostinelli s, E. Cunego t, P. Del Grillo b.
16	II	»	Rigoletto	A. Padovani: G. Pareto s, M. Lucci ms, C. Broccardi t, L. Nicoletti-Kormann bs.
18	II	MADRID *Palacio Real*	*Concert*	

Date of First Performance		City/Theater	Opera and Other Performances	Conductor: Principal Soloists
1916				
20	II	BARCELONA Liceo	Il barbiere di Siviglia	A. Padovani: G. Pareto s, C. Hackett t, L. Nicoletti-Kormann bs, C. Paterna bs.
23	II	»	Pagliacci	A. Padovani: P. Barti s, E. Cunego t, R. Rasponi bs.
28	II	VALENCIA Principal	Hamlet (4)	A. Padovani: G. Pareto s, N. Frascani ms, L. Nicoletti-Kormann bs.
12	III	MADRID Zarzuela	Pagliacci	A. Padovani: A. Agostinelli s, J. Elias t.
15	III	»	Il barbiere di Siviglia	A. Padovani: R. D'Ory s, Kasadei/C. Hackett t, L. Nicoletti-Kormann bs, F. Puíggener bs.
18	III	»	Hamlet	A. Padovani: R. D'Ory s, N. Frascani ms, L. Nicoletti-Kormann bs.
20	V	BUENOS AIRES Colón	**Boris Godunov** (2)	G. Baroni: A. Agostinelli s, P. Navia t, A. Algos t, M. Gaudio bs.
3	VI	»	Andrea Chénier (3)	G. Baroni: G. Dalla Rizza s, E. Johnson t.
11	VI	»	Rigoletto (4)	G. Baroni: M. Capsir/E. Clasenti s, E. Barsanti ms, P. Navia t, M. Journet bs.
29	VI	»	Hamlet (4)	G. Baroni: M. Barrientos/ M. Capsir s, J. Royer ms, M. Journet bs.
3	VII	»	Pagliacci (3)	G. Baroni: A. Agostinelli/ N. Vallin Pardo s, G. Crimi t, A. Bettazzoni b.
14	VII	CORDOVA Rivera Indarte	Andrea Chénier	G. Baroni: A. Agostinelli s, E. Johnson t.
16	VII	»	Rigoletto	G. Baroni: S. Santangelo s, A. Frabetti ms, N. del Rex t, Melachi bs.

Date of First Performance	City/Theater	Opera and Other Performances	Conductor: Principal Soloists
1916			
27 VII	BUENOS AIRES Colón	**Falstaff** (3)	G. Baroni: R. Raisa s, N. Vallin Pardo s, E. Casazza/G. Bertazzoli ms, T. Schipa t, A. Crabbé b, M. Gaudio bs.
2 VIII	»	Il barbiere di Siviglia (3)	G. Baroni: M. Barrientos s, T. Schipa t, M. Gaudio bs, G. Niola bs.
[a] 14 VIII	[a] Coliseo	[a] *Concert*	[a] A. Agostinelli s.
16 VIII	MONTEVIDEO Solis	Hamlet	:: E. Clasenti s, J. Royer ms, M. Journet bs.
18 VIII	»	Falstaff	:: R. Raisa s, N. Vallin Pardo s, T. Schipa t, A. Crabbé b.
21 VIII	»	Il barbiere di Siviglia	:: M. Barrientos s, T. Schipa t, M. Gaudio bs.
24 VIII	»	Rigoletto	:: M. Barrientos s, T. Schipa t.
:: XI	SAINT JEU *Hôpital militaire auxiliare n. 207*	*Benefit concert*	
20 XI	NICE Eldorado[b]	Pagliacci (1)	H. Cas: F. Dereyne s, T. Salignac t, J. Janaur b.
1917			
27 IV	PARIS Opéra-Comique[b]	Pagliacci (1)	P. Vidal: B. Lamare s, C. Fontaine t, M. Bellet b.
1918			
17 XII	MADRID Real	La bohème	G. Falconi: E. Mazzoleni s, P. Barti s, G. Taccani t, L. Nicoletti-Kormann bs.

[a] Following the season in Buenos Aires, T. R. participated in a short tour organized in celebration of the centenary of Argentine independence, singing a total of 9 performances.

[b] For soldiers suffering from tuberculosis.

Date of First Performance		City/Theater	Opera and Other Performances	Conductor: Principal Soloists
1918				
22	XII	MADRID Real	Il barbiere di Siviglia	G. Falconi: J. Dufau s, U. Macnez t, V. Bettoni bs, G. Azzolini bs.
26	XII	»	Andrea Chénier**	G. Falconi: M. Roggero s, B. De Muro t.
::	XII	?	*Benefit concert*	
1919				
6	I	Real	Falstaff	G. Falconi: E. Mazzoleni s, P. Barti s, M. Gay ms, M. Capuana ms, G. Taccani t, G. Giardini b, V. Bettoni bs.
3	III	TRIESTE Verdi	*Concert for civic assistance*ᵃ	L. Mancinelli: L. Tetrazzini s.
29	IV	MEXICO CITY [12] Esperanza Iris	Pagliacci, and La Bohème Acts I & III	G. Polacco: E. Mason s, J. Palet t. G. Polacco: E. Mason s, P. Falco s, J. Palet t.
3	V	»	Il barbiere di Siviglia	:: C. Escobar de Castro s, E. Castellano t.
7	V	»	Rigoletto	G. Polacco: E. Mason s, F. Perini ms, J. Palet t, V. Lazzari bs.
16	V	»	Hamlet	G. Polacco: C. Escobar de Castro s, F. Perini ms, V. Lazzari bs.
18	V	Plaza "El Toreo"	Pagliacci	:: :: :: :: :: :: :: :: :: ::
24	V	Esperanza Iris	Andrea Chénier	G. Polacco: L. Lawrence s, A. Dolci t.
1	VI	Plaza "El Torco"	Hamlet	G. Polacco: C. Escobar de Castro s, F. Perini ms, V. Lazzari bs.
8	VI	»	Un ballo in maschera	G. Polacco: R. Raisa s, F. Perini ms, J. Palet t.
10	VI	Esperanza Iris	Otello	:: :: :: :: :: :: :: :: :: ::

ᵃ*Rigoletto*, Act III, final scene; selections from *Cristoforo Colombo*; "Il Canto del tricolore Trieste" by L. Mancinelli.

Date of First Performance		City/Theater	Opera and Other Performances	Conductor: Principal Soloists
1920				
5	I	CHICAGO Auditorium	Pagliacci (1)	G. Marinuzzi: M. Sharlow s, F. Lamont t.
10	I	»	Rigoletto (1)	G. Marinuzzi: F. Macbeth s, M. Claessens ms, T. Schipa t, V. Arimondi bs.
15	I	»	Hamlet (1)	M. Charlier: F. Macbeth s, C. Van Gordon ms, V. Lazzari bs.
18	I	»	*Concert*	Y. Gall s.
28	I	NEW YORK Lexington[a]	Pagliacci (1)	G. Marinuzzi: M. Santillan/A. Fitziu s, F. Lamont t, D. Defrère b.
1	II	*Hippodrome*	*Concert*	G. Marinuzzi: Y. Gall s.
13	II	Lexington	Hamlet (1)	M. Charlier: F. Macbeth s, C. Van Gordon ms, V. Lazzari bs.
20	II	»	Rigoletto (1)	G. Marinuzzi: A. Galli-Curci/L. Lilpkovska s, M. Claessens ms, T. Schipa t, E. Cotreuil bs.
27	II	*Hotel Commodore*	*Concert*	A. Rubinstein (piano): C. Van Gordon ms, I. Patterson
6	III	BOSTON Boston Opera[a]	Pagliacci	G. Marinuzzi: A. Fitziu s, F. Lamont t.
10	III	»	Rigoletto	G. Marinuzzi: F. Macbeth s, M. Claessens ms, T. Schipa t, E. Cotreuil bs.
1	III	PHILADELPHIA Metropolitan	*Concert*	
18	III	PITTSBURGH Syria Mosque[b]	Pagliacci	:: A. Fitziu s, F. Lamont t.
20	III	CINCINNATI Music Hall[b]	Pagliacci	G. Marinuzzi: A. Fitziu s, F. Lamont t, D. Defrère b.

[a]Chicago Opera Company.

[b]Chicago Opera Company tour.

Date of First Performance		City/Theater	Opera and Other Performances	Conductor: Principal Soloists
1920				
24	III	DETROIT Orchestra Hall[a]	Rigoletto	:: F. Macbeth s, F. Lamont t.
27	III	CLEVELAND Masonic Hall[a]	Pagliacci	:: M. Santillan s, F. Lamont t.
	III-IV	?	*Concert tour*	
1	V	NEW YORK *Hippodrome*	*Concert*	A. Rubinstein (piano): A. Fitziu s.
::	V	SPRINGFIELD (Mass.) ?	*Concert*	
20	X	SPRINGFIELD (Ill.) State Arsenal	Pagliacci	P. Cimini: M. Craft s, F. Lamont t, J. Mojica t, D. Defrère b.
22	X	DES MOINES Coliseum	Pagliacci	P. Cimini: M. Craft s, F. Lamont t.
25	X	SIOUX CITY (Iowa) ?	Pagliacci	:: :: :: :: (unconfirmed)
27	X	SIOUX FALLS (S. Dakota) ?	Pagliacci	:: :: :: :: (unconfirmed)
24	XI	CHICAGO Auditorium	Andrea Chénier (2)	G. Marinuzzi: R. Raisa s, E. Johnson t.
28	XI	»	Rigoletto (1)	G. Marinuzzi: F. Macbeth s, N. Pascova ms, J. Hislop t, V. Lazzari bs.
13	XII	»	**Edipo re***** (3)	G. Marinuzzi: D. Francis s, A. Paillard t, D. Defrère b, T. Dentale bs.
29	XII	»	Otello (1)	P. Cimini: R. Raisa s, C. Marshall t.

[a]Chicago Opera Company tour.

Date of First Performance		City/Theater	Opera and Other Performances	Conductor: Principal Soloists
1921				
19	I	HAVANA Nacional	Otello	A. Padovani: O. Nieto s, M. Salazar t.
22	I	»	Hamlet	A. Padovani: A. Ottein s, N. Lollini ms, R. Diaz t, V. Bettoni bs.
24	I	»	Pagliacci	A. Padovani: O Nieto s, M. Salazar t.
29	I	NEW YORK Manhattan[a]	Rigoletto	G. Marinuzzi: F. Macbeth s, T. Schipa t.
1	II	»	Otello (2)	P. Cimini: R. Raisa s, M. Claessens ms, C. Marshall t, V. Lazzari/T. Dentale bs.
13	II	*Hippodrome*	*Concert*	N. Sokoloff: Cleveland Symphony, M. Piastro
18	II	*Hotel Biltmore*	*Concert "Friday Morning Musicale"*	L. May, R. Vidas
19	II	Manhattan	Pagliacci (1)	P. Cimini: A. Zeppilli/ Maxwell s, E. Johnson t, D. Defrère b.
21	II	»	Edipo re*	G. Marinuzzi: D. Francis s, A. Paillard t, D. Defrère b, T. Dentale bs.
::	II	PHILADELPHIA Metropolitan	*Concert*	
1	III	NEW YORK Manhattan	Il barbiere di Siviglia	G. Marinuzzi: F. Macbeth s, T. Schipa t, V. Lazzari bs, V. Trevisan bs.
5	III	»	Hamlet	P. Cimini: F. Macbeth s, C. Van Gordon ms, J. Mojica t, T. Dentale bs, V. Lazzari bs.
9	III	BALTIMORE Lyric Theater	Otello	:: R. Raisa s, C. Marshall t.
12	III	PITTSBURGH *Syria Mosque*	Rigoletto	:: M. Craft s, A. Bonci t.

[a] Chicago Opera Company.

Date of First Performance		City/Theater	Opera and Other Performances	Conductor: Principal Soloists
1921				
17	III	CLEVELAND B. F. Keith Auditorium	Rigoletto	P. Cimini: M. Craft s, A. Bonci t, V. Lazzari bs.
24	IV	*Hippodrome*	*Concert*	L. Tetrazzini s.
30	X	KANSAS CITY Shubert	*Concert*[a]	
1922				
19	I	NEW YORK Metropolitan	Il barbiere di Siviglia (2)	G. Papi: C. Chase/A. Ottein s, M. Chamlee t, J. Mardones/A. Didur bs, P. Malatesta bs.
28	I	»	Ernani	G. Papi: R. Ponselle s, G. Martinelli t, J. Mardones bs.
31	I	Academy of Music	Il barbiere di Siviglia	G. Papi: A. Galli-Curci s, O. Harrold t, A. Didur bs, P. Ananian bs.
2	II	Metropolitan	Pagliacci (1)	R. Moranzoni: F. Easton s, M. Kingston t, M. Laurenti b.
19	II	*Hippodrome*	*Concert*	F. Hempel s.
5	V	LONDON *Queen's Hall*	*Concert*	
14	V	*Albert Hall*	*Concert*	
17	V	*?*	*Private Concert*	
24	IX	*Albert Hall*	*Concert*	C. Raybould (piano): M. Namara s, M. Bratza (violin).
22	X	BOSTON *Symphony Hall*	*Concert*	Y. D'Arle s.
29	X	NEW YORK *Hippodrome*	*Concert*[b]	A. Sciarretti (piano): Y. D'Arle s.
2	XI	PITTSBURGH *Syria Mosque ?*	*Concert*	
7	XI	PHILADELPHIA Metropolitan	*Concert*	

[a]In honor of General Armando Diaz.

[b]Benefit concert for Bronx Hospital.

Date of First Performance		City/Theater	Opera and Other Performances	Conductor: Principal Soloists
1922				
16	XII	NEW YORK Metropolitan	Ernani (4)	G. Papi: R. Ponselle s, G. Martinelli t, J. Mardones bs.
19	XII	Academy of Music	Pagliacci (1)	R. Moranzoni: E. Rethberg s, M. Kingston t, G. Schützendorf b.
1923				
3	I	Metropolitan	Pagliacci (2)	G. Papi: E. Rethberg s, E. Johnson t, V. Reschiglian b.
18	I	»	Aida (1)	R. Moranzoni: E. Rethberg s, J. Gordon ms, G. Martinelli t, J. Mardones bs.
29	I	»	Il barbiere di Siviglia (2)	G. Papi: A. Galli-Curci s, M. Chamlee t, A. Didur bs, P. Malatesta bs.
::	II	CHICAGO ?	*Concert*	Y. D'Arle s, F. Renk (violin).
::	III/IV	LOS ANGELES *Philharmonic Auditorium*	*Concert*	
::	III/IV	SAN FRANCISCO *Exposition Auditorium*	*Concert (2)*	
::	III/IV	SEATTLE *Arena*	*Concert*	
::	III/IV	PORTLAND *Auditorium*	*Concert*	
::	III/IV	SAVANNAH *Auditorium*	*Concert*	
24	IV	HAVANA[a] Nacional	Il barbiere di Siviglia	C. Peroni: J. Lucchese s, T. Schipa t, P. Ludikar bs, N. Cervi bs.

[a]San Carlo Opera Company of America.

Date of First Performance		City/Theater	Opera and Other Performances	Conductor: Principal Soloists
1923				
		HAVANA[a]		
26	IV	Nacional	Otello	C. Peroni: A. Fitziu s, A. Paoli t.
3	V	»	Aida	C. Peroni: M. Rappold s, S. De Mette ms, G. Martinelli t, N. Cervi bs, De Biasi bs.
6	V	»	Hamlet	C. Peroni: J. Lucchese s, S. De Mette ms, P. Ludikar bs.
12	V	»	Carmen	C. Peroni: M. Kuznetsov ms, Y. D'Arle s, G. Martinelli t.
14	V	»	La bohème	C. Peroni: L. Bori s, Y. D'Arle s, G. Martinelli t, D. Biasi bs.
15	V	»	Pagliacci	C. Peroni: L. Bori s, G. Martinelli t.
23	V	?	*Concert*	A. Bovi (piano).
		NEW YORK		
17	XII	Metropolitan	Andrea Chénier (1)	R. Moranzoni: R. Ponselle s, B. Gigli t.
25	XII	Academy of Music	Ernani (1)	G. Papi: R. Ponselle s, G. Martinelli t, J. Mardones bs.
28	XII	Metropolitan	Ernani (1)	G. Papi: R. Ponselle s, G. Martinelli t, J. Mardones bs.
1924				
		NEW YORK		
3	I	Metropolitan	Pagliacci (1)	G. Papi: L. Bori s, M. Fleta t, L. Tibbett b.
		HAVANA		
15	I	Nacional	Andrea Chénier	G. Soriente: O. Carrara s, A. Cortis t.
17	I	»	Tosca (1)	G. Soriente: O. Carrara s, A. Cortis t.
24	I	*Sala Payret*	*Concert*	

[a]San Carlo Opera Company of America.

Date of First Performance		City/Theater	Opera and Other Performances	Conductor: Principal Soloists
1924				
26	I	CIENFUEGOS Terry	Hamlet (1)	G. Soriente: P. Garavelli s, A. Salori ms, V. Bettoni bs.
28	I	»	La bohème (1)	G. Soriente: O. Carrara s, P. Garavelli s, A. Cortis t.
31	I	CAMAGUEY ::	Hamlet (1)	G. Soriente: P. Garavelli s, A. Salori ms, V. Bettoni bs.
3	II	SANTIAGO (Cuba) Oriente	Hamlet (1)	G. Soriente: P. Garavelli s, A. Salori ms, V. Bettoni bs.
15	II	S. JUAN DE PUERTO RICO Municipal	Hamlet (1)	G. Soriente: P. Garavelli s, A. Salori ms, V. Bettoni bs.
17	II	»	Il barbiere di Siviglia (1)	G. Soriente: P. Garavelli s, A. Pintucci t, V. Bettoni bs, V. Baldo bs.
20	II	»	Pagliacci (1)	G. Soriente: Y. D'Arle s, A. Cortis t, G. Puliti b.
22	II	PONCE Broadway	Hamlet (1)	G. Soriente; P. Garavelli s, A. Salori ms, V. Bettoni bs.
25	II	»	La bohème (1)	G. Soriente: O. Carrara s, P. Garavelli s, A. Cortis t.
27	II	S. JUAN DE PUERTO RICO Broadway	La bohème (1)	G. Soriente: O. Carrara s, P. Garavelli s, A. Cortis t.
8	III	CARACAS Municipal	Hamlet (1)	G. Soriente: P. Garavelli s, A. Salori ms, V. Bettoni bs.
11	III	»	Andrea Chénier (1)	G. Soriente: O. Carrara s, A. Cortis t.
13	III	»	Il barbiere di Siviglia (1)	G. Soriente: P. Garavelli s, A. Pintucci t, V. Bettoni bs, V. Baldo bs.

Date of First Performance		City/Theater	Opera and Other Performances	Conductor: Principal Soloists
1924				
16	III	CARACAS Municipal	Tosca (1)	G. Soriente: O. Carrara s, A. Cortis t.
20	III	»	Pagliacci (2)	G. Soriente: Y. D'Arle s, A. Cortis t, G. Puliti b.
14	IV	CARTAGENA Municipal	Hamlet (2)	G. Soriente: P. Garavelli s, A. Salori ms, V. Bettoni bs.
29	IV	BARRAN- QUILLA Cisneros	Hamlet (1)	G. Soriente: P. Garavelli s, A. Salori s, V. Bettoni bs.
11	V	BOGOTÀ Colón	Hamlet (1)	G. Soriente: P. Garavelli s, A. Salori ms, V. Bettoni bs.
15	V	»	Pagliacci (2)	G. Soriente: Y. D'Arle s, A. Cortis t, G. Puliti b.
17	V	»	Tosca (1)	G. Soriente: O. Carrara s, A. Cortis t.
22	V	»	Il barbiere di Siviglia (3)	G. Soriente: P. Garavelli s, A. Pintucci t, V. Bettoni bs, V. Baldo bs.
23	V	»	Aida (2)	G. Soriente: O. Carrara s, A. Salori ms, A. Cortis t, V. Bettoni bs.
3	VI	»	Rigoletto (2)	G. Soriente: P. Garavelli s, A. Salori ms, A. Pintucci t, V. Bettoni bs.
15	XII	NEW YORK Metropolitan	Andrea Chénier (1)[a]	T. Serafin: R. Ponselle s, B. Gigli t.
23	XII	Academy of Music	La Gioconda (1)	T. Serafin: F. Easton s, J. Gordon ms, M. Alcock ms, B. Gigli t, J. Mardones bs.

[a]Special performance for the Italian Hospital.

Date of First Performance		City/Theater	Opera and Other Performances	Conductor: Principal Soloists
1925				
2	I	NEW YORK Metropolitan	Aida (1)	G. Bamboschek: R. Ponselle s, J. Gordon ms, M. Fleta t, J. Mardones bs.
9	I	»	La Gioconda (1)	T. Serafin: R. Ponselle s, J. Gordon ms, M. Alcock ms, B. Gigli t, J. Mardones bs.
12	I	»	Il barbiere di Siviglia (1)	G. Papi: A. Galli-Curci s, R. Errolle t, A. Didur bs, P. Malatesta bs.
4	IV	BUDAPEST Operaház	Il barbiere di Siviglia (1)	D. Márkus: E. Sándor s, J. Somló t, B. Venczell bs, F. Hegedüs bs.
8	IV	»	Hamlet (1)	R. Máder: E. Sándor s, M. Basilides ms, B. Venczell bs.
13	IV	»	Rigoletto (1)	D. Márkus: E. Sándor s, R. Maraschalkó ms, K. Pataky t, M. Székely bs.
17	IV	BERLIN *Philharmonic*	*Concert*	
22	IV	Volksoper im Th. des Westens	Rigoletto (1)	I. Dobrowen: :: :: :: :: ::
5	V	BUDAPEST Városi Szinház	Tosca	E. Ábrányi: R. Walter s, J. Halmos t.
8	V	»	Pagliacci *(Concert of Italian songs between Acts I & II)*	E. Ábrányi: T. Köszegi s, K. Ocskay t, I. Balla b.
11	X	PISA Verdi	Hamlet (2)[a]	E. Mascheroni: A. Bucciantini s, F. Perini ms, N. Marotta bs.
7	XI	BARCELONA Liceo	**La cena delle beffe****	F. Paolantonio: H. Spani s, C. Folco Bottaro t.
11	XI	»	Tosca	F. Paolantonio: O. Carrara s, M. Fleta t.

[a]Benefit performances.

Date of First Performance		City/Theater	Opera and Other Performances	Conductor: Principal Soloists
1925				
11	XII	NEW YORK Metropolitan	La Gioconda (1)	G. Setti: R. Ponselle s, J. Gordon ms, M. Alcock ms, B. Gigli t, J. Mardones bs.
16	XII	»	Andrea Chénier (1)	G. Bamboschek: R. Ponselle s, B. Gigli t.
18	XII	»	Pagliacci (2)	G. Papi: Q. Mario s, E. Johnson/A. Tokatyan t, L. Tibbett/M. Picco b.
1926				
2	I	»	La cena delle beffe** (2)	T. Serafin: F. Alda s, B. Gigli t.
5	I	PHILADELPHIA Metropolitan	La cena delle beffe (1)	T. Serafin: F. Alda s, B. Gigli t.
20	I	CHICAGO Auditorium	Otello (1)	R. Moranzoni: A. Fitziu s, C. Marshall t.
30	I	BOSTON Boston Opera	Un ballo in maschera	G. Polacco: R. Raisa s, C. Van Gordon ms, C. Marshall t.
15	II	CLEVELAND Keith Palace	Tosca (1)	R. Moranzoni: C. Muzio s, C. Hackett t.
19	II	»	Otello F(1)	R. Moranzoni: R. Raisa s, C. Marshall t.
2	III	BIRMINGHAM Municipal Auditorium	La traviata (1)	R. Moranzoni: C. Muzio s, C. Hackett t.
5	III	MEMPHIS Auditorium	La traviata (1)	R. Moranzoni: C. Muzio s, C. Hackett t.
10	III	MIAMI Coral Gables Stadium	La traviata (1)	R. Moranzoni: C. Muzio s, A. Cortis t.
29	V	BUENOS AIRES Colón	Hamlet (5)	G. Marinuzzi: G. Pareto/ N. Morgana s, F. Anitúa/ A. Buades ms, E. Pinza bs.

Date of First Performance	City/Theater	Opera and Other Performances	Conductor: Principal Soloists
1926			
	BUENOS AIRES		
6 VI	Colón	Andrea Chénier (1)	G. Santini: C. Muzio s, G. Lauri-Volpi t.
18 VI	»	Pagliacci (3)	G. Santini: R. Pampanini s, A. Pertile t, G. Vanelli b.
5 VII	»	Tosca (2)	G. Santini: C. Muzio s, G. Lauri-Volpi t.
8 VII	*Coliseo*	*Benefit concert*	
14 VII	Colón	Il barbiere di Siviglia (3)	G. Santini: G. Pareto/N. Morgana s, R. D'Alessio t, E. Pinza/T. Pasero bs, G. Azzolini bs.
5 VIII	»	La bohème (1)	G. Marinuzzi: I. Marengo s, A. Morelli s, A. Pertile t, R. Rasponi b, E. Pinza bs.
	RIO DE JANEIRO		
17 VIII	Lyrico	Hamlet	G. Marinuzzi: G. Pareto s, A. Buades ms, E. Pinza bs.
22 VIII	»	Tosca (2)	G. Santini: C. Muzio s, G. Lauri-Volpi t.
25? VIII	»	Il barbiere di Siviglia	G. Santini: G. Pareto s, R. D'Alessio t, E. Pinza bs, G. Azzolini bs.
	NEW YORK		
12 XI	*WEAF Studio*	*Concert (broadcast)*	
10 XII	Metropolitan	La cena delle beffe (2)	T. Serafin: F. Alda s, B. Gigli t.
	PHILADELPHIA		
14 XII	Academy of Music[a]	Andrea Chénier (1)	T. Serafin: E. Rethberg s, G. Lauri-Volpi t.
	NEW YORK		
23 XII	Metropolitan	La Gioconda (1)	T. Serafin: R. Ponselle s, C. Van Gordon ms, M. Alcock ms, B. Gigli t, E. Pinza bs.
26 XII	»	*Benefit concert*[b]	G. Bamboschek: M. Talley s, M. Alcock ms, B. Gigli t.

[a]Metropolitan Opera Company.

[b]Selections from *Patrie* and *Rigoletto*.

Date of First Performance		City/Theater	Opera and Other Performances	Conductor: Principal Soloists
1927				
5	I	NEW YORK Metropolitan	Pagliacci (2)	V. Bellezza: Q. Mario s, G. Martinelli/V. Fullin t, G. Cehanovsky/L. Tibbett b.
8	I	*Mecca Temple*	*Concert*	
11	I	PHILADELPHIA Academy of Music[a]	La cena delle beffe (1)	T. Serafin: F. Alda s, B. Gigli t.
18	I	PITTSBURGH Syria Mosque[b]	Pagliacci (2)	P. Paci: F. Campiña s, J. De Gaviria t.
22	I	»	Tosca (1)	P. Paci: F. Campiña s, J. De Gaviria t.
29	I	PHILADELPHIA Metropolitan[b]	Otello	P. Paci: M. Cianci s, F. De Angelis t.
6	II	CLEVELAND *WTAM Studio*	*Concert (Broadcast)*	
31	V	PARIS Opéra	*Concert*	
10	VI	Opéra-Comique	Tosca (1)	A. Messager: C. Victrix s, A. Villabella t.
14	VII	*Salon des Ambassadeurs*	*Concert*[c]	
::	VII	DEAUVILLE Casino	La bohème (2)	:: :: :: :: :: :: :: :: :: ::
26	VIII	OSTENDE *Kursaal*	*Concert*	
19	IX	BERLIN Philharmonie	*Concert*	M. Raucheisen (piano)
16	XI	PHILADELPHIA Metropolitan[d]	Hamlet	W. Grigaitis: P. Garavelli s, R. Toniolo ms, M. Fat- tori bs.
30	XI	»	Otello	A. Rodzinski: M. Micketa s, F. De Angelis t.

[a]Metropolitan Opera Company.

[b]Philadelphia La Scala Company.

[c]Benefit concert sponsored by the President of the Republic.

[d]Pennsylvania Opera Company.

Date of First Performance		City/Theater	Opera and Other Performances	Conductor: Principal Soloists
1927				
		NEW YORK		
5	XII	Metropolitan	Andrea Chénier (2)	T. Serafin: F. Easton/R. Ponselle s, B. Gigli t.
14	XII	»	Aida (1)	T. Serafin: G. Stückgold s, L. Homer ms, G. Martinelli t, E. Pinza bs.
16	XII	»	Pagliacci (1)	V. Bellezza: Q. Mario s, G. Martinelli t, E. Marshall b.
29	XII	»	La Gioconda (1)	T. Serafin: R. Ponselle s, L. Homer ms, M. Alcock ms, B. Gigli t, L. Rothier bs.
1928				
2	I	»	Il barbiere di Siviglia (3)	V. Bellezza: A. Galli-Curci s, M. Chamlee t, E. Pinza/L. Rothier bs, P. Malatesta bs.
9	I	*WEAF Studio*	*Concert (broadcast)*	
		PHILADELPHIA		
8	II	Metropolitan[a]	Tosca (1)	A. Rodzinski: M. Sharlow s, G. Zenatello t.
		NEW YORK		
22	II	*Carnegie Hall*	*Concert*	
		PHILADELPHIA		
29	II	Metropolitan[a]	Andrea Chénier	A. Rodzinski: M. Sharlow s, G. Zenatello t.
		BUDAPEST		
27	IV	Városi Szinház	Tosca (1) *Concert* (after Tosca)	D. Márkus: X. Ragowska s, J. Halmos t.
30	IV	»	Il barbiere di Siviglia (1) *Concert* (in Act II of Barbiere)	D. Márkus: I. Zoltán s, M. Szedö t, Pajor J. Vermes, Medveczky.
		PARIS		
7	V	Champs-Elysées	*Concert*	
		SANTIAGO		
4	IX	Municipal	Hamlet (1)	G. Falconi: L. Pasini s, E. Casazza ms, M. Gaudio bs.

[a]Pennsylvania Opera Company.

Date of First Performance		City/Theater	Opera and Other Performances	Conductor: Principal Soloists
1928				
9	IX	SANTIAGO Municipal	Il barbiere di Siviglia (1)	G. Falconi: L. Pasini s, D. Borgioli t, M. Gaudio bs.
16	IX	»	Tosca (1)	G. Falconi: G. Cobelli s, A. Cortis t.
21	IX	»	Otello (1)	G. Falconi: G. Cobelli s, R. Zanelli t.
29	IX	VALPARAISO La Victoria	Hamlet (1)	G. Falconi: L. Pasini s, E. Casazza ms, M. Gaudio bs.
3	X	»	Tosca (1)	G. Falconi: G. Cobelli s, A. Cortis t.
14	X	BUENOS AIRES Colón	Hamlet, Act I and «Brindisi»[a]	A. De Angelis: L. Romelli s, E. Casazza ms, J. Lanskoy bs.
18	X	»	Il barbiere di Siviglia, Acts II & III[a]	C.A. Stiattesi: B. Sayão s, C. Rodriguez t, J. Lanskoy bs, A. Pacini bs.
23	X	»	Otello (1)	A. De Angelis: I. Alfani-Tellini s, R. Zanelli t.
27	X	»	Hamlet (1)	A. De Angelis: L. Romelli s, E. Casazza ms, J. Lanskoy bs.
31	X	MONTEVIDEO Solis	*Concert*	
6	XI	RIO DE JANEIRO *Palacio*	*Concert*	
8	XII	NEW YORK Metropolitan	Andrea Chénier (1)	T. Serafin: R. Ponselle s, G. Martinelli t.
17	XII	»	Ernani (1)	V. Bellezza: R. Ponselle s, G. Martinelli t, E. Pinza bs.

[a]Performance given in honor of the foreign ambassadors, on the occasion of the inauguration of H. Irigoyen as President of the Republic.

Date of First Performance		City/Theater	Opera and Other Performances	Conductor: Principal Soloists
1929				
1	I	»	Il barbiere di Siviglia (2)	V. Bellezza/G. Bamboschek: A. Galli-Curci s, A. Tokatyan t, E. Pinza/L. Rothier bs, P. Malatesta bs.
21	I	»	Pagliacci (1)	G. Bamboschek: N. Guilford s, E. Johnson t, E. Marshall b.
29	I	PHILADELPHIA Metropolitan	Il barbiere di Siviglia (1)	G. Bamboschek: A. Galli-Curci s, A. Tokatyan t, E. Pinza bs., P. Malatesta bs.
1	II	NEW YORK Metropolitan	Aida (2)	T. Serafin: M. Müller/L. Corona s, K. Branzell ms, G. Martinelli/G. Lauri-Volpi t, P. Ludikar bs.
3	III	Motion picture *Sam H. Harris*	Il Barbiere di Siviglia, "Largo al factotum" & Otello, "Credo"[a]	
24	VIII	OSTENDE *Kursaal*	*Concert*	
1930				
25	II	VIENNA *Grosser Konzerthaus*	*Concert*	P. Sirota (piano)
1	III	PARIS *Salle Pleyel*	*Concert*	
7	III	BRUSSELS *Palais des Beaux-Arts*	*Concert*	
18	III	WARSAW *Filharmonji*	*Concert*	
25	III	BUCHAREST *Opera Romãna*	Il barbiere di Siviglia (1)	:: Metaxas s, Oprisan t, N. Basu bs, Chicideanu bs.

[a] Produced by "Metro-Movietone" and projected for the first time in synchronized sound in the film *Madame X* OF M-G-M. The sound track has been released on Lp: "The Golden Age of Opera" EJS 142-A.

Date of First Performance		City/Theater	Opera and Other Performances	Conductor: Principal Soloists
1930				
17	VI	**ATHENS** *Olympia*	Il barbiere di Siviglia	A. Kiparissis: L. Perpinia s, M. Tomakos t, M. Blakopoilos bs, G. Moilas bs.
19	IX	**STOCKHOLM** Stadsteatern	*Concert*	K. Vehanen (piano)
21	IX	»	*Concert*	K. Vehanen (piano)
1	X	**COPENHAGEN** *Odd Fellows Palacet*	*Concert*	K. Vehanen (piano)
11	XII	**AMSTERDAM** *Concertgebouw*	*Concert*	
15	XII	**THE HAGUE** *Gebouw v.K. & W.*	*Concert*	
1931				
8	I	**NICE** Casino de la Je-tée-Promenade	*Concert*	
18	I	»	*Concert*	
4	II	**CANNES** Casino Municipal	Tosca	:: :: :: :: :: :: :: :: :: ::
9	II	**NICE** Casino de la Je-tée-Promenade	*Concert*	
11	II	**PAU** Nouveau Casino Municipal	*Concert*	
14	II	**CANNES** Casino Municipal	Hamlet	J. Spaandermann: M. Gallyot s, I. Gregoire ms.
18	II	**MARSEILLE** Casino Municipal	Il barbiere di Siviglia (1)	F. Melli: M. Gentile s, L. Cecil t, Billot bs, Enryale bs.
25	V	**BUENOS AIRES** Colón	Hamlet (3)	F. Calusio: I. Marengo s, Y. Allard ms, E. Pinza bs.
14	VI	»	*Concert*	
23	VI	»	Tosca (5)	F. Calusio: G. Gobelli s, G. Thill t.

Date of First Performance		City/Theater	Opera and Other Performances	Conductor: Principal Soloists
1931				
4	XII	GENEVA *Victoria-Hall*	*Concert*	
11	XII	AMSTERDAM *Concertgebouw*	*Concert*	
1932				
7	I	PARIS Salle Pleyel	*Concert*	M. Foa (piano): B. Sayão s.
20	I	MADRID *Avenida*	*Concert*	
26	I	»	*Concert*	
16	II	BARCELONA *Palau de la musica catalana*	*Concert*	P. Sirota (piano): G. Fisher s.
::	III	PARIS *Salle Gaveau*	*Concert*	
27	XII	NEW YORK *Radio City Music Hall*	Carmen (excerpts)	D. Defrère: C. Glade ms, A. Lindi t.
1933				
21	XI	LONDON ?	*Concert*	
1934				
25	II	NICE Casino de la Je-tée-Promenade	*Concert*	
8	III	»	*Concert*	
10	III	»	Hamlet, Act I, Scene 2, and Act III	H. Mario: M. Germain s, S. Joris ms, A. Philippe bs.
::	III	Eldorado	*Concert*	
24	III	PARIS ?	*Concert*	
1935				
2	II	CANNES Casino Municipal	*Concert*	

APPENDIX B

Repertory

RUFFO TITTA, JR.

Operatic Repertory

Operas Performed

OPERA	*COMPOSER*	*ROLE/YEAR FIRST PERFORMED*
Adriana Lecouvreur	F. Cilea	Michonnet/1904
Africaine, L'	G. Meyerbeer	Nelusko/1900
Aida	G. Verdi	Amonasro/1900
Andrea Chénier	U. Giordano	Carlo Gérard/1900
Aurora	H. Panizza	Don Ignazio Dal Puente/1908
Ballo in masachera, Un	G. Verdi	Renato/1899
Barbiere di Siviglia, Il	G. Rossini	Figaro/1903
Bohème, La	G. Puccini	Marcello/1899
Boris Godunov	M. Mussorgski	title role/1916
Carmen	G. Bizet	Escamillo/1899
Cavalleria rusticana	P. Mascagni	Alfio/1899
Cena delle beffe, La	U. Giordano	Neri Chiaramantesi/1925
Cristoforo Colombo	A. Franchetti	title role/1909
Demon	A. G. Rubinstein	title role/1905
Don Carlo	G. Verdi	Rodrigo/1911
Don Giovanni	W.A. Mozart	title role/1908
Don Pasquale	G. Donizetti	Dottor Malatesta/1907
Edipo re	R. Leoncavallo	title role/1920
Ernani	G. Verdi	Don Carlo/1900
Evgenii Onegin	P.I. Chaikovskii	title role/1911
Falstaff	G. Verdi	title role/1916
Fanciulla del West, La	G. Puccini	Jack Rance/1911

OPERA	COMPOSER	ROLE/YEAR FIRST PERFORMED
Faust	C. Gounod	Valentin/1899
»	»	Méphistophélès/1913
Favorita, La	G. Donizetti	Alfonso XI/1899
Fedora	U. Giordano	De Siriex/1901
Forza del destino, La	G. Verdi	Don Carlo di Vargas/1898
Germania	A. Franchetti	Carlo Worms/1904
Gioconda, La	A. Ponchielli	Barnaba/1899
Griselda	J. Massenet	Marquis de Saluzzo/1904
Hamlet	A. Thomas	title role/1907
Iris (?)	P. Mascagni	Kyoto/1901
Jongleur de Nôtre-Dame, Le	J. Massenet	Frère Boniface/1905
Linda di Chamonix	G. Donizetti	Antonio/1906
Lohengrin	R. Wagner	Heerrufer (Herald)/1898
»	»	Friedrich von Telramund/1903
Lucia di Lammermoor	G. Donizetti	Lord Enrico Ashton/1898
Manon Lescaut	G. Puccini	Lescaut/1899
Nabucco	G. Verdi	title role/1901
Otello	G. Verdi	Jago/1900
Pagliacci	R. Leoncavallo	Tonio/1899
Paolo e Francesca	L. Mancinelli	Gianciotto/1908
Proserpina	C. Saint-Saëns	Squarrocca/1903
Rigoletto	G. Verdi	title role/1898
Ruy Blas	F. Marchetti	Don Sallustio/1898
Salinara, La	D. Brescia	Toni/1900
Samson et Dalila	C. Saint-Saëns	Le Grand-Prêtre/1901
Santo, Il	F. Ghin	Publio-Satana/1903
Siberia	U. Giordano	Gléby/1904
Thaïs	J. Massenet	Athanael/1911
Tosca	G. Puccini	Scarpia/1901
Traviata, La	G. Verdi	Giorgio Germont/1900
Tristan und Isolde	R. Wagner	Kurwenal/1903
Trovatore, Il	G. Verdi	Il conte di Luna/1898
Zazà	R. Leoncavallo	Cascart/1902

Religious Works Performed

OPERA	COMPOSER	ROLE/YEAR FIRST PERFORMED
Risurrezione di Lazzaro, La[a]	L. Perosi	Cristo/1899
Messa	L. Barrella	?/1899
Immacolata, L'	G. Mattioli	?/1904

[a] Oratorio

Operas Studied But Not Performed

OPERA	COMPOSER	ROLE
Amica	P. Mascagni	Rinaldo
Antonio e Cleopatra	E. F. de Wittgenstein	?
Bohème, La	R. Leoncavallo	Schaunard
Chatterton	R. Leoncavallo	title role[a]
Crispino e la comare	F. and L. Ricci	Fabrizio
Damnation de Faust, La	H. Berlioz	Méphistophélès
Dinorah	G. Meyerbeer	Hoel
Enoch Arden	G. Coronaro	title role
Fliegende Holländer, Der	R. Wagner	title role
Loreley	A. Catalani	Hermann
Manon	J. Massenet	Lescaut
Papà Martin	A. Cagnoni	title role
Siegfried	R. Wagner	Der Wanderer
Tannhäuser	R. Wagner	Wolfram von Eschenbach
Walküre, Die	R. Wagner	Wotan

Note: Compiled from scores and contracts.

Concert Repertory

Opera Arias

L'Africaine (Meyerbeer): Adamastor
Andrea Chénier (Giordano): Son sessant'anni; Nemico della patria
Un ballo in maschera (Verdi): Eri tu
Carmen (Bizet): Toreador song
Chatatterton[a] (Leoncavallo): Tu sola a me rimani
Cristoforo Colombo (Franchetti): Notturno
Demon (Rubinstein): Aria
Dinorah (Meyerbeer): Sei vendicata assai
Don Carlo (Verdi): Per me giunto
Don Giovanni (Mozart): Finch'han dal vino; Deh, vieni alla finestra
Falstaff (Verdi): Quand'ero paggio
La forza del destino (Verdi): Urna fatale
Hamlet (Thomas): Drinking song
Le jongleur de Notre-Dame (Massenet): Légende de la Sauge
Macbeth (Verdi): Son lontano
Pagliacci (Leoncavallo): Prologue
Patrie (E. Paladilhe): Pauvre martyr obscur
Panurge (Massenet): Chanson de la Touraine
I puritani (Bellini): Ah, per sempre
Tizianello (V. Billi): Canzone pastorale

[a] The role was composed for tenor, but Leoncavallo decided to rewrite it for baritone expressly for Titta Ruffo who, although he had studied the role, never performed it on stage.

Songs

Die beiden Grenadiere (R. Schumann)
Chitarrata abruzzese (F. P. Tosti)
Credo du paysan (G. Goublier)
Cubanita (J. Huarte)
La danza: tarantella napoletana (G. Rossini)
E suonan le campane (E. Titta)
Giovanottino (canzone toscana)
Inno di Mameli (M. Novaro)
Inno di Oberdan (A. Buzzi Peccia)
Lolita (A. Buzzi Peccia)
Marechiare (F. P. Tosti)
Maria, Marì! (E. Di Capua)
La Marseillaise (C. J. Rouget de Lisle)
Mattutino (P. M. Costa)
Oh, che m'importa (E. Titta)
Meriggiata (R. Leoncavallo)
Munasterio (P. M. Costa)
Novembre (E. Tremisot)
El perjuro (M. Tejada)
Querida (A. Seismit-Doda)
El relicario (J. Padilla)
Santa Lucia (T. Cottrau)
Sei morta nella vita mia (P. M. Costa)
Siamo in maggio (E. Titta)
Suonn'e fantasia (G. Capolongo)
Torna a Surriento (E. De Curtis)
Until (J. Sanderson)
Visione veneziana (R. Brogi)

APPENDIX C

Theaters

RUFFO TITTA, JR.

Europe		
COUNTRY	*CITY*	*THEATER—YEAR(S)*
AUSTRIA	Vienna	Hofoper—1906
		Grosser Konzerthaus—1930
BELGIUM	Brussels	Palais des Beaux-Arts—1930
	Ostende	Kursaal—1914, 1927, 1929
DENMARK	Copenhagen	Odd Fellows Palacet—1930
ENGLAND	London	Albert Hall—1922
		Covent Garden—1903
		Grosvenor Square 33—1903
		Lady Kleinwort's Palace—1909
		Queen's Hall—1922
		?—1933
FRANCE	Cannes	Casino Municipal—1931, 1935
	Deauville	Casino—1912, 1927
	Marseille	Casino Municipal—1931
	Nice	Casino de la Jetée-Promenade—1931, 1934
		Eldorado—1916, 1934
		Vaisseau Amiral "Patrie"—1909
	Paris	Champs-Elysées—1913, 1928
		Opéra—1911, 1912, 1927
		Opéra-Comique—1917, 1927
		Palais Comtesse Château—1905
		Palais Stern—1909

COUNTRY	CITY	THEATER—YEAR(S)
FRANCE	Paris	Rue Nitot 31—1912
		Salle Gaveau—1932
		Salle Pleyel—1930, 1932
		Salon des Ambassadeurs—1927
		Sarah Bernhardt—1905
		Trocadéro—1905, 1911
		?—1934
	Pau	Nouveau Casino Municipal—1931
	Saint Jeu	Hôpital Militaire Auxiliaire—1916
GERMANY	Berlin	Königliches Opernhaus—1907
		Philharmonie—1925, 1927
		Volksoper im Theater des Westens—1925
GREECE	Athens	Olympia—1930
HUNGARY	Budapest	Operaház—1912, 1925
		Népopera—1913
		Városi Szinház—1925, 1928
ITALY	Acireale	Bellini—1899
	Bergamo	Donizetti—1904
	Bologna	Corso—1914
		Duse—1899, 1900
	Catania	Chiesa dei Benedettini—1899
		Nazionale—1899
	Catanzaro	Comunale—1898, 1899
	Ferrara	Tosi-Borghi—1900
	Florence	La Pergola—1904
		Verdi—1912, 1914
	Genoa	Carlo Felice—1900
		Politeama Genovese—1915
	Livorno	Arena Alfieri—1898
		Bagni Pancaldi—1898
		Goldoni—1901
	Milan	Carcano—1914
		Famiglia Artistica Milanese—1904
		Lirico—1904, 1905, 1906, 1907
		La Scala—1904
	Naples	Circolo Artistico—1910
		Politeama Giacosa—1911
		San Carlo—1908, 1909, 1910, 1911
	Padua	Garibaldi—1899
	Palermo	Massimo—1901
	Parma	Regio—1900
	Pisa	Politeama—1898
		R. Teatro Nuovo—1901
		Verdi—1925
	Racconigi	Castello Reale—1909
	Rome	Costanzi—1898, 1909, 1910, 1911
	Salerno	Duomo—1899
		Municipale—1899

COUNTRY	CITY	THEATER—YEAR(S)
ITALY	Salsomaggiore	Ferrario—1902
	Siena	dei Rinnovati—1901
	Syracuse	Massimo—1899
	Trieste	La Fenice—1901
		Verdi—1919
	Venice	La Fenice—1903, 1912
		Rossini—1903
MONACO	Monte Carlo	Grand-Théâtre—1907, 1908, 1909, 1910, 1911, 1912
NETHERLANDS	Amsterdam	Concertgebouw—1930, 1931
	The Hague	Gebouw v. K. & W.—1930, 1931
POLAND	Warsaw	Filharmonji—1907, 1930
		Wielki—1907
PORTUGAL	Lisbon	São Carlos—1907, 1908
RUMANIA	Bucharest	National—1907
		Opera Românâ—1930
RUSSIA	Khar'kov	Municipal—1906
	Kiev	Solovzov—1906
	Moscow	Imperial (Bol'shoi)—1905, 1906, 1907
	Odessa	Municipal—1905, 1906
		Sibiriak?—1906
	Petersburg	Aquarium—1906
		Hall of the Cadets—1906
		Imperial?—1906
		New Conservatory—1905, 1906, 1907
		New Opera?—1906
		Nikolai I. Orphanage—1906
		School of Technology—1907
SPAIN	Barcelona	Liceo—1908, 1913, 1916, 1925
		Palau de la Musica Catalana—1932
	Madrid	Avenida—1932
		Palacio Real—1908, 1909, 1910, 1916
		Real—1908, 1910, 1911, 1912, 1913, 1918, 1919
		Zarzuela—1916
	San Sebastiano	Gran Teatro Circo—1913
	Valencia	Principal—1908, 1909, 1913, 1916
SWEDEN	Stockholm	Stadsteatern—1930
SWITZERLAND	Geneva	Victoria Hall—1931
	Lucerne	Kursaal—1900

Africa

EGYPT	Alexandria	Zizinia—1902, 1903
	Cairo	Khedival—1901, 1902, 1903

North America

COUNTRY	CITY	THEATER—YEAR(S)
CANADA	Toronto	Massen Hall—1914
CUBA	Havana	Nacional—1915, 1921, 1923, 1924
		Sala Payret—1924
	Camaguey	?—1924
	Cienfuegos	Terry—1924
	Matanzas	Sauto—1915
	Ponce	Broadway—1924
	Santiago	Oriente—1924
MEXICO	Mexico City	Esperanza Iris—1919
		Nacional—1921
		Plaza "El Toreo"—1919
PUERTO RICO	Ponce	Broadway—1924
	San Juan	Municipal—1924
UNITED STATES	Baltimore	Ford's Grand Opera?—1913
		Lyric Theater—1921
	Birmingham	Municipal Auditorium—1926
	Boston	?—1914
		Boston Opera—1920, 1926
		Symphony Hall—1922
	Buffalo	Broadway—1914
	Chicago	Auditorium—1912, 1913, 1920, 1926
		?—1914, 1923
	Cincinnati	Music Hall—1914, 1920
	Cleveland	B. F. Keith Auditorium—1921
		Keith Palace—1926
		Masonic Hall—1920
		WTAM Studio—1927
	Columbus	?—1914
	Dallas	Coliseum—1914
	Denver	Auditorium—1914
	Des Moines	Coliseum—1920
	Detroit	Armory—1914
		Orchestra Hall—1920
	Kansas City	Shubert—1921
	Los Angeles	Philharmonic Auditorium—1914, 1923
	Memphis	Auditorium—1926
	Miami	Coral Gables Stadium—1926
	Minneapolis	Armory—1914
	New York	Academy of Music (Brooklyn)—1922, 1923, 1924
		Carnegie Hall—1912
		Hippodrome—1912, 1914, 1920, 1921, 1922
		Hotel Biltmore—1920
		Hotel Commodore—1920
		Lexington—1920

COUNTRY	CITY	THEATER—YEAR(S)
UNITED STATES	New York	Manhattan—1915, 1921
		Mecca Temple—1927
		Metropolitan—1912, 1922, 1923, 1924, 1925, 1926, 1927, 1928, 1929
		Radio City Music Hall—1932
		St. Denis—1914
		WEAF Studio—1926, 1928
	Paterson	Regent—1914
	Philadelphia	Academy of Music—1926, 1927, 1929
		Metropolitan—1912, 1913, 1914, 1920, 1921, 1922, 1926, 1927, 1928, 1929
	Pittsburgh	Syria Mosque—1920, 1921, 1922, 1927
	Portland	Auditorium—1923
		Orpheum—1914
	St. Louis	Odeon—1914
	St. Paul	Auditorium—1914
	San Francisco	Exposition Auditorium—1923
	Savannah	Auditorium—1923
	Seattle	Arena—1923
		Orpheum—1914
	Sioux City (Iowa)	?—1920
	Sioux Falls (S. Dakota)	?—1920
	Springfield (Ill.)	State Arsenal—1920
	Springfield (Mass.)	?—1920
	Toledo	?—1914
	Washington, D.C.	Vanderbilt's—1914

South America

COUNTRY	CITY	THEATER—YEAR(S)
ARGENTINA	Buenos Aires	La Argentina—1908
		Avenida—1910
		Coliseo—1916, 1926
		Colón—1908, 1909, 1910, 1911, 1915, 1916, 1926, 1928, 1931
		Odeón—1909
		La Opera—1902
		Palacio de Castellis—1910
		Palacio Mihanovich—1910
	Córdova	Rivera Indarte—1916
	La Plata	Argentino—1908
	Rosario di Santa Fe	Colón—1911, 1916
	Tucumán	Odeón—1916
BRAZIL	Rio de Janeiro	Lyrico—1911, 1926
		Municipal—1915

COUNTRY	CITY	THEATER—YEAR(S)
BRAZIL	Rio de Janeiro	Palacio—1928
	São Paulo	Municipal—1911, 1915
CHILE	Santiago	Municipal—1900, 1928
	Valparaiso	Victoria—1900, 1928
COLOMBIA	Barranquilla	Cisneros—1924
	Bogotá	Colón—1924
	Cartagena	Municipal—1924
URUGUAY	Montevideo	Solis—1902, 1908, 1916, 1928
		Urquiza—1909, 1910, 1911, 1915, 1916
VENEZUELA	Caracas	Municipal—1924

The Recordings of Titta Ruffo—
A Discography

WILLIAM R. MORAN

Dedicated to the memory of RICHARD BONELLI (1889-1980):
one of Ruffo's greatest admirers and a true successor

The recording career of Tita Ruffo covered some thirty years and clearly defines the parabolic trace of his artistic career which he himself so clearly recognized. His first group of recordings were made in Paris in the year 1904 for the Pathé Frères Company. These were originally recorded on wax cylinders, and were sold in that form as well as vertical cut discs, the latter made from the original master cylinders by a pantograph process. In their early form the discs came in several sizes, from 8 to 14 inches in diameter, first single faced, and later coupled in various combinations. The titles were etched in the centers, and the records played from the inside to the outer rim, at speeds around 90 revolutions per minute. Cylinders and early discs all bore the master cylinder number (4200 through 4213 and 4260) and all were announced by the artist. In the 'teens and twenties the same recordings were made available in a new form: The size was standardized at about 11½ inches, playing speeds were fairly well established at 80 rpm, the recordings played from the outside in, and the original spoken announcements were removed. The discs were still vertical cut ("hill-and-dale"), and special reproducers were required to play them on most machines. Fortunately for today's listeners, many of them have been transcribed to Long Playing recordings, although not all such transcriptions have been made at the proper playing speeds. Correct playing speeds cannot be given for the Pathé records, as the speeds varied from copy to copy of the same selection.

From 1907 to 1933 Ruffo recorded for the Gramophone Company ("His Master's Voice") in Milan and London and its affiliated company, The Victor Talking Machine Co., in New York and Camden, N.J. These records, issued by each company under its own cataloging numbers, are listed together in Part II. of this discography. Through the years, various titles were re-made and substituted. During the period when Ruffo recorded for these two concerns, recording speeds were far from standardized and strangely, no written record was maintained of the turntable speeds used when the records were made. To reproduce these recordings properly, they must be played at the speeds at which they were recorded. The determination of playing speed of each record is a painstaking job requiring much subjective judgement and many hours of study and comparison. The playing speeds given in the discography have been determined by the author from recordings in his personal collection, and are offered as "best judgment" recommendations.

Recordings made in the United States by Victor can be identified by the matrix number letter prefix: B or BVE which indicate 10-inch recordings, the first made by the acoustical process and the latter electrically made. Similarly, C and CVE prefixes indicate 12-inch Victor recordings. All matrix numbers not prefixed as above were made in Europe by the acoustical process, with the exception of the 10-inch electrical recordings made in London in 1933 which have an OB prefix. Those ending in the letters *ai, c, f, i,* and *v* are 12-inch recordings; all others are 10-inches in size.

Exact recording dates for the Victor records, as well as information on unpublished recordings have been obtained from data in the Victor files being compiled at the Stanford Archive of Recorded Sound. The author wishes to express his appreciation to his associate in this work, Mr. Ted Fagan.

Two recordings not of HMV-Victor origin have been included for convenience in Part II.: these are from sound films (see: Discography Nos. 30 and 89).

An asterisk preceding a discography number indicates that there is a note on that recording at the end of this appendix.

The present Discography is a corrected and updated version of the one originally published in the reprint edition of Titta Ruffo: *La mia parabola* (New York: Arno Press, 1977). Dr. Ruffo Titta, the singer's son, and Mr. E. G. Mathews were most helpful with their comments on the first edition. The author wishes to express his appreciation to Mr. Andrew Farkas, editor of this book, for his assistance in the preparation of the Discography.

August, 1980

Part I. Cie. Pathé Frères, Paris, 1904

(All with Piano Accompaniment)

Dis-cog. No. SF & Master Cyl No.	DF Cat. No. Italy	DF Cat. No. France	DF Cat. No. U.K.	DF Cat. No. U.S.A.	Transcriptions to Lateral Cut Discs	
					At 78 rpm	*Long Playing Discs*
1. AMLETO: O vin discaccia la tristezza (Thomas) (I)						
4202	10067	0556	5244	60011	—	TAP 309; Scala 812
2. IL BARBIERE DI SIVIGLIA: Largo al factotum (Rossini) (I)						
4203	10067	0556	5244	60011	—	TAP 309; Scala 812
3. La BOHEME: O Mimì, tu più non torni (Puccini) (w. Amedeo Bassi) (I)						
4260	12569	0559 2582	—	—	—	Scala 812
4. CHATTERTON: Tu sola a me rimani o poesia (Leoncavallo) (I)						
4210	10069	—	—	—	IRCC 3027	TAP 309; Scala 812; HRS 3005
5. DINORAH: Sei vendicata assai (Meyerbeer) (I)						
4212		—	—	—	—	—
6. DON CARLO: Per me giunto (Verdi) (I)						
4211	10069	—	—	—	—	TAP 309; TAP 314; Scala 812; HRS 3005
7. FAUST: Stammi ad udir, Margherita! (Morte di Valentino) (Gounod) (I)						
4208	10286	0558	5245	60038	HRS 1085	TAP 309; Scala 812
8 La FAVORITA: Vien, Leonora (Donizetti) (I)						
4204	10068	—	—	—	IRCC 3110	—

Discog. No.	SF & Master Cyl No.	DF Cat. No. Italy	DF Cat. No. France	DF Cat. No. U.K.	DF Cat. No. U.S.A.	Transcriptions to Lateral Cut Discs	
						At 78 rpm	Long Playing Discs
9.	FEDORA: La donna russa (Giordano) (I) 4209	—	—	—	—	—	HRS 3005; Scala 855
	HAMLET see: AMLETO						
10.	Mia sposa sarà la mia bandiera (A. Rotoli) (I) 4213	—	—	—	—	—	—
11.	SIBERIA: O bella mia (Giordano) (I) 4205	10286	0558	5245	—	HRS 1085	TAP 309; Scala 855
12.	La TRAVIATA: Di Provenza il mar (Verdi) (I) 4207	—	—	—	—	—	TAP 309; Scala 812; HRS 3005
13.	Il TROVATORE: Il balen del suo sorriso (Verdi) (I) 4206	10068	—	—	—	—	TAP 309; HRS 3005
14.	ZAZA: Buona Zazà, del mio buon tempo (Leoncavallo) (I) 4200	10066	—	5677	—	—	TAP 309; Scala 812
15.	ZAZA: Zazà, piccola zingara (Leoncavallo) (I) 4201	10066	—	5677	—	—	TAP 309; Scala 812

Discog. No.	Matrix No.	Date	SF Victor Cat. No.	DF Victor Cat. No.	SF HMV Cat. No.	DF HMV Cat. No.	Special "78" Rpm Issues	Speed of Original	Transcription to Ep or Lp discs
16.	L'AFRICANA: All'erta, Marinar! (Meyerbeer) (I) (Or. Rogers)								
	B-15894-1	14 Apr. '15	87223	817	7-52072	DA 164	—	77.43	LM 20110; VL 47215
17.	L'AFRICANA: Adamastor, re dell'acque profonde (Meyerbeer) (I) (Or. '20 Pasternack; '29 Bourdon)								
	C-23947-1, 2	20 Apr. '20	88622	6262	2-052186	DB 406	—	76.00	VIC 1680; LM 20150; VL 47215
	CVE-23947-3	18 Feb. '29	—	—	—	—	—	77.43	—
	-4	20 Mar. '29	—	7153	(42-736)	DB 1397	—	—	—
18.	AMLETO: Apparizione dello Spettro ("Angels and ministers of grace defend us!") (Shakespeare) (Spoken, in Italian)								
	1467u	? '14	87381	985	51097	DA 352	—	76.60?	—
*19.	AMLETO: Essere o non essere ("To be, or not to be...") (Shakespeare) (Spoken, in Italian)								
	1463u	? '14	87382	985	51098	DA 170	—	76.60?	—
	OB-5470-1	24 Nov. '33	—	—	—	—	—	—	—
20.	AMLETO: Nega se puoi la luce (Thomas) (w. Maria Galvany) (I) (Or. Sabaino)								
	1312½c	? '07	92500	8055	054180	—	—	74.23	Rococo R16; ORL 217; Scala 855; COLH 155
21.	AMLETO: Spettro infernal, immagin venerata (Thomas) (I) (Or. Sabaino)								
	10898½ b	? '07	87153	935	2-52622	DA 170	AGSA 16	74.23	Rococo R16; ORL 217; Scala 855; COLH 155

Dis-cog. No.	Matrix No.	Date	SF Victor Cat. No.	DF Victor Cat.No.	SF HMV Cat.No.	DF HMV Cat.No.	Special "78" Rpm Issues	Speed of Original	Transcription to Ep or Lp discs
22.	AMLETO: Spettro santo! ombra vendicatrice (Thomas) (I) (Or. Sabaino)								
	10897b	? '07	87154	935	2-52621	DA 352	AGSA 16	74.23	Rococo R16; ORL 217; Scala 855; COLH 155
*23.	AMLETO: O vin, discaccia la tristezza (Thomas) (I) (Or. '07 Sabaino; '20 Pasternack)								
	1315c	? '07	92037	—	052188	DB 569	—	74.23	Rococo R16; COLH 155; ORL 217
	C-24110-1,-2	13 May, '20	88619	6266 / 18140	—	—	—	76.00	VIC 1394; LM 20150; VL 47216
24.	AMLETO: Essere o non essere (Monologo) (Thomas) (I) (Or. Sabaino)								
	1329c	? '07	92042	6403	052189	—	—	74.23	ORL 217; COLH 155
25.	AMLETO: Com il romito fior (Thomas) (I) (Or. Sabaino)								
	2732f	? Nov. '08	92064	6403	052248	DB 569	—	79.13	Rococo R16; ORL 217; EB 37; Scala 855; COLH 155
26.	ANDREA CHENIER: Son sessant'anni (Giordano) (I) (Or. Pasternack)								
	B-24621-1,-2	11 Oct. '20	87325	817	7-52173	DA 351	—	76.00	VIC 1680; LM 20150; VL 47216
*27.	ANDREA CHENIER: Nemico della patria?!...Un di m'era di gioia (Giordano) (I) (Or. '20 Pasternack; '29 Bourdon)								
	C-24622-1,-2	11 Oct. '20	88626	6262	2-052187	DB 242	—	76.00	VIC 1680; VL 47216

Matrix	Date						Timing	Reissues
CVE-24622-3	18 Feb. '29	—	7153	(42-755)	DB 1397	DB 5386	77.43	17-0047; LM 20110; LCT 1006

28. Un BALLO IN MASCHERA: Alla vita che t'arride (Verdi) (I) (Or. Rogers?)

Matrix	Date						Timing	Reissues
B-12622-1	17 Nov. '12	87113	937	7-52036	DA 358	—	76.60	VL 47215

29. Un BALLO IN MASCHERA: Eri tu che macchiavi quell'anima (Verdi) (I) (Or. Rogers)

Matrix	Date						Timing	Reissues
C-15895-1	14 Apr. '15	88544	6266	2-052170	DB 398	II	77.43	LM 20110; VL 47215

*30. Il BARBIERE DI SIVIGLIA: Largo al factotum (Rossini) (I) (Or. '07 & '12 Sabaino; '20 Pasternack; '26 Bourdon)

Matrix	Date						Timing	Reissues
791 c	? '07	92039	6405	052132	DB 502		77.43	VIC 1680
463ai	? '12	88391		052380		76038	76.00	COLH 155
C-23945-1,-2	19 Apr. '20	88391	6263	2-052184	DB 405	—	76.00	LM 20110; VL 47216
CVE-23945-3,-4	26 Feb. '26							
Sound Film Disc	28 Feb. '29	No. 364-6A	(a-128 - 495 ft.)				33.33	EJS 142

31. Il BARBIERE DI SIVIGLIA: Dunque io son? (Rossini) (w. Maria Galvany) (I) (Or. Sabaino)

Matrix	Date						Timing	Reissues
1328½c	? '07	92501	8054	054181	DB 400	—	74.23	HER 407; TAP 332; Scala 855; VIC 1680

*32. La BOHEME: In un coupè...O Mimì, tu più non torni (Puccini) (w. Beniamino Gigli) (I) (Or. Bourdon)

Matrix	Date						Timing	Reissues
CVE-37320-1,-2	17 Dec. '26					AGSB 56	77.43	EJS 111; LM 20150; VL 47215
-3	17 Dec. '26							49-1422

*33. CARMEN: Ecco alfin ognun si tace (Canzone del Toreador, 2nd verse) (Bizet) (I) (w. Chorus) (Or. '08 Sabaino; '23 Bourdon)

Matrix	Date						Timing	Reissues
2736f	25 Nov. '08	92065	6406	052249	DB 406	DB 5386	79.13	
C-27751-1,-2	11 Apr. '23							—
-3	27 Nov. '23							—

Discog. No.	Matrix No.	Date	SF Victor Cat. No.	DF Victor Cat.No.	SF HMV Cat.No.	DF HMV Cat.No.	Special "78" Rpm Issues	Speed of Original	Transcription to Ep or Lp discs
*34.	CHATTERTON: Tu sola a me rimani o poesia (Leoncavallo) (I) (Or. Sabaino)								
	9228e	25 Nov. '08	87155	—	2-52686	VA 16	—	79.13	Rococo R16
35.	Chitarrata Abruzzese (Abruzzi Serenade) (Riccardo Mazzola—F. Paolo Tosti) (I) (Mandolin, Bianculli; Guitar, E. Cibelli; Or. Bourdon)								
	B-31699-1,-2	21 Jan. '25	—	1076	(7-52332)	DA 769	—	76.00	CL 99-63
36.	Le Credo du Paysan (Borel—Goublier) (F) (Or. Bourdon)								
	B-29035-1,-2,-3	27 Nov. '23	—	1070	(7-52259)	DA 703	—	76.00	—
37.	CRISTOFORO COLOMBO: Perchè piangete ignavi?...Aman lassù le stelle (Franchetti) (I) (Or. Rogers)								
	C-14517-1	26 Feb. '14	88486	—	2-052096	DB 179	AGSB 28	76.00	LM 20110; VL 47216
38.	CRISTOFORO COLOMBO: Dunque ho sognato? (Franchetti) (I) (Or. Pasternack)								
	C-25213-1,-2	14 Apr. '21	88668	6429	(2-052226)	DB 179	AGSB 28	76.00	LM 20110; VL 47216
*39.	Cubanita (Schipa—Huarte) (Spanish) (Or. Bourdon)								
	B-31694-1,-2	21 Jan. '25	—	—		—		76.00	EJS 223
*40.	Dai canti d'amore (Canzone) (Ettore Titta) (I) (Or. Sabaino)								
	464ai	? '12	88395	15-1028	052382	—		76.00	—
*41.	La DANNAZIONE DI FAUST: Che fai tu qui (Serenata di Mefistofele) (Berlioz) (I) (Or. Pasternack)								
	B-27026-1,-2	13 Oct. '22				DA 164		76.00	—
	-3,-4,-5	18 Oct. '22	87369	963	7-52226				
42.	La Danza (Tarantella) (Rossini) (I) (Or. Bourdon)								
	B-31695-1,-2	21 Jan. '25	87370	963	—			76.00	—
43.	DEMON: Do not weep, my child (Arioso) (Rubinstein) (In Russian) (Or. Pasternack)								
	B-27023-1,-2,-3,-4	12 Oct. '22	87370	963				77.43	VIC 1680; LM 20150; VL 47216

44. DINORAH: Sei vendicata assai (Meyerbeer) (I) (Or. Rogers)
C-14279-1 8 Jan. '14 88366 6393 2-052088 DB 178 AGSB 91 76.00 Rococo R16; TAP 324; VL 47215

45. DON CARLO: Felice ancor io son...Per me giunto (Verdi) (I) (Or. Sabaino)
1318c ? '07 92038 15-1028 052190 DB 178 — 73.47 —

46. DON GIOVANNI: Là ci darem la mano (Mozart) (w. Graziella Pareto) (I) (Or. Sabaino)
2728f 21 Nov. '08 92305 8053 054229 DB 875 — 79.13 —

47. DON GIOVANNI: Finch'han dal vino (Mozart) (I) (Or. Rogers)
B-14274-1 7 Jan. '14 87174 938 7-52054 DA 357 — 76.00 —

48. DON GIOVANNI: Deh vieni alla finestra (Serenata) (Mozart) (I) (Or. '07 Sabaino; '12 Rogers?; '20 Pasternack)
10914b ? '07 2-52625 DA 462 73.47 Rococo R16
B-12620-1 17 Nov. '12 87112 — 7-52037 DA 357 76.60 —
-2,-3 19 Apr. '20 87112 818 — 76.00 LM 20110; VL 47216

49. I Due Granatieri (Die beiden Grenadiere) (Robert Schumann, Op. 49, No. 1) (I) (Or. Rogers)
C-15888-1 13 Apr. '15 88527 2-052103 DB 242 77.43 —

E canta il grillo (From TIZIANELLO) (V. Billi—E. Bicci) See: Discography No. 120 and 121

50. E la mia dama (Stornello Toscano) (I) (Or. Sabaino)
9214e 21 Nov. '08 87147 2-52678 DA 169 79.13 CL 99-63

51. Elégie (based on Invocation from Les ERINNYES) (Gallet—Massenet) (F) (Or. Bourdon, Vlc. Lennartz)
C-27750-1 11 Apr. '23 — — — —
B-27750-1 11 Apr. '23 — — — —

52. ERNANI: Lo vedremo, o veglio audace (Verdi) (I) (Or. Pasternack)
B-25215-1,-2 13 Apr. '21 — — — —
-3,-4 14 Apr. '21 87336 818 7-52208 DA 163 76.00 VIC 1680; LM 20150; VL 47216

53. ERNANI: O de' verd'anni miei (Verdi) (I) (Or. Rogers?)
B-12662-1 27 Nov. '12 — — — —

259

Dis-cog. No. / Matrix No.	Date	SF Victor Cat. No.	DF Victor Cat.No.	SF HMV Cat.No.	DF HMV Cat.No.	Special "78" Rpm Issues	Speed of Original	Transcription to Ep or Lp discs
54. ERNANI: Gran Dio! costor sui sepolcrali...O de' verd'anni miei (Verdi) (I) (Or. Pasternack)								
C-25212-**1**,-2	13 Apr. '21	88660	6264	2-052225	DB 398	—	76.00	VIC 1680; LM 20150; VL 47216
*55. E suonan le campane (Ettore Titta) (I) (Or. Rogers)								
B-14269-1	5 Jan. '14	87138	933	7-52049	DA 356	—	76.00	CL 99-63
56. FALSTAFF: L'Onor! Ladri! (Verdi) (I) (Or. Pasternack)								
C-25217-**1**,-2	15 Apr. '21	88637	6264	2-052199	DB 402	—	76.00	LM 20110; VL 47215
57. FALSTAFF: Quand'ero paggio (Verdi) (I) (Or. Pasternack)								
B-27022-1,-2	12 Oct. '22	87360	876	7-52224	DA 396	—	77.43	VIC 1680; LM 20150; VL 47215
-3,-**4**	13 Oct. '22							
*58. a) FALSTAFF: Quand'ero paggio (Verdi) (I); b) Perjura! (Miguel Lerda de Tejada) (Spanish) (Pf. P. B. Kahn or G. Moore)								
OB-5460-1	25 Nov. '33	—	—	—	—	—	—	—
59. FAUST: Dio possente (Gounod) (I) (Or. '07 Sabaino; '15 Rogers; '22 Pasternack)								
792c	? '07	92043	6406	052133	—	—	77.43	Rococo R16; LM 20150
C-15893-1	14 Apr. '15	(88528)	—	2-052104	DB 405	—	76.60	VIC 1680; VL 47216
-**2**,-3	18 Oct. '22	—	6429	—	—	—	76.00	LM 20110
60. FAUST: Rammenta i lieti di quando (Gounod) (I) (Or. Rogers)								
B-15889-1	13 Apr. '15	87166	819	7-52070	DA 360	—	77.43	—
-2	14 Apr. '15							

No. / Title / Matrix	Date						rpm	LP
B-15890-1	13 Apr. '15	87222	819	7-52071	DA 360	---	77.43	LM 20110; VL 47216
-2	14 Apr. '15							
62. La FAVORITA: Vien, Leonora, a piedi tuoi (Donizetti) (I) (Or. Sabaino)								
z6933f	24 Dec. '12			2-052075		AGSB 91	80.00	Rococo R 16
63. La FORZA DEL DESTINO: Solenne in quest'ora (Verdi) (w. Beniamino Gigli) (I) (Or. Bourdon)								
CVE-37319-1,-2,-3	17 Dec. '26					AGSB 49	77.43	EJS 111
*64. La FORZA DEL DESTINO: Urna fatale del mio destino! (Verdi) (I) (Or. Rogers)								
B-15892-1	14 Apr. '15					HRS 2015 / AGSA 10	77.43	Rococo R16
65. La FORZA DEL DESTINO: Le minaccie, i fieri accenti (Verdi) (w. Emanuele Ischierdo) (I) (Or. Sabaino)								
550i	? '07	92504		054102	DB 177		73.47	EB 37
66. La GIOCONDA: Enzo Grimaldo, Principe di Santafior, che pensi? (Ponchielli) (w. Enrico Caruso) (I) (Or. Rogers)								
C-14273-1	8 Jan. '14			---	---			
67. La GIOCONDA: Enzo Grimaldo, Principe di Santafior, che pensi? (Ponchielli) (w. Beniamino Gigli) (I) (Or. Bourdon)								
CVE-37321-1	17 Dec. '26				---	AGSB 49	77.43	EJS 111; 17-0028; LCT 1004; LM 20150
-2	17 Dec. '26				---			
68. La GIOCONDA: O monumento! (Ponchielli) (I) (Or. Sabaino)								
459ai	? Sep. '12	88396	6398	052376	DB 180		79.13	LCT 6701; CSLP 501; VIC 1680
69. La GIOCONDA: Ah! Pescator, affonda l'esca (Barcarola) (Ponchielli) (I) (w. Chorus) (Or. Sabaino)								
461ai	9 Oct.?'12	88394	6265	052378	DB 180		79.13	LM 20150; VL 47215
70. Il Gitano Re (Alfredo Gandolfi—Anthony F. Paganucci) (I) (Or. Bourdon)								
BVE-49961-1,-2	15 Feb. '29		1401					---
71. GUGLIELMO TELL: Resta immobile (Rossini) (I) (Or. Rogers)								
B-141520-1	26 Feb. '14				---		77.43	CL 99-63
C-14520-1	26 Feb. '14				---			
72. El Guitarrico (Jota de Perico) (A. Perez Soriano) (Spanish) (Or. Rogers)								
B-14275-1	7 Jan. '14	87177	820	7-62013	DA 349		76.00	CL 99-63

Matrix No.	Date	SF Victor Cat. No.	DF Victor Cat.No.	SF HMV Cat.No.	DF HMV Cat.No.	Special "78" Rpm Issues	Speed of Original	Transcription to Ep or Lp discs
*73. El Guitarrico (Jota de Perico) (A. Perez Soriano) (Spanish) (Pf. Percy B. Kahn or Gerald Moore)								
OB-5464-1,-2	25 Nov. '33	—	—	—	—	—		—
HAMLET see: AMLETO								
74. LAKMÉ: Lakmé, ton doux regard se voile (Leo Delibes) (F) (Or. Bourdon)								
B-29037-1,-2	27 Nov. '23		1070	(7-52261)	DA 703	—	76.00	VL 47216
75. Lolita (Serenade) (A. Buzzi-Peccia) (I) (Or. Bourdon)								
B-29034-1,-2	27 Nov. '23	87393	1019	(7-52258)	DA 687	—	76.00	CL 99-63
76. MALENA: Disse il saggio (Ettore Titta) (I) (Or. cond. by composer)								
10549b	? '07	87142		2-52624	DA 162	AGSA 20	80.00	Rococo R16; Scala 855
77. MALENA: Ma tu sfiorata di rugiada gentil (Ettore Titta) (I) (Or. cond. by composer)								
10548b	? '07	87149		2-52623		AGSA 20	80.00	Rococo R16; Scala 855
78. Marechiare (F. Paolo Tosti) (I) (Or. '12 Sabaino; '23 Bourdon)								
465ai	? '12			052383	DB 404	—	76.00	—
B-29038-1,-2	27 Nov. '23	87384	995	(7-52263)	DA 748	—	76.00	—
79. Maria, Marì (Vincenzo Russo—Eduardo di Capua) (Neapolitan) (Or. Sabaino)								
1912ah	? '13	87140	932	2-52829	DA 353	—	80.00	CL 99-63
80. MARTA: Chi mi dirà (Canzone del porter) (Flotow) (I) (Or. Pasternack)								
B-25951-1,-2	12 Jan. '22	—	—	—	—	—		—
B-27024-1,-2,-3	12 Oct. '22	87352	876	7-52225	DA 396	—	77.43	VIC 1680; LM 20150; VL 47215
*81. Mattuttino (P. Mario Costa) (I) (Pf. accompaniment by Percy B. Kahn or Gerald Moore)								
OB-5462-1,-2	25 Nov. '33	—	—	—	—	—		EJS 223
82. Meriggiata (Leoncavallo) (I) (Or. Sabaino)								
9224e	24 Nov. '08	87150		2-52685	DA 351	—	79.13	Rococo R16; CL 99-63

No.	Title / Recording details	Matrix	Date				Catalog		Price	Other issues
83.	Mia sposa sarà la mia bandiera (A. Rotoli) (I) (Or. Bourdon)									
	B-31696-1,-2	21 Jan. '25		1076	(7-32093)	DA 748	—	76.00	CL 99-63
84.	Munasterio (Salvatore de Giacomo—P. Mario Costa) (Neapolitan) (Or. Pasternak)									
	B-24111-?	13 May, '20	87323	821	(7-52169)	DA 350	—	76.00	—
*85.	NABUCCO: Che tenti?...Oh trema insano!...Tremin gl'insani del mio furore (Verdi) (I) (Or. Rogers)									
	B-14518-?	26 Feb. '14	87194	—	7-52063	DA 358	AGSA 10	76.00	Rococo R 16; VIC 1680; VL 47215
86.	Non penso a Lei (Ferradini) (I) (Or. '08 Sabaino; '12 Rogers?)									
	9229e	25 Nov. '08	87152	—	2-52680	—	—	79.13	—
	B-12623-1	17 Nov. '12	87121	933	7-52040	DA 348	—	76.60	—
87.	Novembre (Paul Bourget—Edouard Trémisot) (F) (Or. Pasternack, Pf. Bourdon)									
	B-24112-1	13 May '20	87343	820	7-32039	DA 348	—	76.00	CL 99-63
88.	Oh che m'importa? (Ettore Titta) (I) (Or. Rogers)									
	B-14519-1	26 Feb. '14	87195	—	7-52062	DA 356	—	76.00	—
*89.	OTELLO: Credo in un Dio crudel (Verdi) (I) (Or. Rogers)									
	C-14278-1	8 Jan. '14	88466	6267	2-052090	DK 114	—	76.00	LM 20110; VL 47216
				8045				33.33	EJS 142
	Sound Film Disc	8 Mar. '29 No. Scene 1, 381-7 (a-134) 550 ft.							
90.	OTELLO: E qual certezza sognate...Era la notte (Verdi) (I) (Or. Pasternack)									
	C-23948-1,-2	20 Apr. '20	88621	6267	2-052181	DB 404	—	76.00	LM 20110; VL 47216
91.	OTELLO: Oh! mostruosa colpa!...Sì, pel ciel marmoreo giuro! (Verdi) (w. Enrico Caruso) (I) (Or. Rogers)									
	C-14272-1	8 Jan. '14	89075	8045	2-054049	DK 114	—	76.00	17-0025; LCT 1001; LCT 1004; CSLP 510; SP 33-75; RB 16128; LM 6056; ORL 312; VL 47216

Discog. No.	Matrix No.	Date	SF Victor Cat. No.	DF Victor Cat.No.	SF HMV Cat.No.	DF HMV Cat.No.	Special "78" Rpm Issues	Speed of Original	Transcription to Ep or Lp discs
92.	I PAGLIACCI: Si può? si può? (Prologo, Part I.) (Leoncavallo) (I) (Or. Sabaino)								
	462ai	? Sep. '12	88392	6268	052381	DB 464	—	76.00	COLH 155
*93.	I PAGLIACCI: Un nido di memorie (Prologo, Part II.) (Leoncavallo) (I) (Or. '07 & '12 Sabaino; '26 Bourdon)								
	1341c	? '07	92040	6405	052192	—	—	74.23	—
	467ai	? Sep. '12	88393	6268	052379	DB 464	—	76.00	COLH 155
	CVE-34918-1,-2	26 Feb. '26	—	—	—	—	—		
94.	I PAGLIACCI: Si può?...Un nido di memorie (Prologo, Parts I & II.) (Leoncavallo) (I) (Or. Pasternack)								
	C-24113-1	13 May '20	—	—	—	—	—		—
95.	PANURGE: Je suis né...Touraine est un pays (Massenet) (F) (Or. Bourdon)								
	B-27749-1,-2	11 Apr. '23	—	—	—	—	—		—
	BVE-49966-1	18 Feb. '29	—	—	—	—	—		EJS 223
*96.	PANURGE: Je suis né...Touraine est un pays (Massenet) (F) (Pf. Percy B. Kahn or Gerald Moore)								
	OB-5467-1	25 No. '33	—	—	—	—	—		—
97.	PATRIE: Pauvre martyr obscur (Emile Paladilhe) (F) (Or. Pasternack)								
	C-24620-1,-2	11 Oct. '20	88643	—	2-032063	DB 401	—	76.00	—
98.	Perjura! (Miguel Lerda de Tejada) (Spanish) (Or. Pasternack)								
	B-27025-1,-2,-3,-4	12 Oct. '22	87349	1019	7-62053	DA 347	—	77.43	—
	Perjura! (Miguel Lerda de Tejada) (Spanish) (Pf. P. B. Kahn or G. Moore). See: Discography No. 58								
99.	I PURITANI: Suoni la tromba e intrepido (Bellini) (w. Andrés Perello de Segurola) (I) (Or. Sabaino)								
	10906b	? '07	87158 / 87564		54360	VA 16	—	73.47	Rococco R16; TAP 321
100.	Querida (Sigmund Spaeth, trans. George Godoy—Albano Seismit-Doda) (Spanish) (Or. Pasternack)								
	B-25214-1,-2,-3	13 Apr. '21	87331	822	(7-62031)	DA 769	—	76.00	CL 99-63
101.	Il RE DI LAHORE: Le barbare tribù...O casto fior (Massenet) (I) (Or. Pasternack)								
	C-24623-1	11 Oct. '20	88639	6265	2-052190	DB 401	—	76.00	VIC 1680; LM 20150; VL 47215

No.	Title	Matrix	Date				Cat.		Timing	Labels
102.	El Relicario (José Padilla) (Spanish) (Or. Pasternack)	B-25950-1,-2,-3,-4,-5	12 Jan. '22	87341	822	7-62050	DA 349	—	77.43	CL 99-63
103.	RIGOLETTO: Pari siamo (Verdi) (Or. '07 Sabaino; '20 Pasternack)	1330c	? '07	92041	——	052191	DB 502	—	74.23	COLH 155; ORL 217
		C-23946-1,2	19 Apr. '20	88618	6263	2-052185	DB 402	—	76.00	17-0363; LCT 1039; HER 403; LM 20110; VL 47215
104.	RIGOLETTO: Ah! Deh non parlare al misero (Verdi) (w. Giuseppina Finzi-Magrini) (I) (Or. Sabaino)	02535v	? '12	89058	8059	054396	DB 175	—	80.00	COLH 155
105.	RIGOLETTO: Veglia o donna (Verdi) (w. Maria Galvany) (I) (Or. Sabaino)	4727h	? '07	91500	3033	54315	DA 564	—	73.47	ORL 217, EB 37 & 78; Scala 855; ATL 4051; COLH 155
106.	RIGOLETTO: Povero Rigoletto! La rà, la rà...Cortigiani, vil razza dannata (Verdi) (w. La Scala Chorus) (I) (Or. Sabaino)	2735f	25? Nov. '08	92066	8054	052251	DB 175	—	79.13	ORL 217; COLH 155
107.	RIGOLETTO: Miei signori, perdono (Verdi) (I) (Or. Sabaino)	4733h	? '07	87151	937	2-52555	DA 165	—	73.47	ORL 217; EB 78; Scala 855; ATL 4051; COLH 155
108.	RIGOLETTO: Ah! Piangi, piangi fanciulla (Verdi) (w. Maria Galvany) (I) (Or. Sabaino)	545i	? '07	92502	8059	054100	DB 177	—	73.47	HER 403; ORL 217; Scala 855; ATL 4051; COLH 155

Dis-cog. No.	Matrix No.	Date	SF Victor Cat. No.	DF Victor Cat.No.	SF HMV Cat.No.	DF HMV Cat.No.	Special "78" Rpm Issues	Speed of Original	Transcription to Ep or Lp discs
109. RIGOLETTO: No, vecchio t'inganni...Si, vendetta, tremenda vendetta! (Verdi) (w. Maria Galvany) (I) (Or. Sabaino)									
	4730h	?.'07	91501	3033	54316	DA 564	—	73.47	HER 403; EB 78; COLH 155; ORL 217
110. RIGOLETTO: Oh mia Gilda! fanciulla...a me rispondi!...Lassù in cielo (Verdi) (w. Graziella Pareto) (I) (Or. Sabaino)									
	2733f	?. Nov. '08	92506	8053	054228	DB 176	—	79.13	HER 403; ORL 217; EB 78; Scala 855; ATL 4051; COLH 155
*111. Ruffo speaks: Mock conversation with Chaliapin (In Italian; Ruffo speaks both parts)									
	OB-5468-1	24 Nov. '33					—		EJS 223
	OB-5469-1	24 Nov. '33					—		—
112. Santa Lucia (Folk song) (I) (Or. Bourdon)									
	B-29036-1,-2	27 Nov. '23	87383	995	(7-52260)	DA 687		76.00	—
113. Sei morta nella vita mia! (Guglielmo Capitelli—P. Mario Costa) (I) (Or. '20 Pasternack; '29 Bourdon)									
	B-24109-1,-2	13 May '20	87342	821	7-52168	DA 347	—	76.00	CL 99-63
	BVE-24109-3	18 Feb. '29		1460	(40-2197)	DA 1120	VA 55	77.43	—
*114. Sei morta nella vita mia! (Guglielmo Capitelli—P. Mario Costa) (I) (Pf. Percy B. Kahn or Gerald Moore)									
	OB-5463-1,-2	25 Nov. '33					—		—
*115. Suonno 'e fantasia (La Canzonetta) (Genise—Capolongo) (I) (Or. '12 Rogers?: '29 Bourdon)									
	B-12658-1	27 Nov. '12	87123	823	7-52029	DA 162	—	76.60	CL 99-63
	BVE-12658-2,-3	15 Feb. '29		1388	(7-52429)	DA 1049	—	77.43	—
*116. Suonno 'e fantasia (La Canzonetta) (Genise—Capolongo) (I) (Pf. Percy B. Kahn or Gerald Moore)									
	OB-5466-1	25 Nov. '33					—		—

117. TANNHAUSER: Forier di morte, già il crepusco cade...Oh! tu bell'astro incantator (Wagner) (I) (Or. Pasternack)

C-25216-1,-2,-3	15 Apr. '21		—	—			—

118. THAIS: No, il cuore tieni amarezza...Ahimè! fanciullo ancora di rugiada gentil (Massenet) (I) (Or. Rogers)

B-14267-1	5 Jan. '14	934	7-52048	DA 354		76.00	VL 47216

119. THAIS: Ecco dunque l'orribil città (Massenet) (I) (Or. Rogers)

B-14268-1	5 Jan. '14	934	7-52050	DA 354		76.00	VL 47216

120. TIZIANELLO: E canta il grillo (Pastorale) (V. Billi—E. Bicci) (I) (Or. '08 Sabaino; '29 Bourdon)

9215e	23 Nov. '08	87145	2-52679	DA 169		79.13	CL 99-63
BVE-49960-1	15 Feb. '29	—	(40-2196)	DA 1120	VA 55	77.43	

*121. TIZIANELLO: E canta il grillo (Pastorale) (V. Billi—E. Bicci) (I) (Pf. Percy B. Kahn or Gerald Moore)

OB-5459-1	25 Nov. '33	1460	—				—

122. Torna a Surriento (Ernesto de Curtis) (Neapolitan) (Or. '13 Sabaino; '29 Bourdon)

1911ah	? '13	932	2-52828	DA 353		80.00	
BVE-50959-1,-**2**	20 Mar. '29	1401	—	—		77.43	—

123. TOSCA: Già, mi dicon venal (Puccini) (I) (Or. Rogers)

B-15891-1	14 Apr. '15	938	7-52143	DA 163		77.43	LCT 6701; CSLP 501; VIC 1680; LM 20150; VL 47219

124. La TRAVIATA: Dite alla giovine (Verdi) (w. Maria Galvany) (I) (Or. Sabaino)

54oi	? '07	92503	054101	DB 176		73.47	HER 408; Scala 855; ATL 4053
		8055					

125. La TRAVIATA: Di Provenza il mar (Verdi) (I) (Or. Sabaino)

9060b	? '07	87141	936	2-52529	DA 165	78.26	Rococo R16

*126. Il TROVATORE: Di geloso amor sprezzato (Verdi) (w. Fosca Titta & Emanuele Ischierdo) (I) (Or. Sabaino)

10900½b	? '07	87157	54359	DA 462		73.47	OPS 401

127. Il TROVATORE: Il balen del suo sorriso (Verdi) (I) (Or. Sabaino)

9059b	? '07	87148	936	2-52528	DA 163	78.26	Rococo R16
B-12661-1	27 Nov. '12	—		—			—

Matrix No.	Date	SF Victor Cat. No.	DF Victor Cat.No.	SF HMV Cat.No.	DF HMV Cat.No.	Special "78" Rpm Issues	Speed of Original	Transcription to Ep or Lp discs
128. Il TROVATORE: Per me ora fatale (Verdi) (w. La Scala Chorus) (I) (Or. Sabaino; Chor. dir. Venturi)								
9216e	24 Nov. '08							
9217e	24 Nov. '08	87156		2-52687		HRS 2015	79.13	Scala 855
*129. Until (Edward Teschemacher—Wilfrid Sanderson) (E) (Pf. Percy B. Kahn or Gerald Moore)								
OB 5465-1	25 Nov. '33							
*130. Visione Veneziana (Barcarola) (Angiolo Orvieto—Renato Brogi) (I) (Or. '12 Rogers?; '29 Bourdon)								
B-12659-1	27 Nov. '12	87133	823	7-52030	DA 350		76.60	
BVE-12659-2,-3	22 Mar. '26							
-4	15 Feb. '29		1388	(7-52428)	DA 1049		77.43	
*131. Visione Veneziana (Barcarola) (Angiolo Orvieto—Renato Brogi) (I) (Pf. Percy B. Kahn or Gerald Moore)								
OB-5461-1	25 Nov. '33							
Visiting Card to Chaliapin: recitation by Ruffo. See: Discography No. 111								
132. ZAZA: Buona Zazà, del mio buon tempo (Leoncavallo) (I) (Or. Rogers?)								
B-12621-1	17 Nov. '12	87114	824	7-52035	DA 355		76.60	VL 47215
133. ZAZA: Zazà, piccola zingara (Leoncavallo) (I) (Or. Rogers?)								
B-12660-1	27 Nov. '12	87125	824	7-52031	DA 355		76.60	VL 47215

Notes to the Recordings

19. The 1933 recording was made at "His Master's Voice" Abbey Road studios, London.

23. The 1907 recording is with chorus. In the 1920 recording the orchestra includes harp, played by Lapitino, and piano, played by Bourdon.

27. In the New York recording (take 3) the orchestra consists of 4 first violin, 2 second violin, 2 viola, 2 violoncello, 2 clarinet, harp, bassoon, oboe, trombone, 2 cornet, bass, trumpet, tuba; including Schmidt, Lennartz, Keneke, Reitz, Barone, and Lapitino.

30. Ruffo appeared in at least two film shorts, featuring Largo al factotum from Il BARBIERE and the OTELLO Credo. The sound was recorded on 33.33 rpm discs, but these films are not listed in the Library of Congress as part of the Vitaphone Series of 1927-28, which featured such artists as Schumann-Heink, Gigli, Martinelli, Raisa, de Luca, Alda, etc. Numbers given are as shown on the disc.

32. Take 3 was issued on a 45 rpm disc only as a special Christmas gift edition in 1950.

33. The 1908 Milan version contains the second verse only. The 1923 Victor recordings were sung in French, without a chorus, and the orchestra was conducted by Rosario Bourdon.

34. The role of Chatterton was originally written for a tenor. The aria has been transposed down.

39. This recording is known to exist in private pressings.

40. The composer, Ettore Titta, was Ruffo's brother.

41. Sung half tone low to score.

55. Take 3 shown in error on some copies of 933.

58. Recorded at "His Master's Voice" Abbey Road studios, London. The recording books show that both Percy B. Kahn and Gerald Moore took part in the session of 25 Nov., 1933, but do not indicate which artist played for which recording! The recording books show the title *Perjura* but indicate the composer as "Seismit-Doda" who was the composer of another Ruffo favorite, *Querida*. It is presumed that the title listing is correct. One verse of *Perjura* could stand alone as a companion piece to the short FALSTAFF excerpt.

64. Sung one whole tone low to score, in E; a standard transposition approved by Verdi. Unpublished, except as a special Club issue. (Ruffo makes some errors in notation near the middle of the aria.)

73. Recorded at "His Master's Voice" Abbey Road studios, London. Both Kahn and Moore were present at the session; the books do not show which played for this recording.

81. Same comments as Note 73.

85. Ruffo opens the record in the role of the High Priest, Zaccaria, sings an exchange of lines between Nabucco and Zaccaria, and concludes with Nabucco's aria, *Tremin gl'insani*.

89. See note to Discography No. 30. Numbers given are as shown on the disc.

93. Late copies of 88393 (those bearing the "Victrola" label) and all copies of 6268-B are mechanical dubbings, bearing the mark S/8, and are inferior to earlier pressings.

96. Same comments as Note 73.

111. This is listed in the recording books as "Visiting Card to Chaliapin." The recordings were made at "His Master's Voice" Abbey Road studio, London. Since two matrix numbers are shown (rather than two takes of the same matrix number), it is assumed that the contents are different. The portion which has been released on Lp (EJS 223) is a delightful bit of fantasy in which Ruffo imitates the speaking voice of Chaliapin in a mock conversation.

114. Same comments as Note 73.

115. The 1929 recording is sung one half tone lower than the 1912 recording.

116. Same comments as Note 73.

121. Same comments as Note 73.

126. Fosca Titta, the soprano in the trio, was Titta Ruffo's sister. Her name, like Ruffo's own, is found occasionally reversed in professional references.

129. Same comments as Note 73.

130. The 1929 recording is sung one half tone lower than the 1912 recording.

131. Same comments as Note 73.

APPENDIX E

The *Szinházi Élet* Court of Justice

This jocular interview was given by Titta Ruffo in Budapest, Hungary, to the prominent magazine reporting on the "theatrical life" of the capital, which is the exact translation of its title, *Szinházi Élet*. It was selected for inclusion not only because its very informality shows the singer at his playful best, but because the seemingly lighthearted tone of his brief and witty replies reveal a great deal of depth. They somehow capture his views, opinions, attitudes, outlook, interests, habits more vividly than many longer interviews in a more formal setting.

ACCUSED: Titta Ruffo
he tells the truth, the whole truth
and nothing but the truth

This week Titta Ruffo is in the dock. The accusation is that with five appearances he has pocketed ten thousand dollars—about three-quarter billion kroners—thereby publicly discrediting the common misconception that Hungary is a poor country.

Your name: Titta Ruffo.

Details, please. Your last name? Titta.

Given name: Ruffo.

Why do you use the two of them always together? Because Titta is always together with Ruffo.

And why do you write your name the Hungarian way, when Italians and most other nations do the reverse, writing the given name first and then the last name? Because I was first Titta and became Ruffo only a few days later.

Your religion? Roman catholic.

Your age? I am 48 years old.

The interview was published in *Szinházi Élet*, Budapest, volume 15, no. 20, May 17-23, 1925. Translated by Andrew Farkas.

Why do you confess it, after all this is the most you look? Because I was born in 1877.

Your occupation? I am an artist, who expresses his art instead of pen and ink, paint and canvas or chisel and marble with voice and acting. It upsets me the most when I am called a baritone.

Where were you born? In Pisa.

Your family? I have been married for 18 years, I have two children. My beautiful 16 year old daughter's name is Velia, my 15 year old son is, of course, Ruffo.

Who discovered you? I did.

With whom did you study? With myself.

At what age? I was sixteen.

From whom did you inherit your talent? My father was an excellent draftsman, but he opposed my stage career. That I became something I can thank my blessed dear mother who encouraged me and secretly helped me.

When was your debut? In 1898.

Where? At the Teatro Costanzi, in Rome.

In which opera? Lohengrin.

Which role? I sang the Herald.

With what success? I became instantly known.

How many roles have you learned since? Another sixtysix, but mostly major roles.

Which is your favorite role? I can name three: Rubinstein's Demon, Leoncavallo's Edipo re and Thomas' Hamlet.

Why? Because I like human tragedy, the weighty spiritual experiences, and I can pour my entire soul into these three roles.

Who is your favorite partner? I had so many that I cannot pick.

Who is your favorite conductor? Certainly not that friendly young German who conducted my recent Rigoletto in Berlin.

Your favorite author? Shakespeare.

Your favorite painter? Zalnaga.

Your favorite sculptor? Rodin.

Your favorite poet? Mazzini, Byron and believe me, I am not trying to be polite, Pétofi.

Perhaps "Petöfi"? Yes, Yes. I can't pronounce his name correctly, but rather his marvelous poems, because those I could enjoy in excellent Italian translation.

How many languages do you speak? Italian, French, Spanish and English.

You don't speak German? I detest the German language.

And the Germans? Not any less.

How many times were you in America? In North and Central America nine times, in South America ten times.

In which countries? In the United States from New York to San Francisco, in Canada, Mexico, Havana, Colombia, Chile, Brazil, Argentina, Uruguay and in many smaller states.

Where did you receive the highest fee? In New York, for one of the Hippodrome concerts.

How much? Four thousand dollars for singing two arias.

Where is your palace? I have a villa in Rome, on the most beautiful spot of that gorgeous city.

When did you have it built? Some fifteen years ago.

Is it true that it is made of marble? You will find some of that among the ingredients.

Do you have a passion? Paintings. I would go to the end of the world for a beautiful modern painting. Wherever I go I first inquire about the galleries. In Budapest too I visited all the museums, exhibits and other collections.

Whom do you know from among the Hungarian painters? Munkácsy the best, by whom I have a few paintings and drawings.

Do you like to go to the opera? Since Caruso died I sat in an audience only for the sake of Chaliapin. I grew tired of the many eyes.

And to concerts? As seldom as possible.

To the movies? As often as possible. It is my favorite pastime.

At what time do you get up? At nine.

When do you go to bed? If possible, at nine.

How do you like the Hungarian cuisine? Unfortunately I only know the hotel fare; the real, spicy dishes I don't know.

Your favorite food? None.

Your favorite beverage? Tea.

Do you drink wine? Never.

Do you smoke? Never.

Do you like to travel? Oh, yes, the only trouble is that even the most wonderful trip ends on some opera stage.

Why do you sing still, if you are so wealthy? I am almost ashamed to admit it: I am driven by ambition.

Have you flown yet? Certainly, more than a hundred times, in the war.

In what capacity? As a corporal on reconnaissance.

How much time did you spend in the service? Three and a half years.

Weren't you concerned about your voice? I wasn't, only others, who succeeded—contrary to my wish—to work out an exemption for me.

Is it good to be world famous? Dreadful.

What is your greatest ambition? To spend twenty-four hours in some city without anyone pointing at me.

What are you doing these days? I read and study.

What are you studying? Benelli's "Cena delle Beffe" which Giordano set to music for me.

Where will you sing it? In New York.

When? This Fall.

Where are you headed now? Home, to Rome, but I will first visit the modern painting exhibit in Venice.

When will you return to Budapest? In the next season, I hope, unless the bet is settled by then.

What bet? A friend of mine from a New York club bet that I will die before
Chaliapin, because I am the more nervous of the two of us. Now I wait to
see who will be right.

These are the kinds of bets friends make in New York? There they only bet on someone's
death, but here they even try to do the killing.

How? With interviews.

What can you bring up in your defense? That I heroically endured this flood of
questions.

Which is your most recent photograph? The one you made of me at the Tosca
rehearsal at the Városi Szinház, my dear Mr. Vasadi.

Bibliography

RUFFO TITTA, JR., AND ANDREW FARKAS

Books and Articles

Aldrich, Richard. *Concert Life in New York, 1902-1923*. New York: G. P. Putnam's Sons, 1941.

Arnosi, Eduardo. *Titta Ruffo, el titán de los baritonos*. Buenos Aires: Ayer y Hoy de la Opera, 1977.

Barrenechea, Mariano Antonio. *Historia estética de la música con dos estudios más sobre consideraciones históricas y téchnicas acerca del arte del canto y la obra maestra del teatro melodramático*. 3rd ed. Buenos Aires: Claridad, 1941.

————. *Titta Ruffo: Notas de psicología artística*. Buenos Aires: Musica, 1911.

Biografía y juicio critico de Titta Ruffo. Madrid: Pérez de Velasco, 1912.

Blyth, Alan. *Opera on Record*. London: Hutchinson, 1979.

Carretero, José Maria. *Galeria: Más de cien vidas extraordinarias contadas por sus protagonistas y comentadas por el Caballero audaz* (pseud.). Madrid: Caballero audaz, 1943.

Castellan, Joëlle. *Spécial Monte-Carlo centenaire de la Salle Garnier, 1879-1979*. Paris: Opéra International, 1979.

Castro Cerquera, Paulo de Oliveira. *Um Século de Opera em São Paulo*. São Paulo, 1954.

Celletti, Rodolfo. "Titta Ruffo." In *Enciclopedia dello spettacolo*. 9 vols. Rome: Le Maschere, 1954.

————. "Titta Ruffo." In *Le grandi voci*. Rome: Istituto per la collaborazione culturale, 1964.

————. "Titta Ruffo." *La Scala*. Milan, October 1958.

Celli, Teodoro. "Ricordo di Titta Ruffo il Caruso dei baritoni." *Epoca*. Milan, March 4, 1973.

————. "Voce di bronzo per personaggi terribili." *Corriere Lombardo*. Milan, July 8-9, 1953.

I Cento anni dei Teatro di Pisa (1867-1967). Pisa: Giardini, 1967.

Chiadò, Michele. "Titta Ruffo, 1877-1977." *Musica*. Milan, October 1977.

Confalonieri, Giulio. "Il figlio del fabbro 'teneva' una nota per quaranta secondi." *Epoca*. Milan, August 6, 1963.

Contreras, Vicente. *Titta Ruffo y su arte: Biografía y estudio crítico en dos idiomas del eminente barítono*. Madrid, 1910.

Cunelli, Georges. *Voice no Mystery*. London: Stainer & Bell, 1973.

D., R. "Titta Ruffo." *Musical Courier*, March 11, 1920.

Davis, Ronald. *Opera in Chicago*. New York: Appleton-Century, 1966.

Della Corte, Andrea: "È morto Titta Ruffo." *La Stampa*. Torino, July 7, 1953.

Duval, John E. *Svengali's Secrets and Memoirs of the Golden Age*. New York: J. T. White, 1958.

Ewen, David. *Musicians since 1900: Performers in Concert and Opera*. New York: H. W. Wilson, 1978.

Favia-Artsay, Aida. "Titta Ruffo." *Hobbies*, Chicago, October 1953.

————. "Titta Ruffo." *The Record Colllector*. Ipswich, June 1951.

Gaisberg, Frederick W. *The Music Goes Round*. New York: Macmillan, 1943.

————. *Music on Record*. London: Hale, 1946. (Same as his *The Music Goes Round*.)

Gara, Eugenio. *Cantarono alla Scala*. Milan: Electa, 1975.

————. "Il nome di Titta Ruffo non fu scritto sull'acqua." *L'Europeo*. Milan, July 14, 1963.

————. "Ritrattino di Titta Ruffo." *Le vie d'Italia*. Milan: TCI, December 12, 1963.

————. "Titta Ruffo, fratello di Amleto." *Corriere della sera*. Milan, July 3, 1955.

Gentili, Alfredo. Cinquant'anni dopo. . .(*Il Regio teatro Verdi nei suoi ricordi*). Pisa, 1915.

Giuntini, Renato. "Sentì una sola volta Turiddu e si scoperse una voce di rara bellezza." *Historia*. Milan, August 1974.

Gobbi, Tito. *My Life*. London: Macdonald and Jane's, 1979; Garden City, N.Y.: Doubleday, 1980.

Gunsbourg, Raoul. *Cent ans de souvenirs. . .ou presque*. Monte Carlo: Rocher, 1959.

Jellinek, George. "Ruffo and Rigoletto." *Metropolitan Opera House Program*. New York, October 1964.

————. "Ruffo in Retrospect." *The Saturday Review*. New York, August 29, 1953.

Kolodin, Irving. *The Metropolitan Opera 1883-1966*. New York: A. A. Knopf, 1966.

Lancelotti, Arturo. *Le voci d'oro*. Rome: Fratelli Palombi, 1942, 1953.

Lauri-Volpi, Giacomo: *A viso aperto*. Rome: "Corbaccio," 1954.

————. *Incontri e scontri*. Rome: Bonavita, 1971.

————. *Voci parallele*. Milan: Garzanti, 1955, 1960. (3rd ed., Bologna: Bongiovanni, 1977.)

Legge, Walter. "Titta Ruffo." Part I, *The Gramophone*. London, October 1928. Part II, *The Gramophone*. London, November 1928.

Less, Aleksandr. "Immortal Recordings of Titta Ruffo." *For Record Lovers*. Moscow, February 8, 1972 (in Russian).

————. "Razgovor s Titta Ruffo." In *Vtoroia stikhiia: Rasskazy*. Moscow, 1969.

Maggiorotti, Aldo. "Opera Stars on the Screen." *Record News*. Toronto, September 1956.

Marchetti, Romeo. *Mezzo secolo: Ricordi di un giornalista caricaturista*. Rome: Vittorio Ferri, 1940.

Mathews, Emerys G. *Titta Ruffo, a Centenary Discography*. Penybanc, Llandeilo: by the author, 1977, 1981.

Meltzer, Charles Henry. "The Real and the Unreal Titta Ruffo." *The Independent and the Weekly Review*, October 8, 1921.

Monaldi, Gino. *Cantanti celebri*. Rome: Tiber, 1929.

Montale, Eugenio. *Prime alla Scala*. Milan: Mondadori, 1981. (Contains his "Un ricordo di Titta Ruffo.")

———. "Un ricordo di Titta Ruffo." *Corriere d'informazioni*. Milan: July 5, 1958.

Moore, Edward C. *Forty Years of Opera in Chicago*. New York: Horace Liveright, 1930.

Moore, Grace. *You Are Only Human Once*. New York: Doubleday, Doran, 1944.

Natan, Alex. *Primo uomo: Grosse Sänger der Oper*. Basel: Basilius, 1963.

Núñez y Dominguez, Roberto. *Descorriendo el telón; cuarenta años de teatro en Mexico*. Madrid: Graficas Editorial Rollán, 1956.

Pahlen, Kurt. *Great Singers from the Seventeenth Century to the Present Day*. Translated by Oliver Coburn. London: W. H. Allen, 1973; New York: Stein and Day, 1974.

Peeler, Clare P. "Ruffo Titta—His Personality." *Musical America*, December 27, 1913.

Pèrez Lugin, Alejandro. *De Titta Ruffo á la Fons pasando por Machaquito*. Madrid: Tovar, 1912.

Pleasants, Henry. *The Great Singers*. New York: Simon & Schuster, 1966; London: Gollancz, 1974.

Ponselle, Rosa, and Drake, James A. *Ponselle: A Singer's Life*. Garden City: Doubleday, 1982.

Roeseler, Albrecht. *Eine kleine Lachmusik: Musikeranekdoten aus unserer Zeit*. Munich: Piper, 1971.

Rosenthal, Harold D. *Two Centuries of Opera at Covent Garden*. London: Putnam, 1958.

Ruffo, Titta. *La mia parabola: Memorie*. Milan: Fratelli Treves, 1937.

———. *La mia parabola: Memorie*. Rome: Staderini, 1977.

———. *Parabola moei zhizni: Vospominaniia*. Translated by A. D. Bushen. Leningrad: Muzyka, 1968.

Saltzman, Leopold. "The Victor Café." *Opera News*, February 19, 1966.

Santi, Piero. "Dieci anni fa moriva Titta Ruffo grandissimo artista e sincero democratico." *Avanti!* Rome, July 6, 1963.

Sassone, Felipe. *La rueda de mi fortuna: Memorias*. Madrid: Aguilar, 1958.

Schauensee, Max de. "The Lion of Pisa." *Opera News*. New York, April 8, 1967.

Schwarzkopf, Elisabeth. *On and off the Record*. New York: Charles Scribner's Sons, 1982. (Contains Part I of Walter Legge's 1928 article—q.v.)

Scott, Michael. *The Record of Singing to 1914*. London: Duckworth, 1977; New York: Scribner's Sons, 1977.

———. *The Record of Singing, Volume Two: 1914-1925*. London: Duckworth, 1979; New York: Holmes & Meier, 1979.

Seltsam, William H. *Metropolitan Opera Annals: A Chronicle of Artists and Perform-
ances*. New York: H. W. Wilson, 1947.
Steane, John. *The Grand Tradition: Seventy Years of Singing on Record*. London:
Duckworth, 1974; New York: Charles Scribner's Sons, 1974.
Tartoni, Guido. "Titta Ruffo, un leone che non belò nemmeno per un milione
di dollari." *Musica e dischi*. Milan, January 1967.
Tegani, Ulderico. *Cantanti di una volta*. Milan: Valsecchi, 1945.
Titta, Ruffo. See Ruffo, Titta.
Vehanen, Kosti. *Rapsodia elämästä*. Porvoo: W. Söderström, 1956.
Walsh, T. J. *Monte Carlo Opera 1879-1909*. Dublin: Gill & Macmillan, 1975.
Wayner, Robert J. *What Did They Sing at the Met?* 3rd ed. New York: Wayner,
1981.
Wolf, Albert. "Titta Ruffo." *The Record Collector*. Ipswich, May 1947.

Commemorative Lectures

Alisedo Gonzales, Horacio; Costa Valenti, Pedro; Serra Lima, Ivan. Buenos
Aires, Teatro Colón, November 7, 1953.
Dell'Ira, Gino. Pisa, Teatro Verdi, July 5, 1973.
Gara, Eugenio. Florence, Teatro Comunale, July 5, 1963 (published in *Discoteca*,
no. 34, 1963).
Gualerzi, Giorgio. Pisa, Teatro Verdi, December 16, 1963.
Mariani, Renato. Pisa, Teatro Verdi, July 5, 1954.
Novotny, Antonin. Prague, January 24 and March 30, 1954.

Record Notes (with LP Record Numbers)

Caputo, Pietro (RCA VL 47216), in Italian.
Celletti, Rodolfo. Titta Ruffo, a Biographical and Critical Memoir (COLH 155).
————. (RCA Victor LM 20110).
Favia-Artsay, Aida (Rococo R 16).
Höslinger, Clemens (Court Opera Classics CO 321-323), in German.
Jellinek, George (RCA VIC 1680).
Lebow, Bernard (Scala 855).
Salwitz, Bruno (EMI 3C 065-00749), in Italian.
Smith, Edward (Top Artist Platters T 309).
Soprano, Franco (RCA LM 20150), in Italian.
Tassart, Maurice (EMI Falp 500039), in French.

Unpublished Books

Less, Aleksandr. "Prisoner of perfection." (In Russian.) Detailed illustrated biography of Titta Ruffo. Unpublished due to the death of the author in

1972, at the time he was about to deliver the manuscript to the printer. The whereabouts of the manuscript is unknown.

Ruffo, Titta. *La mia parabola: Memorie.* English translation completed by George L. Nyklicek (1965). Second English translation completed by Emerys G. Mathews (1982).

Works Based on the Life of Titta Ruffo

Brocchi, Virgilio. *Il posto nel mondo.* Rome and Milan: Mondadori, 1921.

———. "La razza." In *Gioia di raccontare: Due romanzi.* Milan: Mondadori, 1935.

Kuprin, Aleksandr Ivanovich. "Solovei." In *Sobranie sochinenii.* Vol. 6, *Proizvendeniia 1899-1937.* Moscow: Gos. Izd. Khudozhestvennoi Literatury, 1958.

Index

Contributors

EDUARDO ARNOSI, a graduate of the University of Buenos Aires, is Professor of French Literature at the same institution. He is a regent of the Escuela Nacional de Bellas Artes "Manuel Belgrano." As a music critic he is a contributor to *La Prensa, La Nación, Discoteca* and the Buenos Aires correspondent of *Opera* (London). He is also a lecturer on music at the Teatro Colón, Radio Nacional, Radio Municipal of Buenos Aires, and other institutions. He is the author of *Titta Ruffo, el titán de los baritonos* and producer of the record album *Wagner Tenors of the Past.*

TED FAGAN is an Associate of the Archive of Recorded Sound at Stanford University and an Adjunct Professor of Interpretation at the Monterey Institute of International Studies, and he has previously served as Chief Interpreter at the United Nations. He has contributed extensively to *The Record Collector, ARSC Journal, Amberola Graphic,* and other discographical and musical publications. He is co-compiler of *The Encyclopedic Discography of Victor Recordings* published by Greenwood Press.

ANDREW FARKAS is Director of Libraries and Professor of Library Science at the University of North Florida. He was previously Assistant Manager of Walter J. Johnson, Inc., and Chief Bibliographer and Assistant Head of the Acquisitions Department at the University of California Library at Davis. He is the principal co-editor of the *Librarians' Calendar and Pocket Reference,* editor-contributor-compiler of *Opera and Concert Singers: An Annotated International Bibliography of Books* (in production), editor of the anthological volume *Lawrence Tibbett* (in production). A 42-volume reprint series titled *Opera Biographies* was published under his advisory editorship in 1977. He has published articles, reviews, and photography in *Opera* (London), *Opera News, Library Journal, The*

Library Scene, Florida Libraries, Previews and *The Negro Educational Review*. He is currently collaborating with Enrico Caruso, Jr., on a biography of Enrico Caruso and Ada Giachetti.

AIDA FAVIA-ARTSAY is a writer, musician, vocal coach and singer. Her father, Raffaele Favia, was her first voice teacher, himself a student of Guglielmo Vergine, Caruso's teacher. She is the author of the annotated discography *Caruso on Records* which gives the recommended playing speed for each Caruso recording. A prolific writer, her articles have appeared in *Etude, Opera News, The Gramophone, The Record Collector, Musica e Dischi* and other periodicals dealing with music and records. For over two decades she conducted her own monthly "Historical Records" department in *Hobbies* magazine.

GEORGE JELLINEK is Music Director of radio station WQXR and WQXR-FM and host of the nationally syndicated radio program, *The Vocal Scene*, as well as a number of local programs. He is the recipient of several national broadcast awards and has been decorated by the Government of Austria. He is contributing editor to *Stereo Review* and author of *Callas, Portrait of a Prima Donna* (1960), many articles for national magazines, and two opera librettos. He is also a member of the adjunct faculty at New York University and a regular panelist on the Metropolitan Opera national broadcasts.

EUGENIO MONTALE (1896-1981), recipient of the 1975 Nobel Prize for Literature, is considered Italy's foremost twentieth-century poet. The subject of numerous international critical studies, Montale had many important accomplishments during his long and productive life. He served as curator of the Gabinetto Vieusseux library in Florence, a position he lost in 1938, after ten years of service, because of his refusal to join the Fascist party. He was also a well-known essayist, translator of Shakespeare, Corneille, Blake, and other poets, a staff writer of the daily newspaper *Corriere della sera*, and music critic of *Corriere d'informazioni*. His volumes of poetry are the pride of Italian literature and his essays and other writings continue to be collected and published in anthologies.

WILLIAM R. MORAN is Vice President of Exploration for Molycorp, a subsidiary of the Union Oil Company of California, and founder and Honorary Curator of the Stanford Archive of Recorded Sound. He has written *Melba: A Contemporary Review, Geraldine Farrar*, and *The Recordings of Lillian Nordica* and a large number of articles which have appeared in *The Record Collector, Recorded Sound, Record News, High Fidelity* and other journals. He is the producer for RCA Australia of *Nellie Melba: The American Recordings, 1907-1916*, co-compiler with Ted Fagan of *The En-*

cyclopedic Discography of Victor Recordings, associate editor with Andrew Farkas of the 42-volume reprint series of *Opera Biographies*, and the author of over 25 singers' discographies published in books and periodicals. He has been an associate editor of the American Association of Petroleum Geologists' *Bulletin* since 1959, and has contributed many articles, reviews and biographies to technical and scientific journals.

MAX DE SCHAUENSEE (1899-1982) was a man of varied musical interests. The descendent of a titled Swiss family, baptized as Baron Jean Maximilien Meyer de Schauensee, he first made an attempt at a singing career. Following vocal studies with Emilio de Gogorza at the Curtis Institute, he appeared in *Cavalleria rusticana* and *Boris Godunov* in his native Rome. He also sang in the American premieres of *Khovanchina* (1928) and *Demon* (1929), and sang the role of Radames in Atlantic City (1934). However, he was best known for his work as the music critic of the Philadelphia *Evening Bulletin* (1942-78). Author of *The Collector's Verdi and Puccini* (1962), he was also a contributor to *Opera News*, *Musical America* and *High Fidelity*.

RUFFO TITTA, JR., earned his doctorate in the field of Economics. From 1936 onward he worked as an administrator in the Italian electric industry. In 1963 he became the Director of the Finance Section of the newly formed Ente Nazionale per l'Energia Elettrica and later became the Assistant Director of its central administration. Since his retirement in 1975 he has devoted all his time to his special interests: the arts and natural sciences. In 1977 Dr. Titta published the annotated and supplemented edition of his father's autobiography, *La mia parabola*, commemorating the 100th anniversary of his father's birth.